ADA COMPLIANCE GUIDELINES

CALIFORNIA ACCESS CODE

AMERICANS WITH DISABILITIES ACT
TITLE III

CALIFORNIA ACCESS CODE
TITLE 24

Dorothy L. Grant
and
Thomas M. Grant
Daniel S. Grant, A.I.A.
David M. Grant, A.I.A.

Caveat
The American with Disabilities Act, Title III, legislation and the California Code of Regulations, Title 24, are complex. The regulations and guidelines represent issues that may result in conflicting interpretations. The author has taken care and concern for accuracy and completeness in developing this concise manual. The contents are presented with no warranty, either expressed or implied, and the author and publisher assume no responsibility for omissions from the regulations; for the accuracy of the presentations and information contained herein; or for the outcome of decisions, agreements, or obligations made based on this information. The illustrations contained herein represent specific requirements of the ADA and the California Access Code and are intended only as an aid for building design and construction. It is advisable to contact government regulating entities for interpretation prior to any indecisive compliance action.

Published by:
ACR Group
P. O. Box 720808
San Diego, CA 92172

Compiled, written and edited by:

Dorothy L. Grant - General Contractor • Real Estate Broker
Thomas M. Grant - General Contractor • Real Estate Broker
Daniel S. Grant   - Architect • General Contractor
David M. Grant   - Architect

Library of Congress Catalog Card Number 92-73255
ISBN 0-9633709-6-0

Copyright © January, 1993. All rights reserved exclusive of any portion(s) contained herein that constitute U. S. Government material not eligible for copyright protection, if any. No part of this book may be reproduced in any form or incorporated into any information retrieval system without the written permission of the copyright owner.

PREFACE

Over 43 million Americans have physical or mental disabilities. Discrimination against persons with disabilities remain in critical areas such as housing, employment, transportation, public accommodations, education, recreation, and communication. Those individuals encounter barriers of accessibility daily. As a group, they are severely disadvantaged socially, economically, vocationally, and educationally. This book is dedicated to those persons and to those individuals who bring their facilities into compliance with the ADA standards assuring individuals with disabilities equal opportunity and participation in all aspects of our society.

The Americans with Disabilities Act of 1990 mandates non-discrimination on the basis of disability. This book gives a brief overview of the Act with an emphasis on Title III prohibiting discrimination by private entities in places of public accommodation.

New places of public accommodation, commercial facilities, building additions or alterations are to be designed and constructed in compliance with the ADA accessibility standards. Such facilities are to be readily available and accessible to persons with disabilities. Facilities include all private businesses or entities that own, lease or leases to, or operate a business accommodating the public.

The provisions of Title III became effective January 26, 1992. The final rule addresses types of public accommodation and commercial facilities, design standards for new construction, removal of existing barriers, professional and trade courses and exam accessibility, and enforcement procedures. Title III was enacted to ensure that persons with disabilities receive access to buildings and facilities equal or similar to those accommodations available to the general public.

PREFACE

The state of California has set building code standards to conform with the Americans with Disabilities Act and the Fair Housing Amendments. The Office of the State Architect has presented the access code standards to the State Building Standards Commission (SBSC) for adoption as an amendment of Part 2, Title 24 of the California Code of Regulations (CCR). The California Access Code standards will take effect six months subsequent to the approval by the SBSC. The requirements provided herein are based on the code standards presented to the SBSC as of the date of this printing.

The ADA accessibility guidelines are enforceable through civil action. Code compliance in California will be regulated through local building and state governing agencies and will be mandatory for new construction. The ADA guidelines may be more restrictive than the State of California, or vice-versa. The more restrictive requirements should be applied to comply with both entities. This text does not determine the more restrictive requirements due to varying situations for each entity or property. There may be instances of not having to fully comply with the most restrictive measures due to an unreasonable hardship, disproportionate cost, technical infeasibility, or administrative exemption. Therefore, both the ADA and California requirements are fully included.

The intent of this handbook is to inform and provide the public with a concise and easily understood reference manual of the ADA Title III guidelines cross referenced with the California Access Code. The information should be particularly useful to owners of small businesses, professional services, the building trades, government entities, and to building and facility owners and managers. A registration form is provided in the back of this manual to receive periodic updates.

Dorothy Grant

USING HANDBOOK EFFECTIVELY

This handbook has reference numbers for easy access to any information. The book is sectioned in four major categories namely Section A, general information; Section B, ADA accessibility law; Section C, ADA accessibility regulations and design guidelines; and Section D, California accessibility design and building code regulations. Within these sections each information topic has a reference number except for the general information in Section A. The reference numbers are in numerical order within each Section as shown in the Table of Contents.

Quick access to desired information is possible through three options:

OPTION 1
Table of Contents provides an outline of the subject categories with location reference numbers. Each category chosen can be quickly located by its reference number through the tab markers in the margin.

Margin Tab Markers show the section letter and subject reference number from each page. By searching through the margin tabs, you will reach the desired reference number location.

OPTION 2
Index section provides quick access by page number.

OPTION 3
Description Headings are provided on each page. Sections B, C, and D provide the book section title, category, and then topic under that category. Once familiar with the book sections, easy access is available by glancing through the page headings for a desired location.

USING HANDBOOK EFFECTIVELY

Cross Reference is provided between the ADA, Sections B and C, with the California design standards, Section D.

California: Where California regulations are identical to the ADA regulations, California Section D references within the text to the specific ADA requirements in Section C that are required or are in addition to the California requirements.

Related Topics: Related topics are referenced between the ADA Accessibility Design Standards and the California Access Code by the superscription of " ^{CA} " followed by the related California section number or " ^{ADA} " followed by the related ADA section number. These references are provided only for quick cross reference between like subjects in Section C and D and are not additional requirements to the other. This cross reference is particularly useful when applying both the ADA and the California Access Code regulations.

Highlighted words in the text are intended for ease in locating specific compliance topics within various text sections.

Italic text in Section C are recommendations of an advisory nature by the Architectural and Transportation Barriers Compliance Board (ATBCB) and are not architectural guideline specification requirements.

ADA Terminology in Section A provides definitions, explanations, and examples to better understand the ADA covered in this manual. California Access Code terminology is distinguished by " ^{CA} ", written in " this print ", and applies only to the State of California. Reading the terminology will give the reader a better understanding of the ADA law.

USING HANDBOOK EFFECTIVELY

Abbreviations used in this text and their full identification are furnished in Section A as a quick reference source.

Graphic Illustrations provide the minimum technical design requirements in facilitating persons with disabilities and are intended solely as an aid for design and construction. The illustrations are in numerical order as Figures 1 to 100 throughout this manual. A table listing the graphic illustrations, descriptions, and page numbers is furnished following the Table of Contents.

Table Illustrations are listed in a table following the Table of Graphic Illustrations in Section A for a quick reference to identify and locate a specific table. The "table illustrations" are labeled by the section number (A-D), subsection number, and are in alphabetical order. For example, the first table in Section C, subsection 2 would be labeled Table C-2A.

ADA COMPLIANCE GUIDELINES

TABLE OF CONTENTS

Preface
Using Handbook Effectively
Table of Contents
Index of Graphic Illustrations
Index of Table Illustrations

Section A: GENERAL INFORMATION
Introduction
ADA Law and Information Source
Compliance Enactment Schedule
Understanding ADA Terminology
Abbreviations
Barrier Removal Plan Guidelines

Section B: ADA RULES AND REGULATIONS
B-1 COMPLIANCE REQUIREMENTS
    1.1 Obligated Entities
        1.1.1 Public Accommodations
        1.1.2 Commercial Facilities
        1.1.3 Courses • Examinations
        1.1.4 Exceptions
    1.2 Landlord • Tenant
    1.3 Public Accommodations in Residences
    1.4 Insurance
    1.5 Conflicting Laws
B-2 NONDISCRIMINATION
    2.1 Equal Opportunity
    2.2 Equal Participation
    2.3 Equal Benefits

ADA COMPLIANCE GUIDELINES
TABLE OF CONTENTS

- 2.4 Administrative Control
- 2.5 Association
- 2.6 Conduct
- 2.7 Exceptions
  - 2.7.1 Direct Threat
  - 2.7.2 Illegal Drug Use
  - 2.7.3 Smoking
- B-3 ACCESSIBILITY REQUIREMENTS
  - 3.1 General
    - 3.1.1 Maintenance
    - 3.1.2 Safety
    - 3.1.3 Specialized Accommodations
    - 3.1.4 Personal Accommodations
    - 3.1.5 Special Services
  - 3.2 Auxiliary Aids
    - 3.2.1 Aids • Services
    - 3.2.2 Communication
    - 3.2.3 Telecommunication Devices
    - 3.2.4 Closed Caption Decoders
    - 3.2.5 Exception
    - 3.2.6 Alternative Aids and Services
  - 3.3 Assembly Area Seating
    - 3.3.1 Existing Facilities
    - 3.3.2 New Construction
  - 3.4 Courses • Examinations
    - 3.4.1 Application
    - 3.4.2 Examinations
    - 3.4.3 Courses
  - 3.5 Transportation Service
    - 3.5.1 Application
    - 3.5.2 Barrier Removal
    - 3.5.3 Regulation Compliance

ADA COMPLIANCE GUIDELINES
TABLE OF CONTENTS

- 3.6 Modifications
  - 3.6.1 Policies • Procedures
  - 3.6.2 Elements • Services
  - 3.6.3 Service Animals
- 3.7 Barrier Removal
  - 3.7.1 Application
  - 3.7.2 Priorities
  - 3.7.3 Alterations
  - 3.7.4 Limited Obligation
  - 3.7.5 Movable Fixtures
  - 3.7.6 Portable Ramps
  - 3.7.7 Cinemas
  - 3.7.8 Common Remedies
- 3.8 Violation
- B--4 CONSTRUCTION • ALTERATIONS
  - 4.1 Application
  - 4.2 Design Compliance
  - 4.3 New Construction
    - 4.3.1 Discrimination
    - 4.3.2 Responsible Parties
    - 4.3.3 Implementation
    - 4.3.4 Building Accessibility
    - 4.3.5 Exceptions
  - 4.4 Alterations
    - 4.4.1 Application
    - 4.4.2 Path of Travel
      - 4.4.2.1 Landlord • Tenant
      - 4.4.2.2 Disproportionate Cost
      - 4.4.2.3 Accessibility Priority
      - 4.4.2.4 Evading Obligation
    - 4.4.3 Historic Preservation
    - 4.4.4 Residence and Commercial
  - 4.5 Elevators

ADA COMPLIANCE GUIDELINES
TABLE OF CONTENTS

- 4.5.1 Application
- 4.5.2 Exempt Buildings

B-5 ENFORCEMENT
- 5.1 Civil Suit
  - 5.1.1 Complaint
  - 5.1.2 Injunctive Relief
  - 5.1.3 Public Concern
- 5.2 Attorney General
  - 5.2.1 Investigation
  - 5.2.2 Compliance Review
  - 5.2.3 Cause for Action
- 5.3 Authority of the Court
  - 5.3.1 Plaintiff Relief
  - 5.3.2 Punitive Damages
  - 5.3.3 Attorney Fees
  - 5.3.4 Judicial Consideration
- 5.4 Dispute Resolution
- 5.5 Violations
- 5.6 Non-Compliance
- 5.7 Implementation Dates

B-6 BUILDING CODE CERTIFICATION
- 6.1 Submitting Official
- 6.2 Code Application
  - 6.2.1 Filing Procedure
  - 6.2.2 Documentation Submittal
  - 6.2.3 Administrative Entity
  - 6.2.4 Public Notification and Review
- 6.3 Certification Denial
  - 6.3.1 Notification
  - 6.3.2 Supplemental Documentation
  - 6.3.3 Failure to Respond
  - 6.3.4 Certification Re-evaluation

ADA COMPLIANCE GUIDELINES
TABLE OF CONTENTS

      6.3.5 Certification Decision
  6.4 Preliminary Determination
  6.5 Code Certification
  6.6 Model Codes

Section C: ACCESSIBILITY DESIGN STANDARDS
C-1 MINIMUM REQUIREMENTS
    1.1 Buildings • Facilities
        1.1.1 New Design • Construction
        1.1.2 Special Use
        1.1.3 Temporary Structures
        1.1.4 Structural Impracticability
        1.1.5 Elevators
        1.1.6 Employee Areas
        1.1.7 Employee Service Areas
    1.2 Additions • Alterations
        1.2.1 Application
            1.2.1.1 Maximum Extent Feasible
            1.2.1.2 Maximum Requirement
            1.2.1.3 Non-Reduction Accessibility
            1.2.1.4 Route of Travel
            1.2.1.5 Entrances
            1.2.1.6 Altered Areas
            1.2.1.7 Vertical Travel
            1.2.1.8 Egress
            1.2.1.9 Non-Applicable Elements
        1.2.2 Primary Function Area
        1.2.3 Signs
        1.2.4 Seating Areas
        1.2.5 Performing Areas
        1.2.6 Dressing Rooms
        1.2.7 Unisex Toilet / Bathroom
        1.2.8 Toilet Stalls

ADA COMPLIANCE GUIDELINES
TABLE OF CONTENTS

- 1.2.9 Elevators
- 1.2.10 Platform Lifts
- 1.2.11 Ramps
- 1.2.12 Handrails
- 1.2.13 Door Openings
- 1.2.14 Text Telephones
- 1.3 New Construction
  - 1.3.1 Route of Travel
    - 1.3.1.1 Public Locations
    - 1.3.1.2 Buildings and Facilities
    - 1.3.1.3 Protruding Objects
    - 1.3.1.4 Walking Surfaces
  - 1.3.2 Signs
    - 1.3.2.1 International Symbol
    - 1.3.2.2 Permanent
    - 1.3.2.3 Direction • Information
    - 1.3.2.4 Temporary
  - 1.3.3 Parking
    - 1.3.3.1 Loading Zones
    - 1.3.3.2 Valet Parking
    - 1.3.3.3 Parking Lot Spaces
    - 1.3.3.4 Parking Lot Access Aisles
    - 1.3.3.5 Van Accessibility
    - 1.3.3.6 Medical Care Facilities
  - 1.3.4 Entrances
  - 1.3.5 Doors
  - 1.3.6 Stairs
  - 1.3.7 Elevators
  - 1.3.8 Egress
  - 1.3.9 Rescue Assistance
  - 1.3.10 Assembly Areas
    - 1.3.10.1 Wheelchair Spaces
    - 1.3.10.2 Aisle Seats

ADA COMPLIANCE GUIDELINES
TABLE OF CONTENTS

        1.3.10.3 Assistive Listening System
    1.3.11 Fixed Tables • Seating
    1.3.12 Dressing Rooms
    1.3.13 Toilet Facilities
        1.3.13.1 Toilet Rooms
        1.3.13.2 Limited Use
        1.3.13.3 Portable Units
    1.3.14 Bathing Facilities
        1.3.14.1 Bathing Rooms
        1.3.14.2 Portable Units
    1.3.15 Storage
    1.3.16 Merchandise Displays
    1.3.17 Drinking Fountains
    1.3.18 Public Telephones
        1.3.18.1 Accessible Telephones
        1.3.18.2 Volume Controls
        1.3.18.3 Text Telephones
        1.3.18.4 Bank of Telephones
    1.3.19 Controls
    1.3.20 Automated Teller Machines
    1.3.21 Emergency Warning Systems
    1.3.22 Detectable Warning Devices
 1.4 Historic Preservation
    1.4.1 Alterations
    1.4.2 Qualified Historic Buildings
    1.4.3 State Officer
    1.4.4 Minimum Alternatives
        1.4.4.1 Accessible Route
        1.4.4.2 Entrance
        1.4.4.3 Exhibits
        1.4.4.4 Toilet Facilities
C-2 CLEAR SPACES
 2.1 Route of Travel

C

ADA COMPLIANCE GUIDELINES
TABLE OF CONTENTS

    2.1.1 Application
    2.1.2 Surface
    2.1.3 Clear Space
    2.1.4 Doorways
    2.1.5 Locations
    2.1.6 Emergency Egress
        2.1.6.1 Rescue Assistance Areas
        2.1.6.2 Wheelchair Spaces
        2.1.6.3 Stairways
        2.1.6.4 Communication System
        2.1.6.5 Signs
        2.1.6.6 Instructions
  2.2 Protruding Objects
  2.3 Wheelchairs
    2.3.1 Pedestrian Traffic
        2.3.1.1 Straight Passage
        2.3.1.2 Walking Space
        2.3.1.3 Passing
        2.3.1.4 Two-Way Traffic
        2.3.1.5 Turning
    2.3.2 Clear Floor Space
    2.3.3 Reach Limits

C-3 COMMUNICATION MEANS
  3.1 Alarms
    3.1.1 Application
    3.1.2 Audible
    3.1.3 Visual
    3.1.4 Auxiliary
  3.2 Detectable Warnings
    3.2.1 Application
    3.2.2 Walking Surfaces
    3.2.3 Vehicle and Pedestrian Areas
    3.2.4 Reflective Pools

ADA COMPLIANCE GUIDELINES
TABLE OF CONTENTS

- 3.3 Signs
  - 3.3.1 Application
  - 3.3.2 Placement
  - 3.3.3 Accessibility Symbols
  - 3.3.4 Illumination Levels
  - 3.3.5 Finish
  - 3.3.6 Contrast
  - 3.3.7 Character Dimensions
  - 3.3.8 Raised Characters and Symbols
- 3.4 Telephones
  - 3.4.1 Application
  - 3.4.2 Reach Range
  - 3.4.3 Controls
  - 3.4.4 Cord
  - 3.4.5 Books
  - 3.4.6 Protruding Objects
  - 3.4.7 Clear Space
  - 3.4.8 Hearing Assistance
  - 3.4.9 Text Telephones
- C-4 FACILITY AREAS
  - 4.1 Assembly
    - 4.1.1 Application
    - 4.1.2 Wheelchair Locations
      - 4.1.2.1 Accessible Route
      - 4.1.2.2 Companion Seating
      - 4.1.2.3 Capacity
      - 4.1.2.4 Clustered Seating
      - 4.1.2.5 Seating Design
      - 4.1.2.6 Fixed Seats
      - 4.1.2.7 Continental Seating
    - 4.1.3 Clear Floor Space
    - 4.1.4 Floor Surfaces
    - 4.1.5 Access to Performing Areas

ADA COMPLIANCE GUIDELINES
TABLE OF CONTENTS

- 4.1.6 Listening System
  - 4.1.6.1 Placement
  - 4.1.6.2 Types
  - 4.1.6.3 Magnetic Induction Loops
  - 4.1.6.4 Radio Frequency System
  - 4.1.6.5 Interference
  - 4.1.6.6 Technical Assistance
- 4.2 Dressing Rooms
  - 4.2.1 Application
  - 4.2.2 Doors
  - 4.2.3 Mirrors
  - 4.2.4 Bench
  - 4.2.5 Wheelchair Turning Space
- 4.3 Entrances
  - 4.3.1 Application
  - 4.3.2 Route of Travel
  - 4.3.3 Service Entrances
- 4.4 Parking
  - 4.4.1 Application
  - 4.4.2 Passenger Loading Zones
  - 4.4.3 Parking Facilities
  - 4.4.4 Parking Spaces
    - 4.4.4.1 Width
    - 4.4.4.2 Vertical Clearance
    - 4.4.4.3 Ground Surface
    - 4.4.4.4 Access Aisle
    - 4.4.4.5 Route of Travel
    - 4.4.4.6 Van Accessible
    - 4.4.4.7 Universal Parking
  - 4.4.5 Signs
- 4.5 Showers • Bathrooms
  - 4.5.1 Application
  - 4.5.2 Wheelchair Turning Space

ADA COMPLIANCE GUIDELINES
TABLE OF CONTENTS

- 4.5.3 Doors
- 4.5.4 Showers • Bathtubs
- 4.5.5 Urinals
- 4.5.6 Water Closets
- 4.5.7 Toilet Stalls
- 4.5.8 Lavatories • Mirrors
- 4.5.9 Medicine Cabinets
- 4.5.10 Controls • Dispensers
- 4.5.11 Shower Stall Design

4.6 Shower Stalls
- 4.6.1 Application
- 4.6.2 Size
- 4.6.3 Seats
- 4.6.4 Curbs
- 4.6.5 Shower Enclosures
- 4.6.6 Faucets
- 4.6.7 Shower Head
- 4.6.8 Grab Bars

4.7 Storage
- 4.7.1 Application
- 4.7.2 Hardware
- 4.7.3 Floor Space
- 4.7.4 Reach Range

4.8 Toilet Rooms
- 4.8.1 Application
- 4.8.2 Doors
- 4.8.3 Toilet Stalls
- 4.8.4 Water Closets
- 4.8.5 Urinals
- 4.8.6 Lavatories • Mirrors
- 4.8.7 Controls • Dispensers
- 4.8.8 Turning Space
- 4.8.9 Unisex Toilet Rooms

ADA COMPLIANCE GUIDELINES
TABLE OF CONTENTS

- 4.9 Toilet Stalls
    - 4.9.1 Application
    - 4.9.2 Stall Door
    - 4.9.3 Grab Bars
    - 4.9.4 Toe Space
    - 4.9.5 Stall Design
- C-5 FACILITY ELEMENTS
    - 5.1 Curb Ramps
        - 5.1.1 Application
        - 5.1.2 Surface
        - 5.1.3 Slope
        - 5.1.4 Width
        - 5.1.5 Sides
        - 5.1.6 Built-Up Ramp
        - 5.1.7 Warnings
        - 5.1.8 Placement
            - 5.1.8.1 Corner Curb Ramps
            - 5.1.8.2 Crosswalks
            - 5.1.8.3 Islands
    - 5.2 Doors
        - 5.2.1 Application
        - 5.2.2 Double-Leaf Doorways
        - 5.2.3 Automatic • Power Assisted
        - 5.2.4 Revolving Doors • Turnstiles
        - 5.2.5 Gates
        - 5.2.6 Doors in Series
        - 5.2.7 Hardware
        - 5.2.8 Thresholds
        - 5.2.9 Clearances
        - 5.2.10 Clear Space
        - 5.2.11 Closer
        - 5.2.12 Opening force
    - 5.3 Elevators

ADA COMPLIANCE GUIDELINES
TABLE OF CONTENTS

- 5.3.1 Application
- 5.3.2 Illumination
- 5.3.3 Floor Designation
- 5.3.4 Call Buttons
- 5.3.5 Hall Lanterns
- 5.3.6 Control Panel
- 5.3.7 Location Indicator
- 5.3.8 Car Floor Space
- 5.3.9 Floor Surfaces
- 5.3.10 Operation
- 5.3.11 Door and Signal Timing
- 5.3.12 Door Reopening Device
- 5.3.13 Door Delay
- 5.3.14 Emergency Communication

5.4 Floor • Ground Surfaces
- 5.4.1 Application
- 5.4.2 Surface Conditions
- 5.4.3 Static Coefficient
- 5.4.4 Level Change
- 5.4.5 Carpet
- 5.4.6 Gratings

5.5 Platform Lifts
- 5.5.1 Application
- 5.5.2 Operation

5.6 Ramps
- 5.6.1 Application
- 5.6.2 Slope • Rise
- 5.6.3 Surfaces
- 5.6.4 Landings
- 5.6.5 Clear Width
- 5.6.6 Edge Protection
- 5.6.7 Exterior Ramps
- 5.6.8 Handrails

ADA COMPLIANCE GUIDELINES
TABLE OF CONTENTS

- 5.7 Stairs
    - 5.7.1 Application
    - 5.7.2 Riser • Tread
    - 5.7.3 Nosing
    - 5.7.4 Handrails
    - 5.7.5 Exterior Stairways
- 5.8 Windows
    - 5.8.1 Operation
    - 5.8.2 Hardware

C-6 FACILITY FIXTURES
- 6.1 Automated Teller Machines
    - 6.1.1 Application
    - 6.1.2 Controls
    - 6.1.3 Clear Space
    - 6.1.4 Vision Impairments
- 6.2 Bathtubs
    - 6.2.1 Application
    - 6.2.2 Faucets
    - 6.2.3 Shower Head
    - 6.2.4 Seats
    - 6.2.5 Enclosures
    - 6.2.6 Grab Bars
    - 6.2.7 Clear Floor Space
- 6.3 Equipment • Controls
    - 6.3.1 Application
    - 6.3.2 Operation
    - 6.3.3 Clear Space
    - 6.3.4 Height
- 6.4 Drinking Facilities
    - 6.4.1 Application
    - 6.4.2 Spouts
    - 6.4.3 Controls
    - 6.4.4 Clear Space

ADA COMPLIANCE GUIDELINES
TABLE OF CONTENTS

- 6.5 Handrails • Grab Bars • Seats
    - 6.5.1 Application
    - 6.5.2 Size • Spacing
        - 6.5.2.1 Grip Size
        - 6.5.2.2 Safety Clearance
        - 6.5.2.3 Recess Allowance
    - 6.5.3 Surfaces
    - 6.5.4 Structural Strength
        - 6.5.4.1 Shear Force
        - 6.5.4.2 Tensile Force
        - 6.5.4.3 Shear Stress
        - 6.5.4.4 Bending Stress
- 6.6 Lavatories • Mirrors
    - 6.6.1 Application
    - 6.6.2 Height
    - 6.6.3 Faucets
    - 6.6.4 Knee Space
    - 6.6.5 Floor Space
    - 6.6.6 Mirrors
- 6.7 Fixed Tables • Seating
    - 6.7.1 Application
    - 6.7.2 Floor Space
    - 6.7.3 Knee Space
    - 6.7.4 Worktable Height
- 6.8 Sinks
    - 6.8.1 Application
    - 6.8.2 Height
    - 6.8.3 Bowl Depth
    - 6.8.4 Faucets
    - 6.8.5 Knee Space
    - 6.8.6 Floor Space
- 6.9 Urinals
    - 6.9.1 Application

ADA COMPLIANCE GUIDELINES
TABLE OF CONTENTS

    6.9.2 Type
    6.9.3 Flush Device
    6.9.4 Shields
    6.9.5 Clear Space
6.10 Water Closets
    6.10.1 Application
    6.10.2 Height
    6.10.3 Flush Device
    6.10.4 Paper Dispensers
    6.10.5 Grab Bars
    6.10.6 Floor Space

C-7 SPECIFIC OCCUPANCIES
  7.1 Libraries
    7.1.1 Application
    7.1.2 Stacks
    7.1.3 Reading Areas
    7.1.4 Files • Displays
    7.1.5 Check-out Areas
  7.2 Lodging
    7.2.1 Application
        7.2.1.1 Lodging Facilities
        7.2.1.2 Rooms • Units
        7.2.1.3 Passageways
        7.2.1.4 Visual Alarms
        7.2.1.5 Telephones
        7.2.1.6 General Public Areas
    7.2.2 Minimum Requirements
        7.2.2.1 Accessible Route
        7.2.2.2 Accessible Spaces
        7.2.2.3 Maneuvering Space
        7.2.2.4 Doorways
        7.2.2.5 Storage
        7.2.2.6 Accessible Controls

ADA COMPLIANCE GUIDELINES
TABLE OF CONTENTS

       7.2.2.7 Visual Alarms
       7.2.2.8 Kitchens • Wet Bars
   7.2.3 Communication Devices
       7.2.3.1 Telephones
       7.2.3.2 Visual Alarms
       7.2.3.3 Equivalent Facilitation
   7.2.4 Commercial Facilities • Dormitories
       7.2.4.1 Sleeping Accommodations
       7.2.4.2 Accommodation Choice
       7.2.4.3 Roll-in-Shower
       7.2.4.4 Alterations
   7.2.5 Social Service Lodging
       7.2.5.1 Application
       7.2.5.2 New Construction
       7.2.5.3 Alterations
7.3 Medical Care Facilities
   7.3.1 Application
       7.3.1.1 Facility Defined
       7.3.1.2 Design • Construction
   7.3.2 Patient Bedrooms
   7.3.3 Patient Toilet Room
   7.3.4 Facility Entrances
7.4 Mercantile
   7.4.1 Application
   7.4.2 Sales • Service Counters
   7.4.3 Check-Out Aisles
       7.4.3.1 New Construction
       7.4.3.2 Alterations
   7.4.4 Security Bollards
7.5 Restaurants • Cafeterias
   7.5.1 Application
   7.5.2 Counters • Bars
   7.5.3 Dining Area

ADA COMPLIANCE GUIDELINES
TABLE OF CONTENTS

    7.5.4 Aisles
    7.5.5 Food Service Lines
    7.5.6 Self-Service Areas
    7.5.7 Vending Machines • Equipment
    7.5.8 Platforms
  7.6 Transportation

Section D: CALIFORNIA ACCESS CODE
D-1 GENERAL PROVISIONS
  1.1 Purpose
  1.2 Application
    1.2.1 Publicly Funded
    1.2.2 Privately Funded
  1.3 Priority Order
  1.4 Fire Codes
  1.5 Office of the State Architect/AC
  1.6 Administrative Agency
  1.7 Special Provisions
D-2 GROUP OCCUPANCIES
  2.1 General
  2.2 Group A - Assembly Facilities
    2.2.1 Auditoriums • Assembly Halls
      2.2.1.1 Ticket Booths
      2.2.1.2 Seating
      2.2.1.3 Performing Areas
      2.2.1.4 Public Areas
    2.2.2 Sport Facilities
      2.2.2.1 Ticket Booth
      2.2.2.2 Spectator Seating
      2.2.2.3 Participation Areas
      2.2.2.4 Sanitary • Locker Rooms
      2.2.2.5 Club Rooms

ADA COMPLIANCE GUIDELINES
TABLE OF CONTENTS

- 2.2.3 Banquet • Bar Facilities
  - 2.2.3.1 Functional Activity
  - 2.2.3.2 Entrances
  - 2.2.3.3 Seating
  - 2.2.3.4 Self-service Areas
  - 2.2.3.5 Food Service Lines
  - 2.2.3.6 Food Preparation Areas
  - 2.2.3.7 Restrooms
- 2.2.4 Religious Facilities
  - 2.2.4.1 Sanctuary
  - 2.2.4.2 Sanitary Facilities
  - 2.2.4.3 Classrooms • Offices
  - 2.2.4.4 Assembly Areas
  - 2.2.4.5 Assistive-Listening Systems
- 2.3 Group B - Business Facilities
  - 2.3.1 Office • Service Facilities
  - 2.3.2 Specific Facilities • Areas
    - 2.3.2.1 Offices Facilities
    - 2.3.2.2 Retail Facilities
    - 2.3.2.3 Service Facilities
    - 2.3.2.4 Publicly Used Areas
    - 2.3.2.5 Public Service Facilities
    - 2.3.2.6 Factories • Warehouses
    - 2.3.2.7 Assembly Areas
    - 2.3.2.8 Dining • Banquet • Bar
    - 2.3.2.9 General Access Standards
- 2.4 Group E - Educational Facilities
  - 2.4.1 Libraries
  - 2.4.2 Cubicles • Study Carrels
  - 2.4.3 Laboratory Rooms
- 2.5 Group H - Hazardous Materials
- 2.6 Group I - Institutional Facilities
  - 2.6.1 Application

ADA COMPLIANCE GUIDELINES
TABLE OF CONTENTS

    2.6.2 Entrances
    2.6.3 Office • Suites
    2.6.4 Offices • Waiting Areas
    2.6.5 Diagnostic • Treatment Areas
    2.6.6 Patient Rooms
        2.6.6.1 Application
        2.6.6.2 Accessible Patient Rooms
        2.6.6.3 Patient Toilet Rooms
2.7 Group M - Maintenance Facilities
    2.7.1 Parks • Recreation Areas
        2.7.1.1 Highway Rest Areas
        2.7.1.2 Parking Lots
        2.7.1.3 Campsites
        2.7.1.4 Beaches • Picnic Areas
        2.7.1.5 Boat Docks
        2.7.1.6 Sanitary Facilities
        2.7.1.7 Trails
        2.7.1.8 Nature Trails
        2.7.1.9 Buildings
2.8 Group R - Residential • Lodging
    2.8.1 Transient Lodging
        2.8.1.1 Guest Rooms • Suites
        2.8.1.2 Dormitory Rooms
        2.8.1.3 Toilet Facilities
        2.8.1.4 Kitchens
        2.8.1.5 Notification devices
        2.8.1.6 Public • Common Areas
        2.8.1.7 Recreational Facilities
    2.8.2 Transient Lodging Bathrooms
    2.8.3 Buildings • Multi-Unit Complexes
        2.8.3.1 Publicly • Private Funded
        2.8.3.2 Multi-Story Buildings
        2.8.3.3 Public • Common Use Areas

ADA COMPLIANCE GUIDELINES
TABLE OF CONTENTS

      2.8.3.4 Adaptable Dwelling Units
  2.8.4 Dwelling Bathrooms
D-3 MINIMUM REQUIREMENTS
  3.1 Application
  3.2 Alterations
    3.2.1 Application
    3.2.2 Limitations
    3.2.3 Undue Hardship
    3.2.4 Buildings Without Elevators
    3.2.5 Exceptions
  3.3 Route of Travel
    3.3.1 Applicable Areas • Elements
    3.3.2 Corridors
    3.3.3 Elevators
    3.3.4 Entrances • Exits
    3.3.5 Ramps
    3.3.6 Exterior Routes
    3.3.7 Multiple Routes
    3.3.8 Signs
    3.3.9 Protruding Objects
    3.3.10 Exceptions
  3.4 Wheelchair Space
  3.5 Rescue Assistance Areas
  3.6 Employee Areas
  3.7 Historic Preservation
  3.8 Alarms
  3.9 Detectable Warnings
  3.10 Signs
    3.10.1 Entrances
    3.10.2 Information
    3.10.3 Traffic Control Devices
  3.11 Telephones

ADA COMPLIANCE GUIDELINES
TABLE OF CONTENTS

- 3.12 Parking
    - 3.12.1 Application
    - 3.12.2 Health Care Facilities
    - 3.12.3 Passenger Loading Zones
    - 3.12.4 Valet Parking
- 3.13 Shower • Bathrooms
- 3.14 Storage
- 3.15 Toilet Rooms
- 3.16 Doors
- 3.17 Floors • Levels

D-4 ROUTE OF TRAVEL
- 4.1 Corridors
- 4.2 Elevators
    - 4.2.1 Cars
    - 4.2.2 Doors
    - 4.2.3 Controls
    - 4.2.4 Lanterns
    - 4.2.5 Jamb Symbols
    - 4.2.6 Intercommunication
    - 4.2.7 Lobby Enclosures
    - 4.2.8 Smoke-Detection
    - 4.2.9 Standby Power
    - 4.2.10 Wheelchair Lifts
- 4.3 Ramps
    - 4.3.1 Primary Entrance
    - 4.3.2 Slope
    - 4.3.3 Landings
    - 4.3.4 Handrails
- 4.4 Curb Ramps
    - 4.4.1 Ramp
    - 4.4.2 Grade Separations

ADA COMPLIANCE GUIDELINES
TABLE OF CONTENTS

- D-5 COMMUNICATIONS
  - 5.1 Alarms
    - 5.1.1 Visual
    - 5.1.2 Audible
  - 5.2 Detectable Warnings
    - 5.2.1 Texture
    - 5.2.2 Vehicular Areas
    - 5.2.3 Curb Ramps
    - 5.2.4 Transit Boarding Platforms
  - 5.3 Signs
    - 5.3.1 International Symbol
    - 5.3.2 Specifications
    - 5.3.3 Braille Symbols
    - 5.3.4 Placement
    - 5.3.5 Information Signs
    - 5.3.6 Entrance Signs
    - 5.3.7 Traffic Control Devices
  - 5.4 Telephones
    - 5.4.1 Height
    - 5.4.2 Enclosures
    - 5.4.3 Text Telephones
- D-6 FACILITY AREAS
  - 6.1 Parking
    - 6.1.1 Spaces
    - 6.1.2 Structures
    - 6.1.3 Signs
  - 6.2 Shower • Bath
    - 6.2.1 Application
    - 6.2.2 Bathtubs
    - 6.2.3 Showers
    - 6.2.4 Open Showers
    - 6.2.5 Shower • Bathtub Enclosures
    - 6.2.6 Lockers

ADA COMPLIANCE GUIDELINES
TABLE OF CONTENTS

- 6.3 Toilet Rooms
  - 6.3.1 Application
  - 6.3.2 Identification Symbols
  - 6.3.3 Passageway
  - 6.3.4 Single Accommodation
  - 6.3.5 Multiple Accommodation
  - 6.3.6 Grab Bars
  - 6.3.7 Fixtures • Accessories
- D-7 BUILDING ELEMENTS
  - 7.1 Doors
    - 7.1.1 Application
    - 7.1.2 Doors
    - 7.1.3 Door Hardware
    - 7.1.4 Landings
    - 7.1.5 Thresholds
    - 7.1.6 Operation
    - 7.1.7 Design
    - 7.1.8 Turnstiles
    - 7.1.9 Exceptions
  - 7.2 Stairs
    - 7.2.1 Steps
    - 7.2.2 Striping
    - 7.2.3 Handrails
    - 7.2.4 Signs
- D-8 FIXTURES
  - 8.1 Automated Teller Machines
  - 8.2 Controls
  - 8.3 Drinking Fountains
  - 8.4 Fixed Seating • Counters
  - 8.5 Vending Machines

ADA COMPLIANCE GUIDELINES
GRAPHIC ILLUSTRATIONS

ADA ACCESSIBILITY GUIDELINES			
Illustration #		Description	Page #
		C-2 Clear Spaces	
1	a,b	Accessible Route Minimum Clearance	106
2	a,b	Walking Parallel to a Wall	110
3		Wall-Mounted Objects	111
4	a	Protruding Stair Hazard	111
4	b	Post-Mounted Objects	111
5		Protection Around Wall-Mounted Objects	112
6	a,b	Cane Techniques	112
7		Straight Passage Minimum Clearance	113
8		Two-way Traffic Minimum Clearances	114
9		Wheelchairs Passing	114
10	a,b	Minimum Turning Space	115
11		Recommended Clearance	115
12	a,b	Alcove Space	116
13		Adult Size Wheelchair Dimension	117
14	a,b	Forward Reach	117
15	a,b,c	Side Reach	118
16		Wheelchair Reach Range	119
		C-3 Communication Means	
17	a-d	International Symbols of Accessibility	126

ADA COMPLIANCE GUIDELINES
GRAPHIC ILLUSTRATIONS

Illustration #		Description	Page #
18	a,b	Telephone Placement	132
		C-4 Facility Areas	
19	a,b	Wheelchair Seating Spaces in Series	138
20		Loading Zone Access Aisle	144
21		Parking Space Dimensions	146
22		Van Accessible Aisle at End of Row	147
23		Universal Parking Design	148
24	a,b	Roll-in Shower Toilet Rooms	150
25		Shower Seat Design	151
26	a,b	Shower Enclosure Dimensions	152
27	a,b	Shower Grab Bars	153
28	a,b	Storage	155
29	a-d	Toilet Stalls	160-1
		C-5 Facility Elements	
30		Curb Ramp Slope Measurement	163
31		Flared Sides	164
32		Built-up Curb Ramp	164
33		Returned Curb	164
34	a-d	Curb Ramps at Marked Crossings	165
35		Two Hinged Doors in Series	168
36	a,b,c	Doorway Clearance	169

ADA COMPLIANCE GUIDELINES
GRAPHIC ILLUSTRATIONS

Illustration #		Description	Page #
37		Maximum Opening Depth	169
38	a-f	Maneuvering Clearance at Doors	170-1
39		Hoistway and Elevator Entrance	173
40		Elevator Panel Location with Center Door	174
41		Elevator Panel Location with Side Door	174
42		Elevator Control Panel	175
43		Control Panel Height	176
44		Elevator Car Minimum Dimensions	177
45		Timing Equation	178
46		Level Change	180
47		Floor Beveled Edge	181
48		Carpet Height	181
49		Grating	181
50		Grating Orientation	181
51		Single Ramp and Dimensions	183
52	a-d	Edge Protection and Handrail Extensions	185
53		Flush Riser	187
54		Rounded Nosing	187
55	a,b	Stair Handrails	187
56	a,b	Handrail Extensions	188

ADA COMPLIANCE GUIDELINES
GRAPHIC ILLUSTRATIONS

Illustration #		Description	Page #
C-6 Facility Fixtures			
57	a,b	Bathtub Grab Bars	192
58	a,b	Bathtub Clear Floor Space	193
59	a,b	Reach Limitations	194
60		Spout Height and Knee Clearance	195
61		Clear Floor Space	196
62	a,b	Parallel Approach to Drinking Units	197
63	a-e	Rail and Bar Size and Spacing	198
64		Lavatory Clearances	200
65		Accessible Floor Space	201
66	a,b	Wheelchair Seating	202
67	a,b	Water Closet and Grab Bars	206
68	a,b	Water Closet Transfers	207-8
69		Clear Floor Space	208
C-7 Specific Occupancies			
70		Stacks	209
71		Card Catalog	210
72	a,b	Roll-in Shower with Folding Seat	216
73		Restaurant Food Service Lines	226
74		Restaurant Self-Service Areas	227

ADA COMPLIANCE GUIDELINES
GRAPHIC ILLUSTRATIONS

CALIFORNIA ACCESS CODE			
Illustration #		Description	Page #
D-2 Group Occupancies			
75		Restaurant Self-Service Areas	244
D-4 Route of Travel			
76		Corridors over 200 feet	294
77	a,b	Ramps	304
77	c	Ramp Door Landing	305
78	a-d	Curb Ramps	306-7
79	a	Detectable Warning Groove Detail	308
79	b	Recessed Ramp with Grooved Border	308
80		Corner Curb Ramp with Detectable Warning	308
81		Typical Curb Ramp with Detectable Warning	309
82	a,b	Detectable Warnings	309
83	a,b,c	Curb Ramps	310-2
D-5 Communications			
84	a,b	Full-Height Telephone Enclosures	319
D-6 Facility Areas			
85	a,b,c	Parking Spaces	322
86		Bathtub Reinforcement	326
87		Shower Stalls	327
88		Shower Stall Reinforcement	328

xxxvii

ADA COMPLIANCE GUIDELINES
GRAPHIC ILLUSTRATIONS

Illustration #		Description	Page #
89		Open Showers	329
90		Toilet Facility Symbols	330
91		Toilet Rooms	333
92	a,b,c	Accessible Toilet Facilities	334-5
93		Equivalent Facilitation/ Existing Construction	335
94		Reinforcement Areas	336
95	a,b,c	Exit Doors	340-1
		D-7 Building Elements	
96		Threshold Details	341
97		Door Design	342
98		Striping Detail	343
		D-8 Building Fixtures	
99		ATM Reach Range Limits	348
100	a,b	Drinking Fountains	350

ADA COMPLIANCE GUIDELINES
TABLE ILLUSTRATIONS

TABLE #	ACCESSIBILITY TOPICS	SECTION	SECTION #	TABLE	PAGE #
A-A	Public Accommodations	A	-	A	22
C-1A	Parking	C	1	A	91
C-1B	Fixed Seating • Tables	C	1	B	96
C-1C	Telephones	C	1	C	100
C-3A	Alarms	C	3	A	121
C-3B	Signs	C	3	B	128-9
C-4A	Assistive Listening	C	4	A	140-1
C-6A	Work Surface Heights	C	6	A	203
C-7A	Accessible Rooms	C	7	A	214
C-7A	Accessible Elements	C	7	A	214
C-7B	Roll-in Showers	C	7	B	215
C-7C	Check-out Aisles	C	7	C	224
D-2A	Entrances	D	2	A	274-5

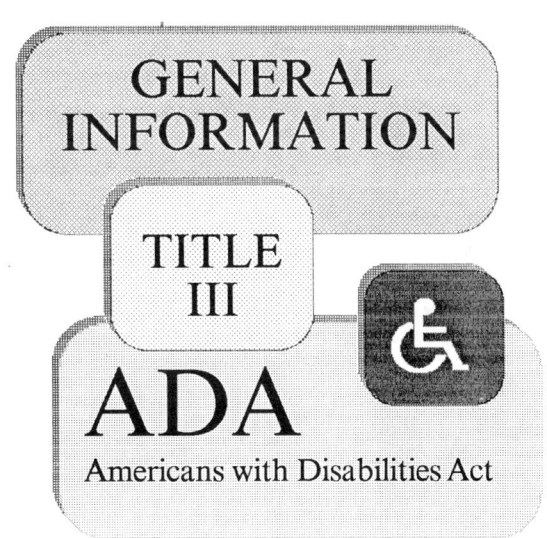

SECTION A

Introductory information helpful in understanding the American with Disabilities Act and requirements.

INTRODUCTION
Americans With Disabilities Act

The Americans with Disabilities Act (ADA) was enacted on July 26, 1990. The ADA contains five major categories prohibiting discrimination. Title I in employment, Title II in public services and transportation, Title III in public accommodations, Title IV in telecommunications, and Title V covers miscellaneous. Title III of the Act was implemented January 26, 1992. Non-compliance of this new law may result in civil actions as well as investigations and litigation conducted by the Attorney General against offenders.

This handbook provides a quick and easy reference to the minimum standard requirements with graphic illustrations in compliance with Title III as well as general information, terminology, and understanding of the ADA. Title III consists of seven sections which include general application, general requirements, specific requirements, new construction and alterations, enforcement, state laws or local building code certification, and accessibility guideline standards for buildings and facilities. The guidelines contained herein are the minimum requirements for accessibility affecting all new construction. The law also requires architectural and communication barriers to be removed in existing public accommodations where "readily achievable". Building permits and certificates of occupancy are no assurance a building complies since state and local building codes may differ from the ADA accessibility requirements. All business and building owners are responsible for carefully assessing, removing, or preparing a plan of action for the removal of existing barriers. The subject matter contained in this handbook was obtained from the Department of Justice's final rules implementing Title III of the ADA printed in the *Federal Register* 28 CFR Part 36, July 26, 1991.

ADA OVERVIEW
Law and Information Source

The American with Disabilities Act (ADA) is designed to extend civil rights protection to persons with disabilities. The Act prohibits discrimination against individuals with disabilities and is defined in five categories. They are employment, public services, public accommodations, telecommunications, and miscellaneous.

TITLE I: Employment

An employer may not discriminate against an individual with a disability in a job application or employment who is otherwise qualified for the job. Reasonable accommodations such as equipment modification and job restructuring must be provided by employers for persons with disabilities. Expense to accommodate an employee with a disability shall not be borne by that employee.
Additional information source:
Equal Employment Opportunity Commission
1801 L Street N.W., Washington, D.C. 20507
Phone: 1-800-669-4000 or 1-800-800-3302 (TDD)

TITLE II: Public Services

Subtitle A: Prohibits discrimination against persons with disabilities by State and local government services.
Subtitle B: Provides accessibility to persons with disabilities on public transportation facilities.
Additional information source:
U.S. Department of Transportation
400 Seventh Street S.W., Washington, D.C. 20590
Phone: 202-366-9305 or 202-755-7687 (TDD)

ADA OVERVIEW
Law and Information Source

TITLE III: Public Accommodations

Prohibits discrimination against persons with disabilities in commercial facilities and places of public accommodation. Access and accommodations shall be provided equally or similar to those available for the general public.

Information source:
Office of the Americans with Disabilities Act
Civil Rights Division, U.S. Department of Justice
P.O. Box 66118, Washington, D.C. 20035-6118
Phone: 202-514-0301, or 202-514-0383 (TDD)

Technical accessibility information source:
US Architectural & Transportation Barriers Compliance Board
1111 18th Street N.W., Suite 501, Washington, D. C. 20036
Phone: 1-800-872-2253 or 202-272-5449 (voice, TDD)

TITLE IV: Telecommunications

Public communication companies shall make telecommunication services and equipment available and accessible to persons with disabilities.

Information source:
Federal Communications Commission
1919 M Street N.W., Washington, D.C. 20554
Phone: 202-632-7260 or 202-632-1836 (TDD)

TITLE V: Miscellaneous

COMPLIANCE ENACTMENT SCHEDULE

AMERICAN WITH DISABILITIES ACT
TITLE III

July 26, 1990 - The President signed the ADA.

July 26, 1991 - ADA final regulations were issued.

January 26, 1992 - ADA regulations became effective.
- Existing barriers should be removed.
- All construction alteration projects must comply.
- Civil action could not be filed against businesses with 25 or fewer employees and gross receipts of $1,000,000 or less prior to this date.

January 26, 1993 -
- Design and new construction must comply when (1) the last building permit or extension is filed after January 26, 1992, or (2) the first certificate of occupancy is issued after January 26, 1993.
- Civil action can not be filed against businesses with 10 or fewer employees and gross receipts of $500,000 or less prior to this date.

CALIFORNIA ACCESS CODE
TITLE 24

The California Access Code is in the process of adoption. The Office of the State Architect projects the SBSC to adopt the new regulations by January, 1993. Once adopted by the SBSC, the accessibility code becomes effective six months after publication.

UNDERSTANDING ADA TERMINOLOGY

The following terminology relates to the Americans with Disabilities Act accessibility guidelines and the California Code of Regulations, Title 24, Access Code. " CA " notes a change, addition, or an individual meaning under California regulations and is shown in "this print".

access aisle
  Adequate space for pedestrian traffic between elements allowing accessibility and usability of those elements.

accessibility
  A site, facility, or portion thereof that complies with the ADA accessibility guideline standards which allows access, circulation, and full use by persons with disabilities.

accessible
  Approachable and usable by persons with disabilities CA in compliance with the California Access Code.

accessible element
  Elements specified by the ADA accessibility guidelines which provide for the usability of particular services, goods, and accommodations by persons with disabilities which would otherwise be a barrier for those persons.
  CA An element specified by the access code regulations adopted by the Office of the State Architect.

accessible route of travel
  A continuous unobstructed pathway conforming to the ADA accessibility guidelines for persons with disabilities which connects all the accessible elements and spaces of an accessible building or facility. CA A path of travel shall be negotiable by persons with severe disabilities using a wheelchair and is safe and usable by others with disabilities.

UNDERSTANDING ADA TERMINOLOGY

accessible space
Any space that is in compliance with the ADA accessibility guideline standards. ^{CA} Space complying with the access code regulations adopted by the Office of the State Architect.

ADA
Americans with Disabilities Act, or "the Act", giving persons with disabilities comprehensive civil rights protection in places of public accommodation, employment, telecommunication, and in state and local governments.

ADAAG
Americans with Disabilities Act Accessibility Guidelines

adaptability
The capability to alter or add elements, modify spaces or facilities to meet the needs of a person or group of persons.

adaptable dwelling units
^{CA} Dwelling units that comply with the adoptable requirements of the California Access Code, Section 3103.

administrative authority
A government agency that adopts or enforces building regulations and guidelines.

alteration
A change to an existing building, facility, or a part thereof that affects or may affect its usability. For clarification of usage with the ADA, an alteration does not fall within normal maintenance improvements. Alterations fall within the categories of remodeling, reconstruction, restorations, renovations, rehabilitations, rearrangements, or changes of walls and other structural elements. A "substantial alteration" is where the total cost of all alterations within a

UNDERSTANDING ADA TERMINOLOGY

twelve month period is 50 percent or greater than the assessed value of the building or facility being altered.

CA Any change, addition, or modification in construction or occupancy.

architectural barrier
An object that blocks the access of a person with a disability to facilities which are available to the public and accessible by persons without disabilities.

area of rescue assistance
An area protected from fire and smoke having direct access to an exit where people not capable of using stairs may wait in safety for assistance during an emergency evacuation.

assembly building
CA A building or portion thereof, used or intended to be used, for the gathering of 50 or more people for a specific purpose or use, or used for showing motion pictures with a gathering of 10 or more people when open to the public and an admission is charged.

automatic door
A power-operated door equipped with opening and closing controls actuated by a signal from a floor mat, manual switch, photoelectric device, or other mechanism.

automatic teller machine (ATM)
CA Any electronic information processing device, including a point of sale machine, for the purpose of executing financial transactions between a business entity or financial institution and its customers. An ATM does not include card reading devices at vehicle facilities and fuel pumps.

auxiliary aids
A means of providing aid in communication to those with physical impairments. Public accommodations are to provide auxiliary aids and services to ensure effective commu-

UNDERSTANDING ADA TERMINOLOGY

nication where individuals with disabilities are not excluded or denied their services or the use of their facilities.

barrier removal
Architectural and communication barriers are to be removed in existing facilities if readily achievable with minimal difficulty or expense. Modification of compliance regulations may be available for existing accommodations that are not available for new construction. The established order of priority to remove barriers in the path of travel is as follows: first, the facility access; second, the facility areas providing goods and services; and third, the facility restrooms. ADA compliance places a continuing obligation on public accommodations to assess and remove accessibility barriers.

barrier removal alternatives
Where a barrier removal is not readily achievable, the public accommodation must provide an alternative method of accommodation to individuals with disabilities such as display rearrangement, curb service, home delivery or other services which are readily achievable.

building code certification
The Attorney General may certify a state or local building code which meets or exceeds the minimum ADA accessibility requirements. Certification reapplication is required on any amendment to a certified code. In enforcement proceedings, certification constitutes rebuttable evidence that a code meets or exceeds the ADA requirements.

building official
CA An officer, designated authority, or their representative charged with the administration and enforcement of the California Building Code.

UNDERSTANDING ADA TERMINOLOGY

building owner / tenant responsibility
 Both the landlord and the tenant are subject to the ADA requirements. The statutory language places an equal responsibility on both parties with allocation of liability in accordance to their lease agreement provisions. The landlord generally provides services in the common area, and tenants provide services in their place of public accommodation.

certificate of equivalency
 Certification that a code meets or exceeds the ADA minimum standard requirements for accessibility and usability of facilities covered by Title III of the ADA.

circulation path
 An interior or exterior pedestrian passageway, or combination thereof, connecting one place to another.

civil rights legislation
 The ADA is enforceable under the civil rights laws. It is not a building code.

clear floor space
 The minimum unobstructed floor area needed to accommodate a person in a wheelchair.

closed circuit telephone
 A telephone line or network within and for the sole purpose of a particular building or facility.

code
 Applicable to the ADA, a code is a law, local building code or similar ordinance, or a part thereof that establishes an accessibility requirement.

UNDERSTANDING ADA TERMINOLOGY

commerce
Trade, commerce, communication, transportation, travel, or traffic conducted between two states, within the same state through another state or foreign country, or between a state and a foreign country or its territory.

commerce clause
"Operations affect commerce" includes local business operations which affect interstate commerce through the purchase or sale of products manufactured in other states. This includes retail activities, providing services, and recreation facilities.

commercial facility
A facility used by a private entity for nonresidential purposes that affects commerce. For ADA purposes, a commercial facility does not fall within the definition of the dictionary or as commonly used in industry. Commercial facility covers a broader range to include all types of activities under the Constitution's commerce clause. It also includes facilities in which employment may occur. Airports operated by public entities are covered by Title II of the Act. Places of public accommodation located within airports are included in Title III. Facilities covered or exempted under the Fair Housing Act of 1968 are exempt from Title III.

common use
Space or elements available and for the use of a restricted group of people.

communication barrier
A facility's failure to provide the means necessary for a person with a disability to receive the necessary and pertinent information allowing that individual the full use of a facil-

UNDERSTANDING ADA TERMINOLOGY

ity or accessibility to its provisions.

congregate residence
^{CA} The term "congregate residence" replaces the term "dormitory" in the California Building Code.

construction standards
The Americans with Disabilities Act Accessibility Guidelines (ADAAG) has been published by the Architectural and Transportation Barriers Compliance Board and adopted as the minimum accessibility standards to ensure that buildings and facilities are accessible in terms of architecture, design, and communication to persons with disabilities. Alternatives to the ADA requirement standards may be permitted when determined as equal in accessibility and usability.

cross slope
A slope perpendicular to the direction of travel.

curb cut
An interruption in a curb at a pedestrian way allowing for a curb ramp.

curb ramp
A sloped surface built-up to a curb or cut through a curb that separates two ground levels providing a consistent walking surface with a gradual grade transition between the levels.

detectable warning
A standard element or texture applied or built into walking surfaces that is detectable by visually impaired individuals to warn them of hazards within the walkway.

UNDERSTANDING ADA TERMINOLOGY

disability
A limitation on one or more of life's primary activities due to a physical or mental impairment, having a record of impairment, or perceived as having an impairment. Such a person is considered to be an individual with a "disability" and is protected under the ADA. Impairments may be a physical disability in walking, seeing, vocal, hearing, respiratory, or cardiovascular; or a mental disability in learning, retardation, emotional or mental illness. A primary life activity includes such things as caring for oneself, walking, seeing, speaking, breathing, learning, and performing manual tasks.

disproportionate costs
Providing a path of travel to an altered area will be deemed disproportionate when the cost exceeds 20 percent of the primary function area's overall alteration cost.

dormitory
A room occupied by more than two people.

dwelling unit
A unit containing space for living, bathing, sleeping and food preparation. Within the ADA guidelines, a dwelling unit does not imply its use as a residence.

egress route
A means of egress by way of a continuous and unobstructed travel route to a public way from any point within a building or facility including vertical travel. An accessible egress route or means also complies with the ADA accessibility guideline standards and does not include inaccessible features such as stairs or escalators.

UNDERSTANDING ADA TERMINOLOGY

element
An architectural, mechanical, or landscaping component of a building, facility, or site.

elevator bank
A bank of elevators is a single or group of elevators that respond to a single call button. There is no limit in the number of cars in a bank, but no more than four cars shall be in a common hoistway.

enforcement
A person may file a lawsuit for preventive relief when such person is subject to discrimination or has reasonable belief there is "about to be" discrimination based on their disability. The court may appoint an attorney for the complainant and authorize civil action without payment of fees. The Attorney General is expected to engage in active enforcement with sufficient resources.

enforcing agency
  CA A department or agency designated by statute.

entrance
The passageway and elements which lead to and access through a point of entry or series of entries to access a building, a place of accommodation, or a commercial facility.

equivalent facilitation
An alternate means of ADAAG compliance with like or similar results. Alternative designs and technologies may be permitted when equivalent accessibility and usability of another facility or site is provided.

UNDERSTANDING ADA TERMINOLOGY

facility
All or part of a structure or group of structures, parking lot, passageway, equipment, rolling stock or other conveyance, or other real or personal property including the location site for which a private entity can exercise control and where a commercial facility or place of public accommodation is located.

fire-resistive
A construction means that resists the spread of fire.

"good faith" effort
The court will give consideration to any good faith effort to comply with the law in assessing an owner's actions. No building or business owner is excused or relieved of their responsibility from ADA compliance for lack of knowledge, not receiving technical assistance, or who has not willfully, intentionally, or recklessly disregarded the law. Implementation of a plan to remove existing accessibility barriers for persons with disabilities could be considered a "good faith" effort in complying with the ADA.

grab bar
A bar that can be grasped with the hand for support.

ground floor
Any floor of a building or facility that has direct access to the exterior ground level and is less than one story above or below grade.

guard rail
A vertical barrier placed along an unprotected edge of an elevated area.

health care provider
A person or entity regulated by a state that offers

UNDERSTANDING ADA TERMINOLOGY

professional services to the public for individuals seeking physical or mental health care.

hertz
A unit of frequency equal to one cycle per second.

historic property
A qualified historic building or facility that is listed or eligible for listing in the National Register of Historic Places or is designated as historic under appropriate state or local laws. Altering a qualified historic building or facility may be subject to the ADA guidelines and to the state and local historic preservation statutes. A person should consult with the Advisory Council on Historic Preservation when subject to the National Historic Preservation Act or with the State Historic Preservation Officer to determine if an alteration would threaten or destroy the historic significance of the facility. The ADA shall be complied with to the maximum extent feasible.

International Symbol of Accessibility
The symbol adopted by the Rehabilitation International 11th World Congress is internationally recognized as the symbol which signifies that a building or facility is accessible to persons with disabilities.

kick plate
A plate affixed to the bottom portion of a door that protects its surface.

lift *see platform lift*

marked crossings
A walkway identified with markings that indicates a pedestrian zone for crossing vehicular traffic lanes.

UNDERSTANDING ADA TERMINOLOGY

maximum extent feasible
In a planned alteration, compliance with the ADA accessibility guideline standards shall be provided to the maximum physical accessibility that is possible when it is virtually impossible to fully comply due to the nature of an existing building or facility. If persons with certain disabilities cannot be accommodated, the facility shall accommodate persons with other disabilities that are feasible.

mezzanine
An occupiable intermediate floor level between two consecutive floors of a building or within one story consisting of a partial floor level or balcony.

model code
A nationally recognized document developed by a private entity that is intended for incorporation or adoption for use by state and local governing agencies in developing code standards within their jurisdiction.

multi-family dwelling
Any building containing three or more dwelling units.

multiple-accommodation toilet facility
CA A room containing more than one toilet fixture intended for multiple and simultaneous use with separation compartments for privacy.

new construction • alterations
Full accessibility to persons with disabilities is required for building permits issued after January 26, 1992, and for first occupancies which occur after January 26, 1993. Compliance is required on alterations after January 26, 1992, and the related path of travel, if applicable. Alterations may include remodeling, renovations, rehabilitation, historic restoration, or structural element rearrangement. Normal maintenance such as painting, wallpapering, roof-

UNDERSTANDING ADA TERMINOLOGY

ing replacement, asbestos removal, or changes to mechanical or electrical systems are not considered alterations unless they affect the facility's use.

non-ambulatory
The inability of an individual to be mobile and unassisted. Persons that depend on mechanical aids ususaly need emergency assistance in building evacuations where stairways impede their exit.

occupiable space
An enclosed space designed for human occupancy being equipped with light, ventilation, and a means to enter and exit.

operable part
A part of equipment or an appliance that activates or deactivates, inserts or withdraws objects, or makes adjustments.

passage door
CA Any door used to pass through other than an exit door.

path of travel
An unobstructed and continuous pedestrian pathway that connects altered spaces with the exterior approaches, entrances, exits, restrooms, telephones, and drinking fountains serving the altered space including vertical accessibility where applicable.

pedestrian
CA A person who moves within a walking area with or without walking aids.

pedestrian grade separation
A structure used by pedestrians to cross over or under an obstacle or traffic way.

UNDERSTANDING ADA TERMINOLOGY

pedestrian walkway
Traffic pathway used exclusively by pedestrians.

penalties
Several types of legal remedies are available. The court will mandate injunctive relief on proven discrimination. The Justice Department can also file suit where there is reasonable cause to believe someone has engaged in a pattern or practice of discrimination in violation of the ADA. Up to $50,000 penalty on the first violation and up to $100,000 on subsequent violations may be accessed along with the correction of the violation. Civil Action may take place subsequent to January 26, 1992. Qualified small businesses have been provided an additional six to twelve months to achieve compliance. This additional time period does not apply to new construction. The courts are authorized to award attorney fees and litigation expenses to the prevailing party. Consideration will be given to an offender for any "good faith" effort in complying with the Act.

place of public accommodation
A privately operated facility is one in which the operation affects commerce and falls within one or more of the following twelve categories: places of lodging; exhibition or entertainment; education; public gathering; recreation and parks; public display of collection; or establishments of service, sales, or rental; serving food or drink; recreation exercise; social service center; specific public transportation stations; ^{CA} church; office building; and a public curb or sidewalk. "Affects commerce" clause is not applicable in the CCR.

power-assisted door
A passage door with a mechanism that assists in opening a door or relieves the opening resistance from the activation of an applied force to the door or from a switch.

UNDERSTANDING ADA TERMINOLOGY

preliminary determination of equivalency
Determination that a code appears to meet or exceed the ADA Title III minimum requirements for accessibility and usability of facilities.

primary entrance
A facility entrance that services the majority of the pedestrian traffic to a primary function area.

primary entry level
CA The floor or level where the primary entrance is located.

primary function area
A primary function area is the facility space holding the major activity for which the facility is intended. Such activity may include the providing of goods, services, privileges, or accommodations.

private club
A club is exempt from coverage under Title II of the Civil Rights Act of 1964 when the club is not open to the public other than to its members. Private club qualification is based on various factors.

private entity
Any individual or entity other than a public entity.

privately funded
CA Construction or alteration projects not funded in whole, in part, directly, or indirectly with municipal, county, or state funds. Private funding provided to home owners by a public agency for individual homes. This also includes the Cal Vet financing program.

public accommodation
A private entity that owns, leases or leases to, or operates a place of public accommodation. See following Table A-A.

UNDERSTANDING ADA TERMINOLOGY
PUBLIC ACCOMMODATIONS

A The following are lists of common types of public accommodations subject to ADA requirements but are not limited to these examples.

TABLE A-A			
LODGING	**FOOD · DRINK**	**EXHIBITION ENTERTAINMENT**	**PUBLIC GATHERING**
• Hotel • Motel • Inn • Dormitory • Resort • Group Home • Halfway House	• Restaurant • Cafeteria • Bar • Fast Food • Specialty Shop • Night Club	• Cinema • Stadium • Concert Hall • Theater • Arena • Race Track • Circus	• Shopping Mall • Auditorium • Lecture Hall • Convention Center • Church [CA] • Meeting Room
RETAIL STORES RENTALS	**SERVICES OFFICES · SHOPS**	**PUBLIC TRANSPORTATION**	**PUBLIC DISPLAY COLLECTIONS**
• Clothing • Grocery • Hardware • Bakery • Lumber Yard • Specialty Shop • Office Supply	• Professional • Bank • Barber/Beauty • Hospital • Funeral Parlor • Dry-cleaner • Gas Station	• Bus Depot • Train Station • Aerial Terminal • Boarding Dock	• Library • Museum • Gallery • Aquarium • Observatory • Historic Place
RECREATION	**EDUCATION**	**SOCIAL SERVICES**	**EXERCISE**
• Park • Zoo • Amusement Park • Beach • Picnic Area	• Public School • Private School • College • University • Nursery • Pre-school • Special Course	• Day Care Center • Seniors Center • Homeless Shelter • Adoption Center • Food Bank • Work Shelter	• Gymnasium • Swimming Pool • Bowling Alley • Golf Course • Health Spa • Tennis Court • Ski Resort

UNDERSTANDING ADA TERMINOLOGY

public entity
Any state or local government; any department, agency, special purpose district, or other instrumentality of a state, states, or local government; and the National Railroad Passenger Corporation and any commuter authority as defined in section 103-8 of the Rail Passenger Service Act. Actions of public entities are covered by Title II of the ADA.

publicly funded construction
   CA Construction and alteration projects subsidized in whole or in part by state, county, or municipal funds or funds of any political subdivision of the state, county, or municipality.

public use
Space or area available to and usable by the general public.

qualified interpreter
An interpreter who is capable of both receptive and expressive interpretation in an accurate, effective, and impartial manner using the necessary specialized vocabulary.

rail transit boarding platform
   CA Horizontal surface raised, recessed, or level with a transit rail from which passengers enter or exit a transit vehicle.

ramp
A walking surface with a running slope greater than 1:20.

readily achievable
Easy to accomplish without much difficulty or expense. Determination factors to consider are:
1. The nature of the needed action and the cost.
2. An entity's overall financial resources, number of persons employed, the effect on expenses and resources, legitimate safety requirements including crime pre-

UNDERSTANDING ADA TERMINOLOGY

vention measures, and the impact placed upon the operation of the site.
3. The administrative or fiscal relationship and geographic separateness of any parent corporation or entity.
4. If applicable, any parent corporation or entity's overall financial resources and overall size based on number of employees and the number, type, and location of its facilities.
5. If applicable, the type of operation or any parent corporation operation including the composition, structure, and function of the parent corporation or entity's work force.

Readily achievable is determined on an individual basis. A barrier removal would not be considered readily achievable if (1) the historic significance of a building or facility is threatened or destroyed, (2) a public accommodation's operation results in a significant loss of profit or efficiency, or (3) the result creates a security risk.

religious entity
A religious organization including a place of worship. A public accommodation, which is not a place of worship but leases space on a religious entity's property, is subject to the ADA requirements.

rescue assistance area
see "area of rescue assistance"

riser
The vertical member of a step.

running slope
Slope parallel to the direction of travel.

UNDERSTANDING ADA TERMINOLOGY

service animal
   Any animal individually trained to perform tasks for the benefit of an individual with a disability. Such tasks may include retrieving dropped items, guiding a person with impaired vision, pulling a wheelchair, alerting a hearing impaired person of sounds or an intruder, providing minimal protection, assisting in rescue work, or other tasks.

service entrance
   A building or facility entrance intended for restricted use by an establishment for the delivery of goods and services.

shopping center
   For ADA purposes, a shopping center or mall is a building or series of buildings on a common site developed as one project or a series, connected by a pedestrian access route, has common ownership or control, houses five or more sales or rental establishments, and only includes the floor levels that house at least one such establishment.

signage
   Information displayed in a verbal, pictorial, tactile, symbolic, or a combination thereof.

site
   A parcel of land within a boundary line or a designated portion of a public right-of-way.

site improvement
   Any incorporated element to a site that improves its functional use.

space
   A specific and definable area.

UNDERSTANDING ADA TERMINOLOGY

special access lift
 CA A vertical hoist equipped with a car or platform which carries people or materials and serves two landings of a structure.

specified public transportation
A means of transportation other than aircraft that accommodates the general public on a regular and continuing basis with general or special services such as a charter service. Places of public accommodations within transportation terminal facilities are covered by the ADA regulations. Airports operated by public entities are covered by Title II of the ADA.

state
Each State of the United States, the District of Columbia, Guam, the Commonwealth of Puerto Rico, the Virgin Islands, American Samoa, the Trust Territory of the Pacific Islands, and the Commonwealth of the Northern Mariana Islands.

story
The portion of a building between the floor surface of one level to the floor surface of the next level or the roof directly above. The ADA guidelines do not consider an unoccupiable building level as a story.

structural frame
All supporting members of a building or structure that are essential to its stability.

submitting official
A state or local official who is authorized to administer or submit a code as the representative of a jurisdiction and one who files for certification.

UNDERSTANDING ADA TERMINOLOGY

tactile
An object used for communication through the sense of touch.

tax deductions and credits
A $15,000 income tax deduction per year is allowed for expenses associated with qualified architectural barrier removal. A business with 30 or fewer employees and less than one million in gross receipts may be eligible for a tax credit on costs relating to ADA compliance. Qualifying entities may receive up to 50 percent credit on eligible expenditures that are between $250 and $10,250.

TDD
A telecommunication display device for the deaf that uses the Baudot code. The newer models also transmit in the ASCII code. The ADA uses the term "text telephone" which currently encompasses various types of telecommunication devices and would cover new technology development of broad ranges of devices and formats. TDD is only one type of a text telephone.

technical infeasibility
Structural, site, or an existing physical constraint that prohibits strict and full compliance with the accessibility requirements for alterations or new construction. Alterations are to include the ADA requirements to the maximum extent feasible.

text telephones
Equipment that transmits graphic communication through coded signals across the standard public telephone network. "Text telephones" do not include facsimile equipment.

UNDERSTANDING ADA TERMINOLOGY

transient lodging
A building, facility, or a portion thereof containing one or more dwelling or sleeping units which accommodate short term use or of a nonpermanent nature excluding inpatient medical care facilities.

transportation terminal
Transportation terminal includes all areas of a facility providing passenger services and other common areas open to the public. Such areas must be on an accessible route from an accessible entrance.

tread
The horizontal surface of a step including the nosing.

tread width
The distance from the front edge of a step to the riser or back edge of the tread.

UBC
Most recent edition of the "Uniform Building Code" adopted by the International Conference of Building Officials.

undue burden
Excessive expense or difficulty may create an undue burden. No guideline for an undue burden has been established by the Justice Department. Determination factors which may be considered are the nature and the cost of the action, overall financial resources, number of employees, effect on expenses and resources, site operation impact, various parent corporation relationships, safety requirements, as well as others. The geographic separateness to and operation of the parent corporation or entity relating to administration; overall financial resources; overall size,

UNDERSTANDING ADA TERMINOLOGY

composition, structure, and functions of the work force; and the number, type, and location of its facilities are also factors to be considered.

unreasonable hardship
^{CA} When an enforcing agency determines that compliance with building standards for specific work would be infeasible by the evaluations of the following:
- Overall construction cost
- Cost of providing access
- Nature of accessibility in gains and losses
- Nature of use and availability to persons with disabilities
- Accessibility improvement impact on the project's financial feasibility

vehicular way
A traffic route or lane intended for vehicle use.

wheelchair
A chair mounted on wheels aided by electric power or operated manually by the occupant and conforming to industry standard models.

work station
Area defined by a work surface or equipment used solely by an employee(s).

ABBREVIATIONS

The following is a list of abbreviations for organizations and terminology associated with the American with Disabilities Act and the California building codes.

ADA	Americans with Disabilities Act of 1990
ADAAG	American with Disabilities Act Accessibility Guidelines
AIA	American Institute of Architects
ANSI	American National Standards Institute
ASME	American Society of Mechanical Engineers
ATBCB	Architectural and Transportation Barriers Compliance Board
ATM	Automated Teller Machine
BHMA	Builders Hardware Manufacturers Association
CABO	Council of American Building Officials
CBC	California Building Code
CEC	California Electrical Code
CCR	California Code of Regulations
CPC	California Plumbing Code
MGRAD	Minimum Guidelines and Requirements for Accessible Design
NCSBCS	National Conference of States on Building Codes and Standards
NPRM	Notice of Proposed Rule Making by the ATBCB

ABBREVIATIONS

OSA	Office of the State Architect, California
OSA/AC	Office of the State Architect, Access Compliance
SBSC	State Building Standards Commission
TDD	Telecommunication Display Device
UBC	Uniform Building Code
UFAS	Uniform Federal Accessibility Standards
UBC	Uniform Building Code
UPC	Uniform Plumbing Code

BARRIER REMOVAL PLAN GUIDELINES

Subsequent to January 26, 1992, all public accommodations are required under the American with Disabilities Act to remove barriers that prevent persons with disabilities the equal accessibility and usability to the commodities and services offered to the public. Failure to remove existing barriers results in discrimination and is punishable by fines up to $50,000 for the first offense, $100,000 the second offense, plus remedies, fees, and costs awarded by the Court. Consideration will be given to an offender for any "good faith" effort in complying with the Act. Implementation of a plan to remove existing accessibility barriers could be considered a "good faith" effort by the Court.

The Law is not intended to place a heavy burden on business and building owners. The law allows alternative means and exemptions under certain circumstances. It does not allow an alternative means in lieu of removing a barrier just because it is more convenient and less costly to the owner. It is advisable in choosing an alternative means to remove a barrier that such action is well documented as an undue burden, an exemption, or as being technically infeasible. A documented plan updated periodically is insurance against complaints or charges that may arise. Documentation will show the intent to comply and record one's position, condition, and other factors at the time the decision was made for no action or cause for delay. Disregarding the law, lack of knowledge, or not receiving technical assistance to remove barriers is not excused by the Court. Discrimination is a civil offense and does not cost the complainant. It can be costly to the offender.

Section B-3.7 "Barrier Removal" and Section B-4.4 "Construction and Alterations" provide the basis of responsibilities and requirements relating to the removal of architectural and communication barriers for persons with disabilities. The

BARRIER REMOVAL PLAN GUIDELINES

following guidelines may be useful in developing a plan to remove those barriers. Also see Section B-3.7.

1. **Conduct survey of facilities**
    a. Identify existing barriers
    b. Consult local disability organizations
        1) Solicit suggestions for cost-effective means
        2) Help in allocating scarce resources
        3) Establish priorities
    c. Determine corrective measures
        1) Consult with construction trades personnel
        2) Inquire on types of material and fixtures required
    d. Estimate cost of any removal, alteration, or addition
        1) Itemize all necessary changes to comply
        2) List all action to change each item
        3) Estimate the cost of each item change
        4) Calculate total estimated cost

2. **Determine if readily achievable**
    a. Structurally feasible
        1) Consult professionals
        2) Identify any structural infeasibility
        3) Document structural conditions, if applicable
    b. Economically feasible
        1) Obtain bids
        2) Cost analysis
        3) Tax credit
        4) Integrate with income projections
        5) Identify economic hardship, if applicable
    c. Operation efficiency
        1) Determine loss of revenue, if any
        2) Determine any security risk
        3) Identify loss of efficiency, if applicable

BARRIER REMOVAL PLAN GUIDELINES

3. Identify any undue burden conditions
   a. Document cause of undue burdens
   b. List alternative accommodation measures
      1) Accessibility
      2) Services

4. Identify the barriers to be removed
   a. Review ADA's priority accessibility order
      1) Building access from public sidewalks, streets, parking, and transportation stops
      2) Access to goods and services available to the public
      3) Access to restroom facilities
      4) Access to other goods and services provided
   b. Define a compliance plan and the order of action to be taken
   c. Consult government agencies on plan and specifications, if applicable
   d. Prepare a time schedule for completion

5. Document historic property exemptions, if applicable
   a. Consult with State Historic Preservation Officer
   b. Define cause for exemptions

6. Plan for future review
   a. Develop a schedule for future reviews
   b. Identify barriers to be periodically re-evaluated

SECTION B

Non-discrimination on the Basis of Disability by Public Accommodations and in Commercial Facilities

American with Disabilities Act
Title III
RULES AND REGULATIONS
SECTION B

B-1 COMPLIANCE REQUIREMENTS

The American with Disabilities Act of 1990 prohibits discrimination based on disabilities of individuals by public accommodations. A public accommodation is any person or entity that provides goods, services, use of facilities, privileges, or any other type of accommodation offered to the general public. Places of accommodations and commercial facilities are to be designed, constructed, and altered in compliance with the ADA accessibility guidelines. These guidelines are the minimum design standards necessary for persons with disabilities to access goods, services, and facilities provided by places of public accommodations.

B-1.1 OBLIGATED ENTITIES

B-1.1.1 PUBLIC ACCOMMODATIONS

Public accommodations are subject to the requirements of Sections B-1, B-2, and B-3 with respect to the operation of a place of public accommodation and all of Section B when designed, constructed, or used as a place of public accommodation or commercial facility.

ADA RULES AND REGULATIONS
COMPLIANCE • Landlords • Tenants

B-1.1.2 COMMERCIAL FACILITIES

Commercial facilities are subject to the requirements of Section B-4.

B-1.1.3 COURSES • EXAMINATIONS

A private entity is subject to the requirements of Section B-3.4 when offering courses and examinations to the public for secondary or post-secondary education and for professional or trade purposes.

B-1.1.4 EXCEPTIONS CA: D-2.2.4, D-2.2.5

The requirements of Title III do not apply to religious organizations, public entities, or to private clubs except to the extent where club facilities are made available to members and patrons as a place of public accommodation.

B-1.2 LANDLORD • TENANT

The landlord, who owns the place of public accommodation, and the tenant, who operates the place of public accommodation, are both subject to ADA requirements. The law does not define responsibilities of either party. The compliance obligations of each party can be determined by agreement between the parties and defined in a lease or other contract.

B-1.3 PUBLIC ACCOMMODATIONS IN PRIVATE RESIDENCES

When a private residence houses a place of public accommodation, any portion of the residence used exclusively for

ADA RULES AND REGULATIONS
COMPLIANCE • Insurance

residential purposes is not covered by Section B. Any portion used for operation by a public accommodation is covered and extends to all exterior and interior spaces and elements available to or used by its patrons or clients.

B-1.4 INSURANCE

B-1.4.1 LIABILITY RISK

A public accommodation shall not refuse to offer their services, goods, or facilities to disabled persons based on comparable insurance coverage and rates by providing or not providing accommodations to disabled persons.

B-1.4.2 INSURER

This section shall not be construed to prohibit or restrict the following when based on or not inconsistent with state law:
a) An insurer, an entity that administers benefit plans, or similar organizations from administering, classifying, or underwriting risks; or
b) A person or organization covered by this part from observing, establishing, sponsoring, or administering the terms of a bona fide benefit plan that are based on administering, underwriting, or classifying risks that are not subject to State laws regulating insurance.

The above provisions shall not be used as a pretext to evade the purposes of the Act.

B-1.4.3 POLICIES

Insurance policies must be based on permissible criteria, not on the terms of the insurance contract for exclusions based on disability.

B-1.4.4 CLASSIFICATIONS

Classification risks limiting certain kinds of coverage is allowed. The plan cannot refuse to insure; refuse to continue to insure; limit the amount, extent, or kind of coverage available to an individual; or charge a different rate for the same coverage based on a physical or mental impairment. Underwriting and classification risks must be based on sound actuarial principles or be related to actual or reasonably anticipated experience.

B-1.4.5 DENIED COVERAGE

Insurance shall not be denied or have different terms and conditions applied to a person with a disability solely based on the disability and when the disability does not pose an increased risk.

B-1.5 CONFLICTING LAWS

B-1.5.1 1973 REHABILITATION ACT

Title V
Title III regulations shall not be construed to apply a lesser standard than the standards set under Title V of the Rehabilitation Act of 1973. This also applies to regulations issued by Federal agencies pursuant to Title V except as otherwise provided herein.

Section 504
These regulations do not affect recipients of Federal financial assistance in their obligations to comply with the requirements and regulations of section 504 of the Rehabilitation Act of 1973.

ADA RULES AND REGULATIONS
COMPLIANCE • Conflicting Laws

B-1.5.2 OTHER LAWS

Title III regulations do not invalidate or limit the remedies, rights, and procedures of any other federal, state, or local laws that provide equal or greater protection rights to persons with disabilities.

ADA RULES AND REGULATIONS
NONDISCRIMINATION • Equal Opportunity

B-2 NONDISCRIMINATION

The general principles of nondiscrimination applicable to entities subject to Title III are stated in Section B-2. Title III rules and regulations are patterned after the civil rights laws prohibiting discrimination.

B-2.1 EQUAL OPPORTUNITY

Persons with disabilities shall not be discriminated against in the full participation and equal enjoyment of goods, services, or any other accommodations offered in places of public accommodation by any private entity who owns, leases or leases to, or operates a place of public accommodation. Equal enjoyment means the entitlement to have an equal opportunity to obtain the same results as others to the maximum extent possible under the provisions of the Act. However, it does not mean accomplishing an identical level of achievement as a person without a disability.

B-2.2 EQUAL PARTICIPATION

B-2.2.1 INTEGRATED ENVIRONMENT

Persons with disabilities shall be provided with an integrated environment appropriate to their needs by a public accommodation providing goods, services, use of facilities, privileges, or other accommodations.

ADA RULES AND REGULATIONS
NONDISCRIMINATION • Equal Participation

B-2.2.2 PUBLIC ACCOMMODATIONS

A public accommodation shall not deny any individual or class of individuals having a disability the participation or benefits from the services, goods, use of facilities, privileges, or other accommodations offered in a place of public accommodation based on disabilities.

1. Same and Equal Accommodations
   A public accommodation shall not discriminate against an individual or class of individuals based on their disabilities by denying or providing unequal or different goods and services than those provided to the general public.

2. Eligibility Rules
   A public accommodation shall not set eligibility rules in order to screen or tend to screen out an individual or any class of individuals having disabilities from the full and equal enjoyment of the goods, services, use of facilities, or other accommodations unless such rules are necessary for the provision of those accommodations.

3. Surcharges
   A public accommodation shall not impose a surcharge on particular individuals or any group of individuals with disabilities to cover any accessibility provision costs. Costs may cover such provisions as auxiliary aids, barrier removal or alternatives, or modifications in policies, practices, and procedures.

4. Restrictions in Documents
   An individual or class of individuals having disabilities shall not be denied participation or benefits from the goods, services, use of facilities, privileges, or other accommodations offered by a public accommodation based on their disabilities through any contractual means, licensing, or other similar arrangement.

ADA RULES AND REGULATIONS
NONDISCRIMINATION • Equal Benefits

B-2.2.3 RIGHT TO REFUSE

An individual or class of individuals having disabilities have the right to refuse any accommodation, aid, service, or benefit available under this Section. This Act does not authorize that person's guardian or representative to decline food, water, medical treatment, or medical services for that individual.

B-2.2.4 ACTIVITIES

A public accommodation shall not deny any individual or class of individuals, based on disabilities, the opportunity to participate in programs or activities that are not separate or different from those offered to other individuals unless provided in accordance with the provisions of Section B.

B-2.3 EQUAL BENEFITS

B-2.3.1 UNEQUAL BENEFITS

A public accommodation shall not afford an individual or class of individuals on the basis of disabilities the unequal opportunity to participate or the unequal benefit of goods, services, use of facilities, privileges, or other accommodations offered by a public accommodation to the general public.

B-2.3.2 SEPARATE BENEFITS

Service, goods, facilities, privileges, or other accommodations provided either directly, through contract, licenses, or other arrangement shall not be provided differently or separately based on a person's, or class of persons' disabilities, from that

ADA RULES AND REGULATIONS
NONDISCRIMINATION • Administrative Control

provided to other individuals unless such action is necessary to provide similar and as effective as those accommodations afforded to other individuals.

B-2.4 ADMINISTRATIVE CONTROL

A public accommodation shall not utilize methods of administration that would create discrimination based on a person's disability. They shall not perpetuate the discrimination of an individual who is or may be subject to common administrative control. Such administrative methods shall not be made directly, through contracts, or any other arrangement.

B-2.5 ASSOCIATION

A public accommodation shall not exclude or deny equal services, goods, use of facilities, privileges, or other accommodations to an individual or entity that has a known relationship or association to a person with a disability. The associate individual or entity has an independent right of legal action under the ADA when such discrimination occurs by a public accommodation.

B-2.6 CONDUCT

B-2.6.1 RETALIATION

No private or public entity shall retaliate against:
- An individual who exercises his or her rights under the Act,

ADA RULES AND REGULATIONS
NONDISCRIMINATION • Conduct

- An individual who opposes any act or practice made unlawful by the provisions of Section B, or
- An individual who has made a charge, assisted, or participated in any investigation or action to enforce the Act or the provisions in Section B.

B-2.6.2 INTERFERENCE

No private or public entity shall coerce, intimidate, threaten, or interfere with any individual or group of individuals who has, is, or is encouraged by another in the exercise or enjoyment of any right granted or protected by the Act such as:

- Coercing an individual to deny or limit the benefits, services, or advantages to which that individual is entitled under the Act.
- Interfere, threaten, or intimidate any person with a disability who is attempting to obtain or use the services, goods, facilities, or other accommodations of a public accommodation.
- Intimidate or threaten any person because that person has assisted or encouraged those entitled to a claim or right granted or protected by the Act or in exercise of their rights.

B-2.7 EXCEPTIONS

B-2.7.1 DIRECT THREAT

A direct threat is a significant risk to the health or safety of others that cannot be eliminated through modification of policies, practices, procedures, or by the provision of auxiliary aids or services. When a person poses a direct threat, a public accommodation is not required to allow that person to

ADA RULES AND REGULATIONS
NONDISCRIMINATION • Exceptions

participate and benefit from its goods, services, facilities, or other accommodations. A direct threat must be determined by a public accommodation. An individualized and reasonable assessment can be based on the following:
- Current medical knowledge or alternative objective evidence to ascertain the nature, duration, and severity of risk;
- The probability a potential injury will actually occur; and
- Whether reasonable modifications of policies, procedures, and practices will mitigate the risk.

B-2.7.2 ILLEGAL DRUG USE

This Section does not prohibit discrimination against a person based on that person's current illegal use of drugs except as otherwise provided herein. A public accommodation shall not discriminate on a person's prior illegal use of drugs if that person is currently not using illegal drugs and who
- has been rehabilitated,
- has successfully completed a supervised drug rehabilitation program,
- participates in a supervised rehabilitation program, or
- is erroneously regarded as engaging in the use of illegal drugs.

1. Rehabilitation
A public accommodation shall not deny health or drug rehabilitation services on the basis of current illegal drug use if the individual is otherwise entitled to these services. Individuals currently engaging in the illegal use of drugs may be denied their continued participation in a drug treatment or rehabilitation program.

2. Drug Testing
Drug testing is neither encouraged, prohibited, restricted,

ADA RULES AND REGULATIONS
NONDISCRIMINATION • Exceptions

or authorized under this section. A public accommodation is not prohibited from administering reasonable policies and procedures to ensure that a former illegal drug user is not currently using illegal drugs.

B-2.7.3 SMOKING

Section B-2 does not prevent places of public accommodation from prohibiting or placing restrictions on smoking.

ADA RULES AND REGULATIONS
ACCESSIBILITY • General

B-3 ACCESSIBILITY REQUIREMENTS

B-3.1 GENERAL

B-3.1.1 MAINTENANCE

Equipment and facilities required to be readily accessible and usable by persons with disabilities shall be maintained in operable working condition. Temporary or isolated interruptions of service or access is not prohibited when due to maintenance or repairs.

B-3.1.2 SAFETY

Legitimate safety requirements may be imposed by a public accommodation when based on actual risks and not on speculation or generalizations regarding individuals with disabilities.

B-3.1.3 SPECIALIZED ACCOMMODATIONS

An individual with disabilities seeking or requiring treatment or services outside the specialization of a public accommodation may be referred by that public accommodation to another if the public accommodation in its normal business operation makes referrals under the same or similar circumstances for persons without disabilities.

B-3.1.4 PERSONAL ACCOMMODATIONS

1. Personal Items
A public accommodation is not required to provide their

ADA RULES AND REGULATIONS
ACCESSIBILITY • General

patrons with personal items or devices, such as wheelchairs, or personal services, such as assistance in eating.

2. Personal Services
Public accommodations, such as hospitals or senior citizen centers, that provide personal services to their patrons shall also provide those services to persons with disabilities who use their facility.

3. Operation Modifications
Operation modifications providing minimal assistance to a person with a disability are not considered services of a personal nature such as a bank employee filling out a deposit slip or a chef cutting food into small pieces.

4. Alternative Barrier Removal
Alternative barrier removal measures provided to assist an individual with a disability are not considered personal services such as retrieving items from shelves, providing curb service, or home delivery.

B-3.1.5 SPECIAL SERVICES

A public accommodation does not have to alter its inventory to facilitate persons with disabilities but is required to special order goods upon their request when special ordering is a customary service provided and the items can be obtained from its customary suppliers. Special requests may include such items as Braille literature, books on audio cassettes, closed-caption video tapes, special clothing or food, or any other special items required by persons with disabilities.

B-3.2 AUXILIARY AIDS

A public accommodation has an obligation to communicate effectively with its patrons who have disabilities which affect

ADA RULES AND REGULATIONS
ACCESSIBILITY • Auxiliary Aids

their hearing, vision, or speech by taking the necessary steps to ensure that those persons are not treated differently from other patrons due to the absence of necessary facility auxiliary aids and services which could result in their exclusion, segregation, or inaccessibility to public accommodations.

B-3.2.1 AIDS • SERVICES

Auxiliary aids and services include but are not limited to:
- Braille materials, large print materials, audio recordings, qualified readers, taped texts, or other effective means of providing visually delivered materials available to persons with visual impairments.
- Telephone handset amplifiers, assistive listening devices, assistive listening systems, telephones compatible with hearing aids, qualified interpreters, note takers, written materials, computer-aided transcription services, closed caption decoders, open and closed captioning, video text displays, telecommunication display devices (TDDs) for deaf persons, or other effective means in providing aurally delivered materials available to persons with hearing impairments.
- Acquisition or modification of equipment or devices.
- Other similar services and actions.

B-3.2.2 COMMUNICATION
ADA: C-1.3.18, C-1.3.21, C-3, C-4.1.6, C-5.3.14, C-7.2.1(4,5), C-7.2.2(7), C-7.2.3 CA: D-2.2.4.5, D-2.8.1.5, D-5

Appropriate auxiliary aids and services shall be furnished by public accommodations where necessary to ensure that communication between persons with impairments is as effective as the communication between persons without impairments.

ADA RULES AND REGULATIONS
ACCESSIBILITY • Auxiliary Aids

B-3.2.3 TELECOMMUNICATION DEVICES (TDDs)
ADA: C-1.2.14, C-1.3.18(3), C-3.3.3(3), C-3.4.9 CA: D-5.4.3

When patrons of a public accommodation receive the opportunity to make outgoing telephone calls on more than an incidental basis, the public accommodation shall also make TDDs available upon request and for the use by those with impaired hearing or communication disorder. A TDD is not required for receiving telephone calls or calls incidental to a public accommodation's operation. Applicable situations for providing a TDD or other effective means would be at such places as a hotel front desk or where a facility uses a security entrance telephone.

B-3.2.4 CLOSED CAPTION DECODERS

Lodging facilities providing television in five or more guest rooms or hospitals providing televisions for patients shall provide a means for decoding captions upon request by a person with impaired hearing.

B-3.2.5 EXCEPTION

Provision of a particular auxiliary aid or service that would alter the nature of goods, services, use of facilities, or other accommodations being offered or that would result in an undue burden on the public accommodation.

B-3.2.6 ALTERNATIVE AIDS AND SERVICES

A public accommodation shall provide an alternative auxiliary aid or service when a particular auxiliary aid or service results in a fundamental alteration in the nature of the goods, services, facilities, or other accommodations being offered. When an undue burden is created by providing an auxiliary aid or service, an alternative means of communication or ser-

ADA RULES AND REGULATIONS
ACCESSIBILITY • Assembly Area Seating

vice may be provided that would ensure individuals with disabilities accessibility to those goods, services, and the other accommodations offered by the public accommodation. Such alternatives shall be provided to the maximum extent possible. A public accommodation can choose among various alternatives as long as the result has the same effect. An exception is when there are no alternatives that would not result in a fundamental alteration or an undue burden for which the alternative auxiliary aid or service is intended.

B-3.3 ASSEMBLY AREA SEATING

B-3.3.1 EXISTING FACILITIES
ADA: C-4.1   CA: D-2.2.1.2, D-2.2.2.2, D-2.2.3.3

An assembly area public accommodation shall provide a reasonable number of wheelchair seating spaces and seats with removable aisle-side armrests allowing the transfer of persons from wheelchairs to seats to the extent that is readily achievable. The spaces shall be in locations dispersed throughout the seating area and shall provide lines of sight and choice of admission prices comparable to those provided to the general public. In addition, the spaces shall adjoin an accessible route with an emergency egress and allow wheelchair users to sit with accompanying companions. A portable chair or other means shall be provided for an accompanying companion when the removal of an adjacent seat is not readily achievable. A public accommodation shall provide assistance in handling the wheelchair of a patron that has transferred to an existing seat. Such requirements shall not be interpreted to exceed the ADAAG standards for alterations in Section B.

ADA RULES AND REGULATIONS
ACCESSIBILITY • Courses • Examinations

B-3.3.2 NEW CONSTRUCTION ADA: C-1.3.10

In newly constructed or altered assembly areas, the construction design standards in Section B govern the wheelchair seating provisions and locations.

B-3.4 COURSES • EXAMINATIONS

B-3.4.1 APPLICATION

This Section is intended to ensure that all avenues to education and employment are open to persons with disabilities and to fill any gap created when licensing, certification, and other testing authorities are not covered by Title II or the Rehabilitation Act. Courses and examinations offered by a public entity shall be accessible to persons with disabilities or alternative accessible arrangements for such persons shall be offered. Such services include those related to applications, licensing, certification, or credentialing for secondary or post-secondary education and for professional or trade purposes.

B-3.4.2 EXAMINATIONS

1. Examination Results
In administering an examination to a person with disabilities who has an impairment of their sensory, manual, or speaking skills, the private entity subject to this section and offering the examination must best ensure that the examination results accurately reflect a disabled individual's aptitude, achievement level, or other examination measure factor rather than reflect the individual's impairment. An exception applies where the examination is actually reflecting or measuring the individual's impairment.

ADA RULES AND REGULATIONS
ACCESSIBILITY • Courses • Examinations

2. Testing
An examination designed for individuals with impaired sensory, manual or speaking skills shall be offered at equally convenient locations, as often as other examinations, and administered in facilities accessible to persons with disabilities or alternate accessible arrangements. Modifications to an examination may require changes in the length of time allotted for completion and adaptation in the manner to which the examination is given.

3. Advanced Notice
A public accommodation administering examinations may require an advanced notice of any modifications needed, aids required, and any appropriate documentation of the applicant's disability. Any documentation shall be at the applicant's expense. Such requirements shall not be unreasonable, and the deadline for the information shall not be earlier than the deadline for others applying to take the examination.

4. Auxiliary Aids
The appropriate auxiliary aids for persons with impaired sensory, manual, or speaking skills shall be provided by the private entity offering the examination. Exceptions would be when the offering of a particular auxiliary aid would fundamentally alter the measurement of skill or knowledge the examination is intended to test, or the offering would result in an undue burden to the entity offering the exam. In such cases, alternative accessible arrangements must be provided with comparable conditions as to those provided for individuals without disabilities.

B-3.4.3 COURSES

1. Facilities
Courses must be administered in accessible facilities to persons with disabilities or alternative accessibility and comparable conditions must be provided as those offered to persons without disabilities.

2. Modifications
Any applicable private entity covered by this section must make the necessary modifications to best ensure the place and manner in which a course given is accessible to persons with disabilities. Modifications may include changes in completion time, specific requirement substitutions, or an adaptation of the manner conducted or materials distributed.

3. Auxiliary Aids
The private entity offering the course shall provide the appropriate auxiliary aids for persons with impaired sensory, manual, or speaking skills. An exception would be when the offering of a particular auxiliary aid would fundamentally alter the course or would result in an undue burden.

B-3.5 TRANSPORTATION SERVICE

B-3.5.1 APPLICATION

A public accommodation that provides transportation service to its patrons and is not primarily engaged in the business of transporting people is subject to the general and specific provisions in Sections B-2, B-3, and B-4 for its transportation operation except as provided herein. This section does not apply to transportation services for employees only.

ADA RULES AND REGULATIONS
ACCESSIBILITY • Modifications

When employees, customers, or clients are served by the same transportation system, the requirements of this section apply. Such transportation services include among others:
- student transportation systems
- customer shuttle bus service
- shuttle service between a transportation terminal and a place of public accommodation
- transportation within a recreational facility

B-3.5.2 BARRIER REMOVAL

Transportation barriers in existing vehicles and rail passenger cars used for transporting people shall be removed by public accommodations if readily achievable. Installation of hydraulic or other lifts to remove barriers is not required.

B-3.5.3 REGULATION COMPLIANCE

A public accommodation subject to this section shall comply with the vehicle and transportation system requirements contained in the regulations issued by the Secretary of Transportation.

B-3.6 MODIFICATIONS

B-3.6.1 POLICIES • PROCEDURES

Reasonable modifications shall be made by a public accommodation in its policies, practices, and procedures when it is necessary to make its facilities, services, goods, and other accommodations accessible to persons with disabilities. An exception would be when a modification would alter the nature of the facility or the accommodations.

ADA RULES AND REGULATIONS
ACCESSIBILITY • Barrier Removal

requirements of Section B-4.4 are not readily achievable and do not fully comply with the specified requirements in removing those barriers. However, no alternate measure shall be taken that imposes a significant health or safety risk.

B-3.7.4 LIMITED OBLIGATION

Barrier removal requirements of this section shall not be interpreted to exceed the alteration standards of Section B-4.4. When relevant alterations standards are not provided in Section B-4.4, the requirements shall not be interpreted to exceed the new construction standards of Section B-4.3. The obligation to remove barriers does not extend to facility areas that are used exclusively as employee work areas and which are addressed in Title I of the Act.

A public accommodation shall not fail to provide alternative methods to make its goods, services, facilities, and other accommodations available when a barrier removal has been demonstrated to be not readily achievable. An exception is when there is no alternative method of provision that is readily achievable. Examples of alternatives may be to provide curb service, home delivery, retrieve merchandise from inaccessible shelves, and relocate activities to accessible locations.

B-3.7.5 MOVABLE FIXTURES

In order to provide accessibility, rearrangement of temporary or movable fixtures may be necessary such as furniture, equipment, and display racks. Rearrangement may not be readily achievable if the result is a significant loss of selling or serving space. Alternative methods to remove barriers must be taken to provide accessibility of goods and services in any remaining inaccessible areas.

ADA RULES AND REGULATIONS
ACCESSIBILITY • Barrier Removal

B-3.7.6 PORTABLE RAMPS

Portable ramps should be used only when a permanent ramp installation is not readily achievable. When providing a portable ramp, consideration shall be given to safety features such as nonslip surfaces, railings, anchoring, and the strength of materials to avoid any risk to the health or safety of individuals.

B-3.7.7 CINEMAS [CA: D-2.2.1]

Where a theater provides multi-screen cinema, the theater shall establish a film rotation schedule which provides reasonable access by wheelchair users to all films being shown when it is not readily achievable to remove existing barriers that would allow persons with mobility impairments complete access to each cinema.

B-3.7.8 COMMON REMEDIES

The following list provides a few examples of actions a public accommodation can take in removing common accessibility barriers:
- Create designated accessible parking spaces
- Make curb cuts in sidewalks and entrances
- Install ramps
- Install flashing alarm lights
- Widen doors
- Eliminate a turnstile or provide an alternative accessible path
- Install accessible door hardware
- Install offset hinges to widen doorways
- Increase maneuvering space in stalls by rearranging the stall partitions
- Install grab bars in toilet stalls

sequent to January 26, 1993.

B-4.3.2 RESPONSIBLE PARTIES

Any public accommodation or private entity responsible for design and construction must ensure that facilities conform to the ADA accessibility guidelines. Compliance interpretation by responsible parties for design and construction accessibility shall be consistent with the intent of the Statute.

B-4.3.3 IMPLEMENTATION

Implementation of the ADA regulations went into effect January 26, 1992. New additions and alterations to existing buildings shall be in compliance subsequent to that date. Barriers in existing buildings and facilities shall also be removed. New construction is required to be in compliance with the exception of a granted extension. See the "Compliance Enactment Schedule", Section A. Discrimination occurs with the failure to design, construct, or remove barriers in existing buildings and facilities which would provide accessibility and usability by persons with disabilities.

B-4.3.4 BUILDING ACCESSIBILITY
ADA: C-1.3.1 CA: D-1.1

Newly constructed facilities shall provide an accessible route of travel from the street or parking lot as far as the extent of its control over the route and be in compliance with the Act. In multi-story buildings, ready access from an entrance to a floor level which is above or below the entrance level is not required in buildings where elevators are exempted.

B-4.3.5 EXCEPTIONS

New construction accessibility requirements do not fully

ADA RULES AND REGULATIONS
CONSTRUCTION • Alterations

apply when an entity can establish structural impracticability, when unique characteristics of the terrain prevent incorporating accessibility features, or when the physical integrity of a facility would be destroyed by providing accessibility features. Steep grades on a plot of land do not apply within this exception. Any portion of a facility shall be made accessible to the full range of accessibility requirements which are structurally practicable. Where accessibility by a specific disability is structurally impracticable, accessibility shall still be provided for other types of disabilities.

B-4.4 ALTERATIONS
ADA: C-1.2 CA: D-3.2

B-4.4.1 APPLICATION

Any altered portion or addition to a place of public accommodation or commercial facility started after January 26, 1992, shall be made readily accessible to and usable by persons with disabilities. Any change to a place of public accommodation or commercial facility that does affect or could affect the usability of that building, facility, or a portion thereof is an alteration subject to the regulations of the Act. Each altered existing element, space, or common area shall comply with the applicable regulations of this section. Compliance shall be performed to the maximum extent feasible when it is impossible to fully comply with the accessibility standards.

B-4.4.2 PATH OF TRAVEL
ADA: C-1.2.2, C-1.2.1(4), C-2.1 CA: D-3.3, D-4.1

The path of travel to an altered facility containing a primary function area as well as the restrooms, telephones, and drink-

ADA RULES AND REGULATIONS
CONSTRUCTION • Elevators

B-4.5 ELEVATORS

B-4.5.1 APPLICATION
ADA: C-1.1.5, C-1.2.9, C-1.3.7, C-5.3 CA: D-3.3.3, D-4.2

The statute applies the same to both new construction and alterations of facilities except where an alteration to an existing building is not eligible for the statutory exemption. In such cases, the following circumstances will eliminate the requirement to install an elevator in existing altered facilities.
1. The elevator installation cost is disproportionate in cost and scope to the overall alteration cost.
2. The installation of an elevator is technically infeasible.

B-4.5.2 EXEMPT BUILDINGS ADA: C-1.3.7

Elevators are exempt in buildings less than three stories or with less than 3,000 square feet per story unless the facility houses a shopping center, health care professional office, or transportation terminal. Only the floor levels that include at least one sales office, one rental establishment, or one health care provider and any floor designed, used, or intended for use by at least one health care provider, sales, or rental establishment shall be serviced by an elevator. The elevator exemption does not obviate or limit the obligation to meet all of the other accessibility requirements.

ADA RULES AND REGULATIONS
ENFORCEMENT • Civil Suit

B-5 ENFORCEMENT CA: D-1.6

Any person may file a civil suit for preventive relief who has been subjected to discrimination in violation of the Act or who has reasonable grounds to believe discrimination is about to take place based upon their disability.

B-5.1 CIVIL SUIT

B-5.1.1 COMPLAINT

A complainant may file application to the Court. The Court may authorize and appoint an attorney to initiate a civil action on behalf of the complainant free of any costs, fees, or security.

B-5.1.2 INJUNCTIVE RELIEF

The complainant may file an application with the Court for permanent or temporary injunctive relief. The Court may order the defendant to make alterations to a facility, bring the facility into compliance with the ADAAG standards, or require the provision of an auxiliary aid or service, a modification of policy, an alternative provision, or other similar relief.

B-5.1.3 PUBLIC CONCERN

The Attorney General may intervene in any civil action when the case is of public importance subject to the court's permission.

ADA RULES AND REGULATIONS
ENFORCEMENT • Dispute • Violations • Non-compliance

B-5.4 DISPUTE RESOLUTION

Alternative means of resolving disputes in lieu of a Court action is encouraged where it is appropriate and authorized by law. Resolution can be through negotiation, arbitration, conciliation, mediation, facilitation, fact finding, and mini-trials.

B-5.5 VIOLATIONS

B-5.5.1 VIOLATIONS

All discriminatory acts having occurred are counted as a single violation in the first civil suit. All violations found in a second suit of the same person or entity would cumulatively be considered a "subsequent violation".

B-5.5.2 GOVERNMENT

The United States government shall be liable for violations the same as any private individual.

B-5.6 NON-COMPLIANCE

No person or entity is excused from ADA compliance due to their failure to receive technical assistance including any development or distribution of technical assistance manuals authorized by the Act.

ADA RULES AND REGULATIONS
ENFORCEMENT • Implementation Dates

B-5.7 IMPLEMENTATION DATES

The ADA Title III became effective on January 26, 1992. Civil action cannot be commenced for violations or omission of the Act occurring prior to July 26, 1992, against businesses with 25 or fewer employees and gross receipts of $1,000,000 or less, and prior to January 26, 1993, against business with 10 or fewer employees and gross receipts of $500,000 or less. Subsequent to August 25, 1990, purchased or leased vehicles must be readily accessible to and usable by persons with disabilities including wheelchair users. Also see the "Compliance Enactment Schedule", Section A.

ADA RULES AND REGULATIONS
BUILDING CODE CERTIFICATION • Cetification Denial

Washington, DC; and
- b) at the offices of the state or local agency charged with the administration and enforcement of the code.
2. Adequate public notices
   - a) are published in the relevant jurisdiction of the certification application, and
   - b) identifies the locations where the materials can be reviewed.

B-6.3 CERTIFICATION DENIAL

B-6.3.1 NOTIFICATION

The Assistant Attorney General shall notify the submitting official when he has made a preliminary determination to deny certification. The notification may include specifications required to amend the code to qualify for certification.

B-6.3.2 SUPPLEMENTAL DOCUMENTATION

The submitting official shall be allowed at least 15 days to submit opposing arguments and documentation to the preliminary determination to deny certification.

B-6.3.3 FAILURE TO RESPOND

If the submitting official fails to respond, the Assistant Attorney General shall not be required to take further action.

B-6.3.4 CERTIFICATION RE-EVALUATION

If the submitting official submits additional supporting materials, the Assistant Attorney General will evaluate those materials and any other pertinent information.

B-6.3.5 CERTIFICATION DECISION

The Assistant Attorney General shall make a final denial for certification or a preliminary determination of equivalency.

B-6.4 PRELIMINARY DETERMINATION

The Assistant Attorney General shall make a preliminary determination of a code equivalency or a preliminary determination to deny certification.

Procedure:
The Assistant Attorney General shall:
- Inform the submitting official in writing of the preliminary determination of equivalency.
- Publish a notice in the Federal Register to
  a) advise the public of the preliminary determination of equivalency of the submitted code,
  b) invite public opinion on the certification through written comments, and
  c) advise the public that written comments will be accepted within a 60 day period subsequent to the publication.
- Review public response to the notice.
- Publish a notice and hold an informal hearing in Washington, DC, where interested persons may express their views on the preliminary equivalency determination.
- Issue a certification of equivalency or final determination to deny the request for certification on the basis of the submitted materials, information, and the consultations with the Architectural and Transportation Barriers Compliance Board.
- Publish a notice of the decision in the Federal Register.

Americans with Disabilities Act
Title III
ACCESSIBILITY DESIGN STANDARDS
SECTION C

C-1 MINIMUM REQUIREMENTS

C-1.1 BUILDINGS · FACILITIES

C-1.1.1 NEW DESIGN · CONSTRUCTION [ADA: B-4]

New design, construction, and alterations shall comply with the accessibility guidelines of Sections C-1 through C-6 unless otherwise provided or modified herein. Accessible building and facility alterations shall be in compliance with Section C-1.2. Newly designed or newly constructed buildings and facilities are to be accessible in accordance with the requirements of Section C-1.3.

C-1.1.2 SPECIAL USE

Libraries, lodging, medical care facilities, restaurants, transportation facilities, mercantile and other businesses are to comply with the additional requirements specified in Section C-7. Any part of a multi-use building or facility that accommodates a special use subject to the American with Disabilities Act Accessibility Guidelines (ADAAG) shall comply with the additional requirements for that special use.

ADA ACCESSIBILITY DESIGN STANDARDS
MINIMUM REQUIREMENTS • Additions • Alterations

technically infeasible. Any features or elements being altered that can be made accessible shall be made accessible within the scope of the alteration.

2. **Maximum Requirement**
   No alteration shall impose a greater accessibility requirement in existing facilities than would be required for new construction.

3. **Non-reduction Accessibility**
   No commenced alteration shall reduce the usability and accessibility of a building or facility to less than the accessibility requirements for new construction.

4. **Route of Travel** ADA: B-4.4.2 CA: D-3.3, D-4
   An altered space or element required to be on an accessible route in new construction is not required in alterations except to the extent of complying with the provisions of Section C-1.2.2 for a primary function area.

5. **Entrances**
   An alteration to an entrance does not have to comply with Section C-1.3.4 except to the extent required by Section C-1.2.2 where the building has an accessible entrance. An inaccessible entrance shall have appropriate accessible signs placed at or near the entrance directing persons with disabilities to the nearest accessible entrance. A disabled person shall not have to retrace their approach route from the inaccessible entrance.

6. **Altered Areas**
   An entire space or room shall be made accessible when alterations to single elements within that space are altered creating an altered space or room.

7. **Vertical Travel**
   A vertical accessible means shall be provided that complies with the applicable provisions of Sections C-5.1, C-5.3, C-5.5, and C-5.6 when a stairway or escalator is

ADA ACCESSIBILITY DESIGN STANDARDS
MINIMUM REQUIREMENTS • Additions • Alterations

planned or installed where none exists and major structural modifications are necessary for the installation. The regulations of Section C-1.1.5 apply to elevator exemptions in building and facility alterations.

8. Egress
The egress and rescue assistance area regulations of Sections C-1.3.8, C-1.3.9, and C-2.1.6 do not apply to alterations.

9. Non-applicable Elements
The regulations of Section C-1.2.2 do not apply to alteration work done to the electrical, plumbing, or mechanical system of a building, a hazardous material abatement, the retrofit to an automatic sprinkler system, or to any space or element not requiring accessibility.

C-1.2.2 PRIMARY FUNCTION AREA [ADA: B-4.4.2]

Alterations that affect or could affect the usability or accessibility of a primary function area shall ensure to the maximum extent feasible the accessibility to persons with disabilities on a path of travel, at drinking fountains, at telephones, and in the restrooms serving the altered area. An exception to this rule is when the scope and cost of the alteration to the path of travel is disproportionate to the scope and cost of the overall alteration.

C-1.2.3 SIGNS [CA: D-3.3.8, D-3.10]

Signs in compliance with Sections C-3.3.1, C-3.3.5, C-3.3.6, and C-3.3.7 shall be provided indicating the nearest accessible toilet or bathing facility location when existing toilet or bathing facilities are being altered and cannot be made accessible.

ADA ACCESSIBILITY DESIGN STANDARDS
MINIMUM REQUIREMENTS • Additions • Alterations

C-1.2.11 RAMPS CA: D-3.3.5, D-4.3, D-4.4

A ramp or curb ramp on a site or in an existing facility that is located in a restrictive space preventing the use of a 1:12 slope or less may have a slope between 1:10 and 1:12 with a maximum 6-inch rise or a slope between 1:8 and 1:10 with a maximum 3-inch rise. A 1:8 slope is the maximum slope allowed.

C-1.2.12 HANDRAILS CA: D-7.2.3

Full handrail extensions at stairways are not required where an extension would be hazardous or impossible.

C-1.2.13 DOOR OPENINGS CA: D-3.16, D-7.1

1. Clear Width
A maximum 5/8-inch doorstop projection is allowed on the opening latch side when it is technically impossible to comply with the opening requirement of Section C-5.2.9.

2. Thresholds CA: D-7.1.5
Existing thresholds may remain if they are no more than 3/4 inches high and have a beveled edge on each side.

C-1.2.14 TEXT TELEPHONES CA: D-5.4.3

At least one interior public text telephone shall be provided and comply with Section C-3.4.9 when
a) an alteration to a building or facility increases the total number of public pay telephones to at least four with one at an interior location; or
b) an alteration occurs to at least one interior or exterior public telephone in a building or facility that has at least four public telephones with a minimum of one telephone at an interior location.

ADA ACCESSIBILITY DESIGN STANDARDS
MINIMUM REQUIREMENTS • **New Construction**

C-1.3 NEW CONSTRUCTION

Accessible property sites, buildings, and facilities shall meet the minimum requirements of Section C-1.3.

C-1.3.1 ROUTE OF TRAVEL ADA: B-4.3.4   CA: D-3.3, D-4

All accessible buildings, facilities, elements and spaces shall be connected by an accessible route within a property site and comply with the requirements of Section C-2.1.

1. **Public Locations**
   At least one accessible route within the property site shall be provided to an accessible building or facility entrance from public streets, sidewalks, passenger loading zones, transportation stops, and accessible parking spaces in compliance with Section C-2.1.
2. **Buildings and Facilities**
   All accessible building spaces and elements within a facility shall be connected to the entrances with at least one accessible route that complies with Section C-2.1.
3. **Protruding Objects** CA: D-3.3.9
   Protruding objects in circulation paths shall comply with Section C-2.2.
4. **Walking Surfaces** CA: D-3.17
   The ground and floor surfaces of accessible routes and accessible spaces shall comply with Section C-5.4.

C-1.3.2 SIGNS CA: D-3.3.8, D-3.10, D-5.3

1. **International Symbol**
   The following accessible facility elements and spaces shall be identified by the International Symbol of Accessibility

ADA ACCESSIBILITY DESIGN STANDARDS
MINIMUM REQUIREMENTS • New Construction

and comply with Section C-3.3.3.
- a) Accessible entrances unless all entrances are accessible. (Directional signs to the nearest accessible entrance shall be located at each inaccessible entrance.)
- b) Accessible passenger loading zones.
- c) Reserved accessible parking spaces.
- d) Accessible toilet and bathing facilities, unless all are accessible.

2. Permanent Signs
Signs that designate permanent rooms, spaces, or areas shall comply with Sections C-3.3.1, C-3.3.2, C-3.3.5, and C-3.3.7.

3. Direction • Information Signs CA: D-5.3.6
Signs providing directions to, or information about, functional spaces or areas shall comply with Sections C-3.3.1, C-3.3.5, and C-3.3.6.

4. Temporary Signs
Temporary signs such as menus and building directories are not required to comply.

C-1.3.3 PARKING CA: D-3.12, D-6.1

C 1.3

Accessible properties shall meet at least the following minimum requirements:

1. Loading Zones CA: D-3.12.3
In loading zones, at least one passenger loading space shall comply with Section C-4.4.2.

2. Valet Parking CA: D-3.12.4
Valet parking facilities shall provide at least one passenger loading space that complies with Section C-4.4.2. The space shall be located on an accessible route adjoining an accessible facility entrance. *Valet parking is not always available to persons with disabilities due to a removed*

ADA ACCESSIBILITY DESIGN STANDARDS
MINIMUM REQUIREMENTS • New Construction

driver's seat or special vehicle controls. In such cases, another person cannot park the vehicle. It is recommended that some self-parking spaces be provided at the valet parking facility. The spaces should be located on an accessible route to the entrance.

TABLE C-1A	
Number of Parking Spaces	**Minimum Accessible Parking Spaces**
1 to 100	1 for each 1-25 spaces
101 to 200	4, +1 for each 1-50 spaces
201 to 500	6, +1 for each 1-100 spaces
501 to 1000	2% of total spaces
1001 and over	20, +1 for each 1-100 over 1000

3. **Parking Lot Spaces** CA: D-6.1.1(1,2)
   Self-parking lots for employees or visitors shall provide accessible parking spaces for persons with disabilities and the spaces shall comply with Table C-1A and Section C-4.4.4. Accessible parking spaces may be provided in other equivalent accessible locations.
4. **Parking Lot Access Aisles** CA: D-6.1.1(1)
   Parking lot access aisles adjacent to accessible parking spaces shall have no less than a 5-foot minimum width.
5. **Van Accessibility** CA: D-6.1.1(3)
   A minimum 8-foot wide access aisle shall be provided at one of every eight accessible parking spaces but never less

ADA ACCESSIBILITY DESIGN STANDARDS
MINIMUM REQUIREMENTS • New Construction

than one accessible space. The designated parking spaces shall be identified by a sign stating "van accessible" as required by Section C-4.4.5. The vertical clearance of the space shall comply with Section C-4.4.2. A parking structure may group van accessible spaces together on one level. An exception to the van accessibility requirements occur when all accessible parking spaces are in compliance with the "Universal Parking Design" as illustrated in Figure 23.

6. **Parking at Medical Care Facilities** CA: D-3.12.2

    Medical care facilities for persons with mobility impairments shall comply with the parking requirements of Section C-1.3.3 and C-4.4 and in addition:

    a) 10% of the total parking spaces serving each outpatient facility shall be accessible, and

    b) 20% of the total spaces serving each facility specializing in mobility impairment treatment shall be accessible.

C-1.3.4 ENTRANCES CA: D-2.2.3.2, D-3.3.4

The following are the minimum requirements for public entrances in new construction. Requirement one and two shall be met independently. (Service entrances are not considered public entrances within these guidelines.)

1. Accessible entrances shall be the entrances used by the majority of patrons and employees, when feasible. One entrance may meet more than one of the minimum requirements of (a) through (d).

    a) One public ground floor entrance must be accessible.

    b) At least 50 percent of public entrances must be accessible with the exception of 2(a,b) of this subsection.

    c) Accessible entrances must not be less in number than the exits required by the applicable building and fire codes.

ADA ACCESSIBILITY DESIGN STANDARDS
MINIMUM REQUIREMENTS • New Construction

    d) Provide at least one accessible entrance to each building tenant.
2. In addition to meeting the above requirements, access shall be provided
   a) to at least one direct accessible entrance between a building and an enclosed parking structure that has direct pedestrian access between the two, and
   b) from elevated or enclosed pedestrian passageways by providing at least one accessible entrance to any building or facility for which that passageway accesses.
3. A service entrance shall be accessible when that entrance is the only entrance to a facility.
4. Directional signs shall be placed at inaccessible entrances indicating the nearest accessible entrance and shall comply with Sections C-3.3.1, C-3.3.5, and C-3.3.6.

Making all entrances accessible is preferred since entrances also serve as emergency exits.

C-1.3.5 DOORS CA: D-3.16, D-7.1

The following accessible doors shall be provided and comply with Section C-5.2.
1. At least one accessible door at each accessible building entrance.
2. An accessible egress door as required by Section C-2.1.6.
3. At least one accessible door at each accessible space within a building.
4. An accessible door as an element of an accessible route.

C-1.3.6 STAIRS CA: D-7.2

Interior and exterior stairs shall comply with Section C-5.7 where the stairs connect building levels that have no other vertical means of access.

ADA ACCESSIBILITY DESIGN STANDARDS
MINIMUM REQUIREMENTS • **New Construction**

C-1.3.7 ELEVATORS ADA; B-4.5   CA: D-3.3.3, D-4.2

At least one passenger elevator shall serve each level of a multi-story building and comply with Section C-5.3 requirements. Each full passenger elevator shall comply with Section C-5.3 when multiple elevators are provided. *Equipment and material hoists, dumbwaiters, non-passenger freight elevators, and construction elevators are not covered by these guidelines. A platform lift or other vertical means provided in lieu of an elevator is not required in elevator exempt buildings.*

The following four conditions allow an exemption from the elevator requirement:

1. No elevator is required in facilities less than three stories or less than 3000 square feet per story unless the building contains a shopping center, a professional office for health care, a transportation terminal, or another type as determined by the Attorney General. This elevator exemption does not preclude the obligation to comply with other accessibility requirements of Section C-1.3.7. When facilities are provided or required by the ADAAG on building levels not served by an elevator, those facilities must also be provided on the accessible ground level. If a building qualifies for an elevator exemption but then has a full-passenger elevator installed, the elevator shall serve each building level and comply with Section C-5.3. Other levels of a building are not required to be served by a full passenger elevator when providing service from a garage to one level of a building.

2. Elevator penthouses, mechanical rooms, elevator pits, and piping or equipment catwalks are exempt from this requirement.

ADA ACCESSIBILITY DESIGN STANDARDS
MINIMUM REQUIREMENTS • **New Construction**

3. Platform lifts (wheelchair lifts) which comply with Section C-5.5 and state and local codes may be used in place of an elevator to:
   a) provide access where existing constraints prevent the use of a ramp or an elevator;
   b) provide an accessible route to a performing area of an assembly facility;
   c) comply with the wheelchair line-of-site viewing position and disbursement required by Section C-4.1.2; and
   d) provide access to incidental facility spaces which accommodate no more than five people and are not open to the general public.
4. Accessible ramps may be used in place of an elevator when they comply with Section C-5.6.

C-1.3.8 EGRESS CA: D-3.3.4

A facility shall provide an accessible means of egress to at least the number of exits required by local building and life safety regulations.

C-1.3.9 RESCUE ASSISTANCE CA: D-3.5

Areas of rescue assistance shall comply with Section C-2.1.6 and in the same number as inaccessible exits on each occupied level above or below an accessible exit level. A horizontal exit shall satisfy the requirements for an area of rescue assistance when the exit meets local building and safety regulations. Buildings or facilities with supervised automatic sprinkler systems are not required to have areas of rescue assistance. *Supervised automatic sprinkler systems have a high level of performance and fire response due to their monitoring features.*

ADA ACCESSIBILITY DESIGN STANDARDS
MINIMUM REQUIREMENTS • **New Construction**

TABLE C-1B	
Assembly Area Seating Capacity	Required Wheelchair Locations
4 to 25	1
26 to 50	2
51 to 300	4
301 to 500	6
501 and over	6, + 1 for each 100 increase

C-1.3.10 ASSEMBLY AREAS
CA: D-2.2.1.2, D-2.2.2.2, D-2.2.3.3, D-2.2.4.1, D-2.3.2.7

1. **Wheelchair Spaces**
   Accessible wheelchair locations in assembly areas with fixed seating shall comply with Sections C-4.1.2, C-4.1.3, and C-4.1.4 and Table C-1B. *Removable or folding seating units may be used in lieu of open wheelchair spaces.*

2. **Aisle Seats**
   a) One percent of the fixed seating capacity, but never less than one seat, shall be accessible aisle seats which have folding, removable, or no armrests on the aisle side.
   b) Each accessible seat shall be identified by a sign or marker. *Accessible seat markers should be given consideration in darkened rooms with contrasting colors or reflective material.*
   c) The ticket office shall post a sign notifying patrons of the available accessible seats.
   d) Aisle seats are not required to comply with Section C-4.1.4, floor surface requirements.

3. **Assistive Listening System** CA: D-2.2.4.5
   Assembly areas where audible communications are integral to the use of the space is subject to these require-

ments. The areas shall have a permanently installed assistive listening system that complies with Section C-4.1.6 if

a) the area accommodates at least 50 people or has an audio-amplification system, and

b) fixed seating.

Other assembly areas shall provide a permanently installed assistive listening system or the necessary provisions to support a portable assistive listening system. Receivers equal to at least 4 percent of the total seating shall be provided, but not less than two receivers. Signs that comply with Section C-3.3 shall be placed in the required locations to inform patrons of the availability of a listening system.

C-1.3.11 FIXED TABLES · SEATING
CA: D-2.2.1.2, D-2.2.2.2, D-2.2.2.3, D-2.2.4.1, D-8.4

At least 5 percent, but never less than one, of all public or common area fixed tables or seating in a public or common-use area shall be made accessible, shall be located on an accessible route to and through the area, and shall comply with Section C-6.7.

C-1.3.12 DRESSING ROOMS CA: D-2.3.2.2(7)

At least 5 percent of each type of dressing room, but not less than one of each type, shall be accessible in each cluster when used by the public, employees, or customers. The rooms shall comply with Section C-4.2.

C-1.3.13 TOILET FACILITIES CA: D-3.15, D-6.3

1. Toilet Rooms

Accessible public and common use toilet rooms shall be

ADA ACCESSIBILITY DESIGN STANDARDS
MINIMUM REQUIREMENTS • New Construction

on an accessible route and comply with Section C-4.8 when required or provided.

2. Limited Use
A toilet room provided and used by occupants of a specific space, such as a private office, shall be adaptable.

3. Portable Units
At least 5 percent, but not less than one accessible portable toilet unit, shall be provided in each cluster of portable units, shall be identified with the International Symbol of Accessibility, and shall comply with Section C-4.8. A portable toilet unit used exclusively by construction personnel at a construction site is not required to comply with Section C-1.3.13.

C-1.3.14 BATHING FACILITIES CA: D-3.13, D-6.2

1. Bathing Rooms
Bathing rooms for public and common use shall comply with Section C-4.5 and be located on an accessible route when provided.

2. Portable Units
At least 5 percent, but not less than one accessible portable bathing unit, shall be provided in each cluster of portable bathing units and shall be identified with the International Symbol of Accessibility.

C-1.3.15 STORAGE CA: D-3.14

At least one of each type of fixed or built-in storage facilities provided in accessible spaces shall comply with Section C-4.7 requirements. Additional storage may be provided and need not comply.

ADA ACCESSIBILITY DESIGN STANDARDS
MINIMUM REQUIREMENTS • **New Construction**

C-1.3.16 MERCHANDISE DISPLAYS ^{CA: D-2.3.2.2}

Customer self-service shelves and display units shall be located on an accessible route and comply with Section C-2.1 requirements. Accessible reach requirements do not apply.

C-1.3.17 DRINKING FOUNTAINS ^{CA: D-8.3}

A drinking fountain accessible to persons using wheelchairs and complying with Section C-6.4 shall be provided in addition to a fountain accessible to those with difficulty bending or stooping when only one fountain area is provided per floor. Accommodation can be accomplished by:
 a) a "hi-lo" fountain,
 b) two fountains, one to service each group,
 c) a fountain complying with Section C-6.4 and a water cooler, or
 d) other means equivalent to serving both groups.

At lease half of the total drinking fountains on a floor shall be on an accessible route and comply with Section C-6.4. *If an odd number of fountains are planned or exist, round down and calculate 50 percent of the even number. Multiple accessible fountains should be disbursed evenly throughout a facility.*

C-1.3.18 PUBLIC TELEPHONES ^{CA: D-3.11, D-5.4}

1. **Accessible Telephones**
   Telephones used by the public shall comply with Sections C-3.4.2 through C-3.4.8 and to the extent required by Table C-1C.
2. **Volume Controls**
   All telephones required to be accessible shall have volume controls. Twenty-five percent, but never less than one, of

ADA ACCESSIBILITY DESIGN STANDARDS
MINIMUM REQUIREMENTS • New Construction

TABLE C-1C	
Telephones provided per floor	**Accessible telephones required to comply with Sections C-3.4.2 to C-3.4.8[1]**
single units	1 per floor
one bank[2]	1 per floor
multiple banks[2]	1 per bank • A single accessible unit may be installed near a bank. • At least one shall meet the forward reach requirement for telephones[3].

[1] Accessible telephones may be either forward or side reach telephones unless otherwise specified.
[2] A bank consists of two or more adjacent public telephones that may be as one unit.
[3] Exception: A side reach telephone may be installed at exterior installations in lieu of the required forward reach telephone when the dial tone first service is available.

all other public telephones provided in a building or facility shall be equipped with a volume control. The volume controlled telephones shall be dispersed among all the various types of public telephones provided, including closed circuit telephones. All required signs complying with Section C-3.3 shall be provided. *Volume controls can be installed on any telephone.*

3. **Text Telephones** CA: D-5.4.3

   At least one public text telephone shall be provided at an interior location in compliance with Section C-3.4.9 as follows:

ADA ACCESSIBILITY DESIGN STANDARDS
MINIMUM REQUIREMENTS • New Construction

a) when a total of four or more public pay telephones are provided, at least one shall be at an interior location,
b) at a hospital emergency, recovery, or waiting room where a public pay telephone is provided, and
c) in a stadium, convention center, hotel with a convention center, or a covered mall where at least one interior public pay telephone is provided.

4. Bank of Telephones
A bank of three or more public pay telephones at an interior location requires at least one of those telephones to be designed and equipped with a shelf and outlet for a portable text telephone and shall comply with Section C-3.4.9(3)

C-1.3.19 CONTROLS CA: D-8.2

Accessible fixture and element operating mechanisms located in accessible spaces or along accessible routes shall comply with Section C-6.3.

C-1.3.20 AUTOMATED TELLER MACHINES CA: D-8.1

Automated teller machines shall comply with Section C-6.1. If more than one ATM is provided at one location, then only one ATM must comply. Drive-up-only ATMs are exempt from the requirements of Sections C-6.1.3, C-6.3.3, and C-6.3.4.

C-1.3.21 EMERGENCY WARNING SYSTEMS
CA: D-2.8.1.5, D-3.8, D-5.1

Emergency warning systems shall include both audible and visual alarms and comply with Section C-3.1. Transient lodging sleeping accommodations required by Section C-7.2 shall have an alarm system that complies with Section C-3.1.

ADA ACCESSIBILITY DESIGN STANDARDS
MINIMUM REQUIREMENTS • Historic Preservation

A medical care unit emergency warning system may be modified to meet the standard health care alarm design practice.

C-1.3.22 DETECTABLE WARNING DEVICES
CA: D-3.9, D-4.4.1(6), D-5.2

Detectable warning devices shall be provided according to Section C-3.2.

C-1.4 HISTORIC PRESERVATION
ADA: B-4.4.3
CA: D-3.7

A qualified historic building or facility is one which is listed or is eligible for listing in the National Register of Historic Places or is designated as historic under an appropriate state or local law.

C-1.4.1 ALTERATIONS

Alterations to a qualified historic building or facility shall comply with Section C-1.2, with the applicable technical specifications of Sections C-1 through C-6, and with the applicable requirements of Section C-7. Historic buildings are exempt from alterations if compliance would threaten or destroy the historic significance of the building or facility as determined by the National Historic Preservation Act, Section 106 procedures. In such case, the alternative minimum requirements for historic preservation in Section C-1.4.4 may be used.

C-1.4.2 QUALIFIED HISTORIC BUILDINGS

Qualified historic building and facility alterations are subject to Section 106 of the National Historic Preservation Act. Section 106 requires that the Federal agency with jurisdiction consider the effects of alterations on qualified historic buildings and facilities and give the Advisory Council on Historic Preservation a reasonable opportunity to comment on the alteration prior to approval of the undertaking.

Section 106 of the National Historic Preservation Act procedures are to be followed where alterations are undertaken on a qualified historic building or facility which is subject to Section 106. The alternative minimum requirements of Section C-1.4.4 may be used if the State Historic Preservation Officer or the Advisory Council on Historic Preservation determines that compliance with the requirements for accessible routes, ramps, entrances, or toilets would threaten or destroy the historic significance of the building or facility. The State Historic Preservation Officer should be consulted on alterations to qualified historic buildings and facilities not subject to Section 106 if there is belief that compliance with the requirements for accessible routes, ramps, entrances, or toilets would threaten or destroy the historic significance of the building or facility.

C-1.4.3 STATE OFFICER

The State Historic Preservation Officer may delegate consultation responsibility to a certified local government historic preservation program for the purposes of this section. Interested persons, organizations, and accessibility officials should be invited to participate in the consultation process.

C-1.4.4 MINIMUM ALTERNATIVES

1. **Accessible Route**
   At least one accessible route shall be provided from a site access point to an accessible entrance and shall comply with Section C-2.1. Accessible routes shall be provided

ADA ACCESSIBILITY DESIGN STANDARDS
MINIMUM REQUIREMENTS • Historic Preservation

from an accessible entrance to all publicly used spaces, at least on the accessible entrance level. Access to all levels shall be provided in compliance with Section C-1 when practicable. A ramp may be used as part of an accessible route to an entrance where the slope is no greater than 1:6 for a run not exceeding two feet.

2. Entrance
At least one accessible entrance used by the public shall be provided and shall comply with Section C-4.3. When no public entrance can comply with Section C-4.3, access at an alternative accessible entrance not used by the general public may be used when directional signs to the alternative entrance are placed at the primary entrance. A notification system shall be provided at the alternative accessible entrance signifying a person's presence. A remote monitoring system at that entrance may be used where security is required.

3. Exhibits
Displays and written information should be placed where seated persons may also view them. The top edge of horizontal displays should be no higher than 44 inches above the finished floor.

4. Toilet Facilities
At least one toilet facility in compliance with Sections C-4.8 and C-1.2 shall be provided along an accessible route that complies with Section C-2.1 when toilets are provided. The toilet facility may be unisex in design.

ADA ACCESSIBILITY DESIGN STANDARDS
CLEAR SPACES • Route of Travel

C-2 CLEAR SPACES

C-2.1 ROUTE OF TRAVEL

C-2.1.1 APPLICATION [CA: D-3.3, D-4]

All spaces on an accessible route of travel that are needed to reach other accessible spaces and elements shall comply with Section C-2.1 including all walks, aisles, corridors, hallways, tunnels, skywalks, and other similar spaces. *Persons with mobility impairments move slower and tend to rest frequently. A two minute rest period for every 100 feet can be used to estimate travel times for people with severely limited stamina. This slow progress and periodic resting times can greatly increase a disabled person's exposure to the weather elements.*

C-2.1.2 SURFACE [CA: D-3.17]

Accessible route surfaces shall comply with Section C-5.4.

1. **Slope** [CA: D-4.3]
   Accessible route slopes shall be 1:20 or less with cross slopes not exceeding 1:50. Slopes steeper than 1:20 are considered ramps and shall comply with Section C-5.6. *A level or slope less than 1:20 on an indirect route is sometimes more convenient to a disabled person than the maximum allowable slope in a shorter distance.*

2. **Level Changes**
   Changes in levels along an accessible route shall comply with the floor surface regulations in Section C-5.4.4. A ramp, elevator, or platform lift shall be provided when an

ADA ACCESSIBILITY DESIGN STANDARDS
CLEAR SPACES • Route of Travel

accessible route changes in level greater than one-half inch.

C-2.1.3 CLEAR SPACE ^{CA: D-3.4, D-4.1}

1. **Width**
   An accessible route shall have a minimum 36-inch clear width except at doors. (Fig. 1a) A wheelchair needs additional clear space when making a turn around an obstruction which is less than 48 inches in length as shown in Figure 1(b).

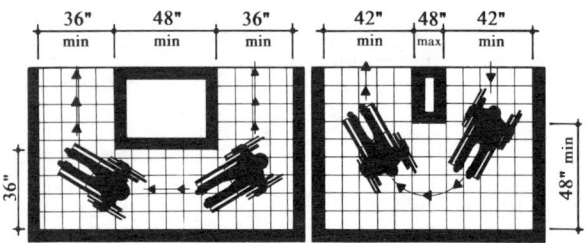

Fig. 1(a)   Fig. 1(b)
Fig. 1 **Accessible Route Minimum Clearance**

2. **Passing Space**
   A 5-foot by 5-foot minimum passing space shall be provided at reasonable intervals of 200 feet or less when an accessible route has less than a 5-foot clear width. A corridor or walkway T-intersection can be used as a passing area.

3. **Height**
   Minimum height clearance shall be at least 80 inches above the floor on accessible routes.

ADA ACCESSIBILITY DESIGN STANDARDS
CLEAR SPACES • Route of Travel

C-2.1.4 DOORWAYS ^{CA: D-3.16, D-3.3.4, D-7.1}

Doors and door openings along an accessible route shall comply with the door regulations in Section C-5.2.

C-2.1.5 LOCATIONS ^{CA: D-3.3}

A minimum of one accessible route within a facility site shall
a) be provided from public streets or sidewalks, passenger loading zones, accessible parking spaces, and public transportation stops to the accessible facility or building entrance served by those areas;
b) connect accessible buildings, facilities, elements, and spaces on the same site;
c) connect accessible building or facility entrances with all accessible spaces, elements, and dwelling units within the facility;
d) connect at least one accessible dwelling unit entrance with the interior and exterior spaces and facilities serving those units; and
e) coincide with the general public route to the maximum extent possible.

C-2.1.6 EMERGENCY EGRESS ^{CA: D-3.3.4}

Accessible routes shall also serve as an emergency egress route or connect to an accessible area of rescue assistance. *Emergency management plans to ensure safe evacuation is essential for life safety for those who are visiting, employed, or residents within the building or facility.*

1. Rescue Assistance Areas ^{CA: D-3.5}
An area of rescue assistance shall be one of the following:
a) A portion of a smoke-proof enclosed stairway landing that meets the local building code requirements.

ADA ACCESSIBILITY DESIGN STANDARDS
CLEAR SPACES • Route of Travel

b) A portion of a stairway landing separated from the building interior, vented to the outside, and separated by at least a one-hour fire-resistant door assembly.

c) A vestibule that is constructed according to the fire-resistant building standards for corridors and openings and which is located adjacent to an exit enclosure.

d) A portion of a one-hour fire-resistant corridor adjacent to an exit enclosure that is in compliance with the local fire-resistant construction and opening protection codes.

e) A portion of an exterior exit balcony which meets the local building code and is adjacent to an exit stairway. Fire protection assemblies having at least a 3/4-hour fire protection rating shall be provided at interior openings of the building within 20 feet of the rescue assistance area.

f) A room or space separated from the rest of the building by a smokeproof barrier. The smokeproof barrier shall have at least a one-hour fire-resistant rating which completely encloses the space. The space shall provide an exit directly to an exit enclosure. Door assemblies shall be smoke and draft controlled, have a fire-protection rating of at least twenty minutes, and be automatic or self-closing. Rooms or areas having direct access to an exit enclosure shall have the same fire resistant construction, opening protection, and rating when that exit enclosure has more than a one-hour rating.

g) An elevator lobby and an elevator shaft that are both pressurized smoke-proof enclosures which
  1) comply with ADA guidelines regarding size, signs, and communication requirements;
  2) have smoke detectors which activate the pressurized system; and

ADA ACCESSIBILITY DESIGN STANDARDS
CLEAR SPACES • Route of Travel

3) have pressurization equipment and duct work separated from the rest of the building by a minimum two-hour fire-resistant construction rating.

Smokeproof enclosures and smoke detectors shall be in approved locations and shall comply with local building codes and regulations.

2. **Wheelchair Spaces**
Each area of rescue assistance shall provide at least two accessible 30 by 48-inch wheelchair spaces and shall not encroach on the width of any required exit route. For every occupant load of 200 persons served by the area of rescue assistance, no less than one wheelchair space per story shall be provided. The minimum number of spaces may be reduced to one by the appropriate local authorities on floors with less than a 200 occupant load.

3. **Stairways**
A 4-foot minimum clear width shall exist between stairway handrails located adjacent to areas of rescue assistance for evacuation of individuals in wheelchairs and others. *This is an adequate path for ambulatory persons.*

4. **Communication System**
A two-way communication system shall be provided between the primary entrance and each area of rescue assistance. An alternative location may be approved by the appropriate local authorities. The system shall have both a visible and audible means of communication for confirming "help is on the way".

5. **Signs**
An "AREA OF RESCUE ASSISTANCE" sign with the International Symbol of Accessibility shall identify each area of rescue assistance. This sign shall also be illuminated when an exit sign is required to be illuminated. Inaccessible exits shall have signs giving direction to the areas of rescue assistance.

ADA ACCESSIBILITY DESIGN STANDARDS
CLEAR SPACES • Protruding Objects

6. Instructions
Emergency instructions on the use of a rescue assistance area shall be posted next to the two-way communication system within the area.

C-2.2 PROTRUDING OBJECTS   CA: D-3.3.9

C-2.2.1 PROJECTION

Protruding objects mounted less than 27 inches above the finished floor do not have protruding restrictions. (Fig 2a) Objects between 27 inches and 80 inches above the finished floor shall not extend more than 4 inches from any vertical surface into walkways. (Fig 2b) Free-standing and wall mounted objects may not exceed a 12-inch overhang between 27 inches and 80 inches above the finished floor. (Figs. 3, 4) The clear width of an accessible route or maneuvering space shall not be reduced by protruding objects. (Fig. 5)

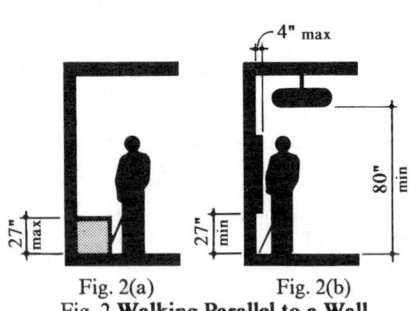

Fig. 2(a)   Fig. 2(b)
Fig. 2 **Walking Parallel to a Wall**

ADA ACCESSIBILITY DESIGN STANDARDS
CLEAR SPACES • Protruding Objects

Fig. 3 **Wall Mounted Objects**

Fig. 4(a) **Protruding Stair Hazard**

This overhang is unrestricted since it cannot be approached from a side direction.

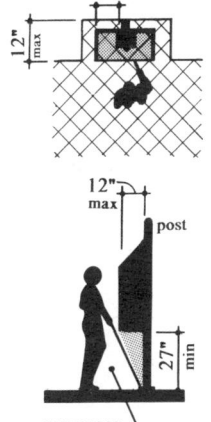

Fig. 4(b) **Post-Mounted Objects**

Cane Techniques

Persons with disabilities using canes as a guide are taught two basic touch techniques: (1) touch technique by swinging the cane in an arc from side to side past the shoulders, and (2) the diagonal technique where the cane is held in a stationary position in front and across the body. (Fig. 6) The grip and the tip are both extended outside each shoulder with the cane tip touching or just above the floor. The touch technique is normally used in unfamiliar surroundings where the diagonal technique is used in more controlled environments and familiar spaces.

Object Awareness

The visually impaired are only aware of potential hazards when they are within the range of the

ADA ACCESSIBILITY DESIGN STANDARDS
CLEAR SPACES • Protruding Objects

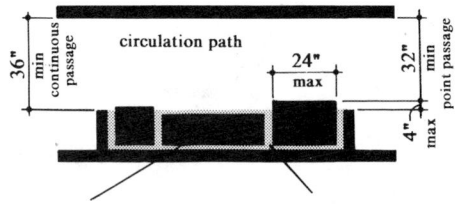

Fig. 5 **Protection Around Wall-Mounted Objects**

cane. (Fig. 6) When walking toward an object, the cane can detect an overhanging object when the lowest surface is not higher than 27 inches above the floor. Protruding objects along-side a passageway are not normally detected. Slight overhangs of less than 4 inches are not hazardous since the swing of the cane normally extends that amount or more past the shoulders.

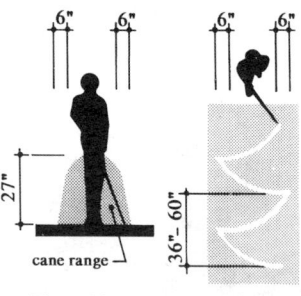

Fig. 6(a)   Fig. 6(b)
Fig. 6 **Cane Techniques**

ADA ACCESSIBILITY DESIGN STANDARDS
CLEAR SPACES • Wheelchairs

C-2.2.2 CLEAR HEIGHT

All circulation areas shall have an 80-inch high clearance above the floor level. (Fig. 2b) When an adjoining area to an accessible route is less than 80 inches above the floor, a barrier shall be provided to warn and protect the visually impaired. (Figs. 4a and 5)

C-2.3 WHEELCHAIRS

C-2.3.1 PEDESTRIAN TRAFFIC CA: D-3.4, D-4.1

1. **Straight Passage**
   The minimum clear width for wheelchairs shall be 32 inches at any one point and 36 inches for a continuous approach. (Fig. 7) *Wheelchairs require a 30-inch clear opening width for straight passage between two points such as a doorway. A 32-inch clear width is usually adequate for varying conditions. Restrictive spaces exceeding 24 inches in length are considered passageways and require a 36-inch clear width.*

2. **Walking Space**
   A person on a walkway needs a 32-inch wide clearance. Persons with a walking-aid need at least 32 inches to clear openings and a 36-inch clear width in passageways and walkways for a comfortable gait and safety allowance.

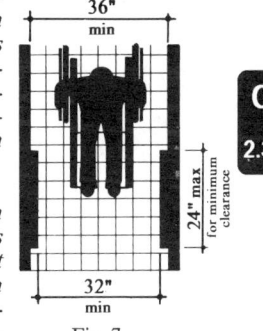

Fig. 7
Minimum Clearance

ADA ACCESSIBILITY DESIGN STANDARDS
CLEAR SPACES • Wheelchairs

3. **Passing**
   The minimum clear width for two passing wheelchairs is 60 inches. (Fig. 9)

4. **Two-way Traffic**
   Two streams of traffic can comfortably pass in a clear 64-inch wide space, whereas a 60-inch space provides a restricted flow. A minimum 48-inch width is needed for ambulatory and non-ambulatory persons to pass each other, but only in a restrictive manner. (Fig. 8)

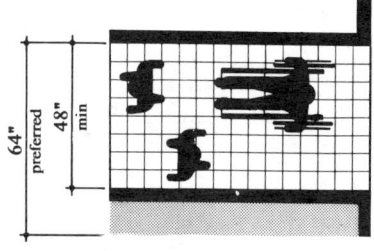

Fig. 8 **Minimum Clearance**

5. **Turning**
   A wheelchair needs a minimum 60-inch diameter (Fig. 10a) or a clear 60 by 60-inch T-shaped space to maneuver turns (Fig. 10b).

   These spaces are usually satisfactory to allow wheelchairs to turn. Less space may cause repeated turns or bumping into objects resulting in less maneuverability.

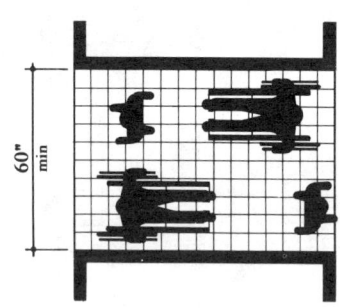

Fig. 9 **Wheelchairs Passing**

ADA ACCESSIBILITY DESIGN STANDARDS
CLEAR SPACES • Wheelchairs

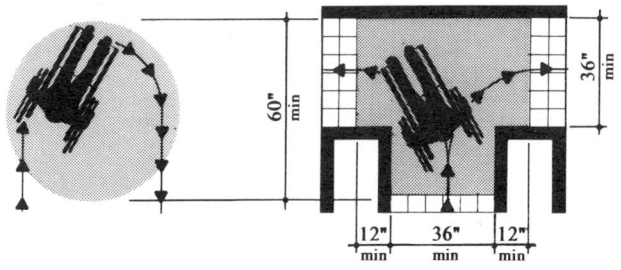

Fig. 10(a)   Fig. 10(b)
Fig. 10 **Minimum Turning Space**

The clear space in Figure 11 is more suitable for turning.

C-2.3.2 CLEAR FLOOR SPACE
CA: D-2.8.2.4, D-2.8.4.1(3), D-3.4, D-6.3.5(1), D-7.1.4(2)

The minimum clear ground space for a stationary wheelchair and occupant is 30 inches by 48 inches. The space may be provided in a forward or parallel approach to an object. Knee space under objects may be used as part of the clear floor space. One full unobstructed side of a wheelchair floor space shall adjoin an accessible route. The space shall overlap the route or adjoin another clear wheelchair floor space.

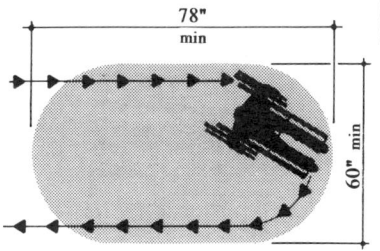

Fig. 11 **Recommended Clearance**

ADA ACCESSIBILITY DESIGN STANDARDS
CLEAR SPACES • Wheelchairs

Additional clearance space shall be provided for alcoves and other areas having all or part of three confined sides. (Figs. 12a, 12b) Clear floor spaces for wheelchairs shall comply with the ground and floor surfaces in Section C-5.4. *Figure 13 shows the dimensions for a typical adult male in a wheelchair and provides a uniform reference for design.*

Fig. 12 **Alcove Space**

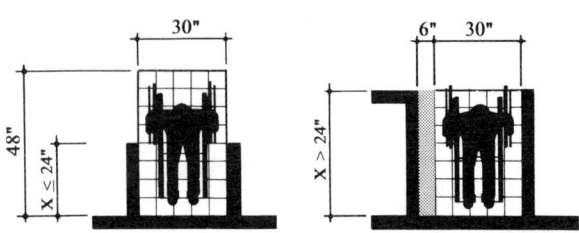

Fig. 12(a) When the "x" measurement is greater than 24", an additional clearance of 6" shall be provided as shown.

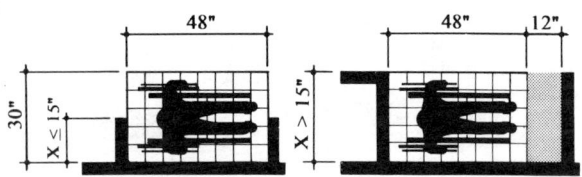

Fig. 12(b) When the "x" measurement is greater than 15", an additional clearance of 12" shall be provided as shown.

ADA ACCESSIBILITY DESIGN STANDARDS
CLEAR SPACES • Wheelchairs

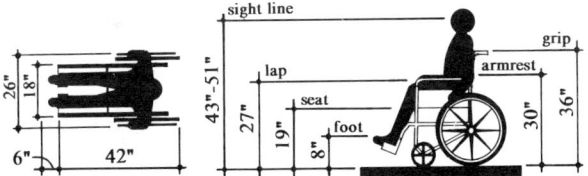

Fig. 13 **Adult Size Wheelchair Dimension**
(The footrest may extend farther for tall people)

C-2.3.3 REACH LIMITS

1. Forward Reach

A forward reach over an obstruction shows the accessible measurement requirements in Figure 14(a). An object which requires a forward approach and reach from a

Fig. 14 **Forward Reach**

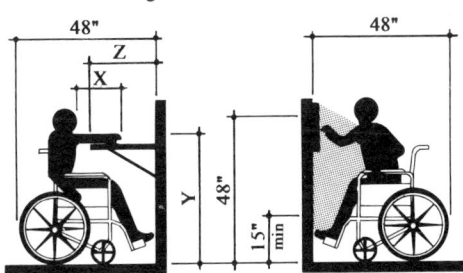

Note: x shall be $\leq 25"$, and z shall be $\geq x$. If $x < 20"$, then y shall be $\leq 48"$. If x is 20"-25", then y shall be $\leq 44"$.

Fig. 14(a) **Over an Obstruction**   Fig. 14(b) **High Reach Limit**

ADA ACCESSIBILITY DESIGN STANDARDS
CLEAR SPACES • Wheelchairs

wheelchair shall not be lower than 15 inches or higher than 48 inches above the floor surface. (Fig. 14b)

2. **Side Reach**
The maximum range for a side reach is shown in Figure 15. The maximum high and low side reach is between 9 inches and 54 inches above the floor surface for a parallel approach. (Fig. 15b) The clearance and reach limit over an obstruction is shown in Figure 15(c).

Fig. 15 **Side Reach**

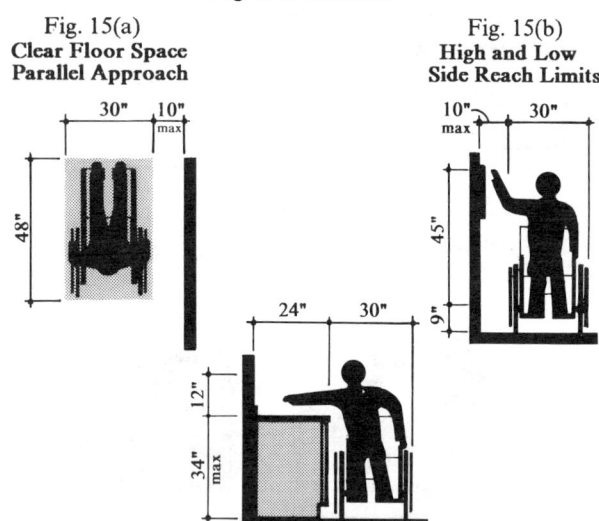

Fig. 15(a) **Clear Floor Space Parallel Approach**

Fig. 15(b) **High and Low Side Reach Limits**

Fig. 15(c) **Side Reach Limit over Obstruction**

ADA ACCESSIBILITY DESIGN STANDARDS
CLEAR SPACES • Wheelchairs

Figure 16 shows the overall reach limitations for persons in wheelchairs.

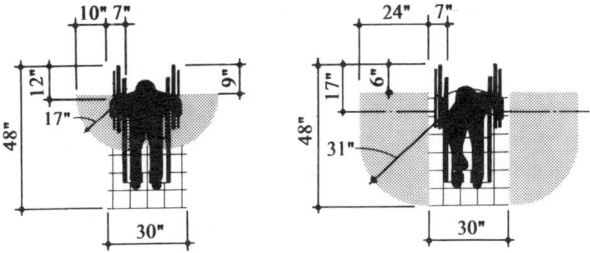

Fig. 16 **Wheelchair Reach Range**

C-3 COMMUNICATION MEANS

C-3.1 ALARMS

C-3.1.1 APPLICATION CA: D-3.8, D-5.1

Notification systems required by Section C-1 shall comply with the requirements of Section C-3.1. Minimum requirements call for visual signal appliances to be provided in building and facility common areas and restrooms.

C-3.1.2 AUDIBLE CA: D-5.1.2

1. **Sound Level**
   The maximum sound pressure level allowed for alarms is 120 dbA. An audible emergency alarm sound shall be at least 15 dbA over the existing sound level within a space or shall exceed the maximum sound level by 5 dbA for at least 60 seconds, whichever is louder.

2. **Effective Signals**
   Audible emergency signals must have an intensity and frequency to bring awareness to persons with hearing impairments. Persons over the age of 60 normally have difficulty perceiving frequencies higher than 10,000 Hz. The best alarm signals are those with a periodic element of individual distinctive tones void of noise in between. Constant or reverberating tones should be avoided.

C-3.1.3 VISUAL CA: D-2.8.1.5, D-5.1.1

A building or facility alarm system shall provide a visual signal. A single station visual alarm signal shall be provided

ADA ACCESSIBILITY DESIGN STANDARDS
COMMUNICATION MEANS • Alarms

when single station audible alarm signals are provided. Visual alarm signals shall have the features shown in Table C-3A. *Zoned or coded alarm systems may be used.*

TABLE C-3A	
FEATURE	**SIGNAL REQUIREMENT**
Lamp	• xenon strobe or equivalent
Color	• clear or nominal white
Intensity	• 75 candela minimum
Flash	• 1 Hz minimum to 3 Hz maximum
Pulse[1]	• duration of .2 seconds • maximum duty cycle of 40 percent
Placement	• lowest position of either 80 inches above the highest floor level or 6 inches below the ceiling • within a 50 feet horizontal plane of any location within the room or space • placed up to 100 feet around the perimeter in large open spaces that exceed 100 feet across and which do not have obstructions more than 6 feet above the finished floor in lieu of suspending appliances from the ceiling • no more than 50 feet from the signal in common corridors and hallways

[1] The pulse duration is the time interval between the initial and final point of 10% of the maximum signal.

ADA ACCESSIBILITY DESIGN STANDARDS
COMMUNICATION MEANS • Alarms

C-3.1.4 AUXILIARY

1. Visual Alarms
Sleeping rooms and units shall either have a visual alarm connected to the building emergency alarm system or shall have a standard 110-volt electrical receptacle into which an auxiliary visual alarm appliance can be connected. This auxiliary alarm shall be triggered by the building emergency alarm system. A visual alarm shall be located where the signal can be viewed from any area of the room or space. Instructions shall be made available on the use of the auxiliary alarm.

2. Light Level
Deaf persons who live or work alone need to be warned by a visual alarm when an emergency alarm is activated. Such appliances must reflect the signal or raise the overall light level sharply throughout a space to be effective. A flashing light at least seven times brighter than the overall light level is usually adequate to awaken sleepers or signal awake persons in a normal daylight room.

3. Vibrator Alarm
Visual alarms alone are not always the best means to alert sleepers. A signal-activated vibrator under the mattress or pillow is found to be much more effective in alerting sleepers. Many alarm appliances are sound-activated by a clock radio or alarm, telephone, or smoke detector. A vibrator can be activated by a signal transmitted through an ordinary 110-volt outlet, or a building alarm system can trigger an auxiliary alarm which activates the vibrator.

ADA ACCESSIBILITY DESIGN STANDARDS
COMMUNICATION MEANS • Detectable Warnings

C-3.2 DETECTABLE WARNINGS

C-3.2.1 APPLICATION CA: D-3.9, D-5.2

Detectable warnings required by Section C-1 shall comply with the regulations of Section C-3.2.

C-3.2.2 WALKING SURFACES CA: D-4.4.1(6), D-5.2.1

Raised truncated domes shall be used for detectable warnings on walking surfaces. The domes shall contrast with adjoining surfaces, light on a dark surface or dark on a light surface. The contrasting materials shall be an integral part of the walking surface

1. **Contrast**
   The contrasting material should differ 70 percent or more. Contrast in percent is determined by:

   $$Contrast = [(A - B) / A] \times 100$$

   A = *light reflectance value (LRV) of the lighter area*
   B = *light reflectance value (LRV) of the darker area*

   Note: *White and black are never absolute. Thus A never equals 100 percent and B is always greater than 0.*

2. **Dimensions**
   Raised truncated domes shall have a nominal 0.9-inch diameter, nominal 0.2-inch height, and a nominal 2.35-inch space from center to center.

3. **Interior Surfaces**
   Adjoining walking surfaces shall differ in resiliency or sound-on-cane contact from the detectable warnings when used on interior walking surfaces.

ADA ACCESSIBILITY DESIGN STANDARDS
COMMUNICATION MEANS • Signs

C-3.2.3 VEHICLE AND PEDESTRIAN AREAS
CA: D-5.2.2

A 36-inch wide continuous detectable warning strip shall be used when a walk crosses or adjoins a vehicular way and where the walking surface of the pedestrian and vehicular areas are not separated by curbs, railings, or other elements. The detectable warnings shall comply with Section C-3.2.2.

C-3.2.4 REFLECTIVE POOLS

Detectable warnings, railings, curbs, or walls shall be used for protection from reflective pool edges. Detectable warnings shall comply with Section C-3.2.2 when provided.

C-3.3 SIGNS

C-3.3.1 APPLICATION CA: D-3.10, D-5.3

Accessible signs required by Section C-1 shall comply with the applicable requirements of Section C-3.3. The following are helpful means to relate information and instructions to the visually impaired:

1. **Auditory Instructions**
   Several maps and auditory instructions have been developed and tested for specific applications for the visually impaired to enable them to find specific locations within building complexes independently. The type of building, the type of user, and the type of information to be communicated determines the kind of map or instructions for use.

2. **Landmark Cues**
   Landmark orientation cues are useful to the visually impaired such as illumination level changes, unique patterns,

COMMUNICATION MEANS • Signs

bright colors, wall murals, special equipment placement, or various architectural features.

3. Peripheral Vision Limitation
Persons with disabilities involving limitation in head movement and reduced peripheral vision are more likely to notice signs placed perpendicular to the path of travel. People can usually distinguish signs within a 30-degree angle to either side of their face centerline without moving their head.

C-3.3.2 PLACEMENT
CA: D-3.3.8, D-3.10, D-5.3.4, D-6.1.3, D-6.3.2, D-7.2.4

Signs shall be mounted 60 inches above the finish floor to the centerline of the sign. A person shall be able to approach a sign to within 3 inches without interference from protruding objects or the swing of a door.

Permanent Room Signs
Permanent identification signs for rooms and spaces shall be placed on walls adjacent to the latch side of the door. Signs shall be placed on the nearest adjacent wall when there is no wall space directly adjacent to the latch side or adjacent to double-leaf doors.

C-3.3.3 ACCESSIBILITY SYMBOLS

1. International Symbol CA: D-5.3.1
The International Symbol of Accessibility shall be used to identify accessible facilities and elements required by Section C-1 and displayed as shown in Figures 17(a,b).

2. Telephone Handset Symbol
Volume control telephones required by Section C-1.3.18 (2) shall be identified by a sign portraying a telephone handset with radiating sound waives.

ADA ACCESSIBILITY DESIGN STANDARDS
COMMUNICATION MEANS • Signs

3. TDD Symbol

Text telephones required by Section C-1.3.18(3) shall be identified by the international TDD symbol. (Fig. 17c) Directional signs shall be provided in facilities with public text telephones and shall include the international TDD symbol. A sign shall be located adjacent to all telephone banks that do not contain a text telephone and shall give directions to the nearest text telephone location. Directional signs shall be placed at building entrances or in building directories of facilities which do not have a bank of telephones.

Fig. 17 **International Symbols of Accessibility**

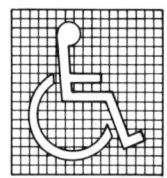

Fig. 17(a) **Proportion**

Fig. 17(b) **Display Choice**

Fig. 17(c) **TDD Symbol**

Fig. 17(d) **Hearing Loss**

ADA ACCESSIBILITY DESIGN STANDARDS
COMMUNICATION MEANS • Signs

4. Hearing Loss Symbol

Signs with the international symbol of access for hearing loss (Fig. 17d) shall be displayed in assembly areas to show the availability of a permanently installed assistive listening system as required by Section C-1.3.10(3).

Different types of listening systems should be indicated by appropriate messages and displayed with the hearing loss symbol of accessibility. For example:

> **INFRARED**
> **ASSISTIVE LISTENING SYSTEM**
> **AVAILABLE**
> ----PLEASE ASK---

> **AUDIO LOOP IN USE**
> **TURN T-SWITCH FOR**
> **BETTER HEARING**
> ----OR ASK FOR HELP---

> **FM**
> **ASSISTIVE LISTENING**
> **SYSTEM AVAILABLE**
> ---PLEASE ASK---

The symbol accompanied by a message may be used to notify persons of other auxiliary aids and services available such as sign language interpreters, oral interpreters, real time captioning, and captioned note taking.

C-3.3.4 ILLUMINATION LEVELS

Sign surface shall have a uniform illumination level and be in the range of 10 to 30 footcandles. The sign shall be located so a light source behind or in front of the sign does not exceed the illumination level on the sign surface.

ADA ACCESSIBILITY DESIGN STANDARDS
COMMUNICATION MEANS • Signs

TABLE C-3B
ACCESSIBILITY SIGN EXAMPLES

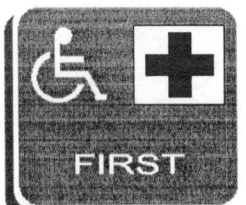 

ADA ACCESSIBILITY DESIGN STANDARDS
COMMUNICATION MEANS • Signs
TABLE C-3B
ACCESSIBILITY SIGN EXAMPLES

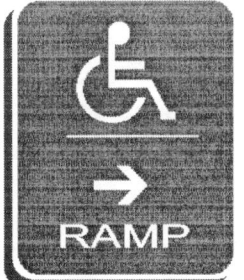
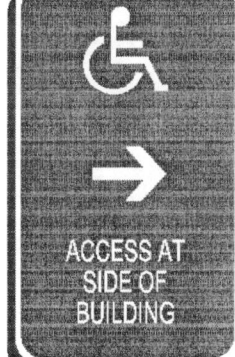

ADA ACCESSIBILITY DESIGN STANDARDS
COMMUNICATION MEANS • Signs

C-3.3.5 FINISH ^{CA: D-5.3.2}

Sign characters and sign background shall be eggshell, matte, or other non-glare finish. *Eggshell finish of 11 to 19 degree gloss on a 60 degree glossmeter is recommended.*

C-3.3.6 CONTRAST ^{CA: D-5.3.2}

Characters and symbols shall contrast with the background by light on dark or dark on light. *A dark background with light-colored characters and symbols usually achieves the greatest readability. Signs are more legible for persons having low vision which have a 70 percent or more contrasting background. Refer to Section C-3.2.2(1) for the contrast percentage formula.*

C-3.3.7 CHARACTER DIMENSIONS ^{CA: D-5.3.2}

The necessary viewing distance shall determine the character and number size. The upper case "X" is the measure used for the minimum height. The use of lower case characters are permitted. The minimum character height is 3 inches. Signs that are suspended or projected overhead shall comply with Section C-2.2.2.

Letter and number size   width-to-height ratio between 3:5 and 1:1 .

Character Stroke   width-to-height ratio between 1:5 and 1:10

Legibility of printed characters depends on:
1. *viewing distance*   2. *character height*
3. *color*   4. *character/background Contrast*
5. *font type*   6. *ratio stroke width/character height*

ADA ACCESSIBILITY DESIGN STANDARDS
COMMUNICATION MEANS • Signs

C-3.3.8 RAISED CHARACTERS AND SYMBOLS
CA: D-5.3.2, D-5.3.3

A pictograph border dimension shall be at least 6 inches in height. Pictographs shall have a verbal description placed directly below them. Letters and numbers shall be upper case sans serif or simple serif font, raised 1/32-inch, and be accompanied with Grade 2 Braille. Raised characters shall be between 5/8-inch and 2 inches in height.

The standard dimensions for literary Braille are:

Dot diameter.. .059 inch
Inter-dot spacing..................................... .090 inch
Horizontal separation between cells........ .241 inch
Vertical separation between cells............. .395 inch

Raised borders should be set far enough apart from raised characters to eliminate confusion in reading. Interpretive guides, audio tape devices, or other methods may prove to be more effective where a sign description may not provide sufficient detailed information for a meaningful understanding.

C-3.4 TELEPHONES

C-3.4.1 APPLICATION CA: D-3.11, D-5.4

Public telephones required to be accessible by Section C-1 shall comply with the requirements of Section C-3.4.

C-3.4.2 REACH RANGE CA: D-5.4.1

Telephones shall be mounted where the highest operable part is within the reach ranges specified in Sections C-2.3.3. *Some coin operated telephones have a dial-tone first system where*

ADA ACCESSIBILITY DESIGN STANDARDS
COMMUNICATION MEANS • Telephones

Fig. 18 **Telephone Placement**

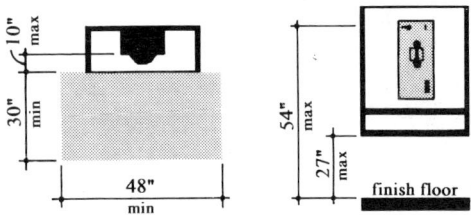

Fig. 18(a) **Side Reach**

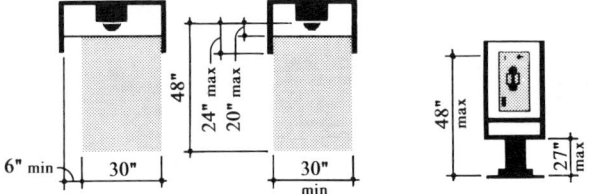

The maximum height of basic telephone operable parts is 48 inches.
Fig. 18 (b) **Forward Reach**

calls can be placed through an operator without inserting coins. The operator button is 46 inches high when the coin slot is at 54 inches. With the coin slot placed at 48 inches high, a universal installation of telephones would be possible if all operable parts were no more than 48 inches high.

ADA ACCESSIBILITY DESIGN STANDARDS
COMMUNICATION MEANS • Telephones

C-3.4.3 CONTROLS

Push button control telephones shall be provided where service is available. The highest operable part shall be within the reach range indicated in Section C-2.3.3.

C-3.4.4 CORD

The telephone cord on handsets shall be at least 29 inches long.

C-3.4.5 BOOKS

When provided, telephone books shall be located within the reach ranges that comply with Section C-2.3.3.

C-3.4.6 PROTRUDING OBJECTS

Telephones shall comply with Section C-2.2.

C-3.4.7 CLEAR SPACE

A 30-inch by 48-inch clear floor space shall be provided at telephones allowing a forward or parallel approach by wheelchair users. (Fig. 18) Such space shall comply with the requirements of Section C-2.3. Bases, enclosures, and fixed seats shall not impede approaches to telephones by persons using wheelchairs.

C-3.4.8 HEARING ASSISTANCE

Telephones shall be compatible with hearing aids. Volume controls shall be provided with capabilities of 12 dbA minimum to a maximum 18dbA above normal and provided as required by Section C-1.3.10(3). The maximum may be exceeded when an automatic reset is provided.

ADA ACCESSIBILITY DESIGN STANDARDS
COMMUNICATION MEANS • Telephones

C-3.4.9 TEXT TELEPHONES CA: D-5.4.3

A public text telephone may be an integrated pay text telephone unit or a portable text telephone permanently attached within or adjacent to a pay telephone enclosure. A text telephone that is not a single integrated text pay telephone unit needs a shelf which is 10 inches wide, 10 inches deep, has a 6-inch minimum vertical clearance, and is accompanied by an electrical outlet and power cord.

1. **Location**
   A text telephone shall be permanently affixed within or adjacent to the telephone enclosure when used with the pay telephone.
2. **Cord**
   The cord shall be long enough to connect the telephone receiver and the text telephone when an acoustic coupler is used.
3. **Portable Text Telephone**
   A pay telephone accommodating a portable text telephone shall have a shelf, electrical outlet within or adjacent to the telephone enclosure, and a handset capable of being placed flush on the shelf surface. The shelf shall sufficiently accommodate a text telephone and have a 6-inch minimum vertical clearance where the text telephone is placed.
4. **Equivalent Facilitation**
   A portable text telephone may be provided as an equivalent facilitation in lieu of a permanently installed text telephone when it is available at a 24-hour service area and can be used at a nearby public pay telephone. The nearby pay telephone shall provide a shelf, electrical outlet, handset, and sufficient cord length to accommodate the portable text telephone and comply with Section C-3.4.

ADA ACCESSIBILITY DESIGN STANDARDS
COMMUNICATION MEANS • Telephones

Signs complying with Section C-3.3.3 shall indicate the text telephone availability and its location. *Equivalent facilitation may be made available with a portable text telephone. The telephone shall be readily available, convenient, and easily accessible. Pocket-type text telephones are not considered equivalent to conventional text telephones since they are not widely used.*

ADA ACCESSIBILITY DESIGN STANDARDS
FACILITY AREAS • Assembly

C-4 FACILITY AREAS

C-4.1 ASSEMBLY

C-4.1.1 APPLICATION ᶜᴬ: D-2.2

Accessible assembly and associated areas required by Section C-1 shall comply with the requirements of Section C-4.1.

C-4.1.2 WHEELCHAIR LOCATIONS
CA: D-2.2.1.2, D-2.2.2.2, D-2.2.3.3, D-2.2.4.1(2), D-3.4, D-8.4

Wheelchair locations shall be an integral part of any fixed seating plan with choices of admission prices and seating locations similar to those offered to the general public. When a wheelchair user is not occupying a designated wheelchair space, that space may have seats which can be removed and replaced to convert the space for use by others.

1. **Accessible Route** ᶜᴬ: D-2.2.1.2(6)
   Wheelchair areas shall connect to an accessible route that also serves as an emergency egress route.
2. **Companion Seating**
   Each wheelchair seating area shall be accompanied by at least one fixed seat for a companion.
3. **Capacity** ᶜᴬ: D-2.2.1.2(3)
   Additional wheelchair spaces shall be provided in more than one location when the seating capacity exceeds 300.
4. **Clustered Seating**
   When the line-of-sight requires a slope in excess of 5 percent, accessible spaces may be clustered for bleachers, balconies, and similar seating areas. Equivalent accessible

ADA ACCESSIBILITY DESIGN STANDARDS
FACILITY AREAS • Assembly

viewing spaces may be located on other levels if they have accessible egress.

5. **Seating Design** CA: D-2.2.1.2(5)
   Wheelchair users can be offered a choice of viewing and prices when wheelchair areas are planned for a variety of locations.

6. **Fixed Seats** CA: D-2.2.1.2(4)
   Building/life safety codes set minimum distances between fixed seating rows. Consideration is given to the number of seats in a row, the exit aisle width and arrangement, and the location of exit doors.

7. **Continental Seating** CA: D-2.2.1.2(2)
   "Continental" seating should be considered when designing spaces with fixed seating. Continental seating provides more seats per row with an increase in row spacing and exit doors. This allows greater ease in accessing mid-row seats and facilitates emergency egress, especially for people with mobility impairments.

C-4.1.3 CLEAR FLOOR SPACE CA: D-2.2.1.2(7)

Figure 19 illustrates the minimum requirements for the clear floor space that shall be provided at each wheelchair location. *An accessible space accommodating two wheelchairs allow persons attending together to sit together.*

C-4.1.4 FLOOR SURFACES CA: D-2.2.1.2(8)

The floor or ground surface at wheelchair locations shall be level and comply with the requirements of Section C-5.4.

C-4.1.5 ACCESS TO PERFORMING AREAS
CA: D-2.2.1.2, D-2.2.1.3, D-2.2.2.2, D-2.2.2.4, D-2.2.4.1

Wheelchair seating locations shall be on an accessible route

ADA ACCESSIBILITY DESIGN STANDARDS
FACILITY AREAS • Assembly

that connects to the areas used by performers such as stages, arena floors, dressing rooms, locker rooms, and similar areas.

Fig. 19 **Wheelchair Seating Spaces in Series**

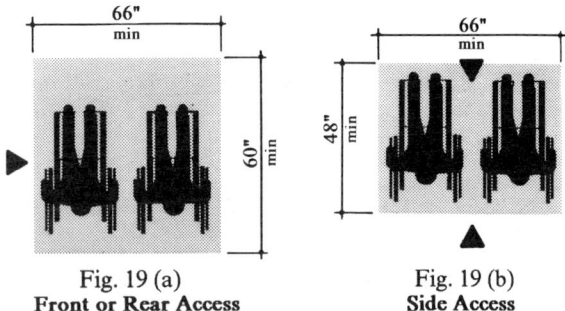

Fig. 19 (a)
Front or Rear Access

Fig. 19 (b)
Side Access

C-4.1.6 LISTENING SYSTEM CA: D-2.2.4.5

1. **Placement** CA: D-2.2.4.5(2)
   Individual fixed seats served by a listening system shall be within 50 feet of the performing area with a full view.

2. **Types** CA: D-2.2.4.5(1)
   Background noise can be filtered or eliminated with an assistive listening system (ALS). These systems provide signals which are received directly by persons with special receivers in their hearing aid which augment standard public address and audio systems. The type of program, the setting, and the intended audience determines the type of assistive listening system appropriate for a particular application. Types of assistive listening systems appropriate for various applications are magnetic induction loops, infrared, and radio frequency systems. Some advantages

ADA ACCESSIBILITY DESIGN STANDARDS
FACILITY AREAS • Assembly

and disadvantages of assistive listening devices are shown in Table C-4A. *An assistive listening system appropriate for groups of people in an assembly area may differ from the system appropriate for a particular individual in providing an auxiliary aid or as an accommodation that meets their individual need and usability. Whereas, the appropriate system for various assembly areas will be focused toward the "average" user or aggregate needs of various individuals. The most flexible way to meet this specification is a listening system that can be used from any seat.*

3. **Magnetic Induction Loops**
   Volume controlled earphone jacks will benefit those with a slight hearing loss but not those using hearing aids. The most feasible type of listening system for people who use hearing aids equipped with "T-coils" are magnetic induction loops. People without hearing aids, or hearing aids not equipped with inductive pick-ups, cannot use them.

4. **Radio Frequency System**
   Radio frequency systems can be very effective and inexpensive, but to use them, hearing aids need a special receiver. Radio frequency systems would be usable by those with or without hearing aids if hearing aids had a jack allowing a by-pass for microphones.

5. **Interference**
   Some listening systems receive interference from other equipment and feedback from hearing aids of those using the system. Careful engineering design could control the interference.

6. **Technical Assistance**
   Technical assistance can be obtained in the selection and installation of appropriate systems through demonstration centers.

ADA ACCESSIBILITY DESIGN STANDARDS
FACILITY AREAS • Assembly

Assistive Listening Devices
Advantages and Disadvantages

TABLE C-4A			
	Induction Loop	**Infrared**	**FM Applications**
Transmitter	Transducer wired to induction loop around listening area.	Emitter and receiver in line-of-sight.	Flashlight-size attached to speaker.
Receiver	Self-contained induction receiver or personal hearing aid with telecoil.	Personal hearing aid via DAI or induction neckloop and telecoil, or self-contained.	With personal hearing aid via DAI or induction neckloop and telecoil, or self-contained with earphone(s).
Application	• Meeting areas • Conference rooms • Theaters • Classrooms • Churches and temples • TV viewing	• Churches and Temples • Theaters • Auditoriums • Meetings requiring confidentiality • TV viewing	• Meeting areas • Classroom • Tour groups • Outdoor events • One-on-one
Continued...			

ADA ACCESSIBILITY DESIGN STANDARDS
FACILITY AREAS • Assembly

	Induction Loop	Infrared	FM
Advantages	• Low maintenance • Cost-effective • Easy to use • Unobtrusive • Some hearing aids can function as receivers • May be possible to integrate into existing public	• Easy to use • Moderate cost • Insures privacy and confidentiality • Can often be integrated into existing public address system.	• High user mobility • Highly portable • Variable for large range of hearing losses • Different channels allow use by different groups within the same room.
Disadvantage	• Susceptible to electrical interference • Inconsistent signal strength • Adjacent room signal spill over • Limited portability • Lack of standards for induction coil performance • Head position affects signal strength	• Limited portability • Ineffective outdoors • Requires installation • Line-of-sight required between emitter and receiver.	• High maintenance • Equipment is fragile • High cost of receivers • Equipment obtrusive • Expensive to maintain • Custom fitting to individual user may be required

Source: <u>Rehab Brief</u> National Institute on Disability and Rehabilitation Research, Washington, DC. Vol. XII, No. 10 (1990).

ADA ACCESSIBILITY DESIGN STANDARDS
FACILITY AREAS • Dressing Rooms

C-4.2 DRESSING ROOMS

C-4.2.1 APPLICATION CA: D-2.3.2.2(7)

Accessible dressing and fitting rooms required by Section C-1 shall comply with Section C-4.2 and shall be on an accessible route.

C-4.2.2 DOORS CA: D-2.3.2.2(7a)

Accessible dressing room doors shall comply with the requirements of Section C-5.2.

C-4.2.3 MIRRORS CA: D-2.3.2.2(7e)

When mirrors are provided in dressing rooms, an accessible dressing room of the same use shall have at least an 18-inch wide by 54-inch high full-length mirror positioned for both a standing view and sitting view from the bench.

C-4.2.4 BENCH CA: D-2.3.2.2(7d)

A 24 by 48-inch fixed bench shall be attached to the longest wall of every accessible dressing room between 17 and 19 inches above the finished floor.

1. **Clear Floor Space** CA: D-2.3.2.2(7c)
   An adjacent clear floor space shall be provided to enable a person in a wheelchair to make a parallel transfer onto the bench.
2. **Structural Strength**
   The bench fasteners and structural strength shall comply with the shear force requirement of Section C-6.5.4.

ADA ACCESSIBILITY DESIGN STANDARDS
FACILITY AREAS • Entrances

3. **Surface**
   Benches in showers, swimming pools, or other wet areas shall have a slip-resistant surface and be designed where water does not accumulate upon the bench surface.

C-4.2.5 WHEELCHAIR TURNING SPACE
CA: D-2.3.2.2(7)

Every accessible dressing room which is accessed through a swinging or sliding door shall have a clear floor space allowing a person using a wheelchair to make a 180-degree turn. The turning space shall not be obstructed by any door swing. A private dressing room does not require a turning space when accessed through a curtained opening at least 32 inches wide. The clear floor space must comply with Section C-2.3.

C-4.3 ENTRANCES

C-4.3.1 APPLICATION CA: D-2.2.3.2, D-3.3.4

Accessible entrances required by Section C-1 shall be part of an accessible route complying with Section C-2.1.

C-4.3.2 ROUTE OF TRAVEL CA: D-3.3, D-4

At least one accessible route of travel shall connect accessible entrances to all accessible spaces or elements in a building or facility, accessible parking and passenger loading zones, and available public streets, sidewalks, and transportation stops.

C-4.3.3 SERVICE ENTRANCES

Service entrances shall not be used as the only accessible entrance unless it is the only entrance.

ADA ACCESSIBILITY DESIGN STANDARDS
FACILITY AREAS • Parking

C-4.4 PARKING

C-4.4.1 APPLICATION ^{CA: D-3.12, D-6.1}

Parking spaces required to be accessible by Section C-1.3.3 shall comply with Sections C-4.4.3, C-4.4.4 and C-4.4.5. Accessible passenger loading zones shall comply with Sections C-4.4.2.

C-4.4.2 PASSENGER LOADING ZONES ^{CA: D-3.12.3}

1. **Access Aisle**
   An access aisle shall be provided adjacent and parallel to the vehicle pull-up space of a passenger loading zone. The aisle shall be a minimum 60 inches wide and 20 feet long as shown in Figure 20.
2. **Vertical Clearance** ^{CA: D-6.1.2}
   The minimum vertical clearance shall be 9 feet 6 inches at accessible loading zones and along at least one vehicle access route from those areas to the site entrance and exit.
3. **Surface**
   Accessible spaces and aisles shall be level and any surface slope shall not exceed 2 percent in all directions.
4. **Curb Ramps**
   Where a curb exists between a pull-up space and an access aisle, a curb ramp shall be pro-

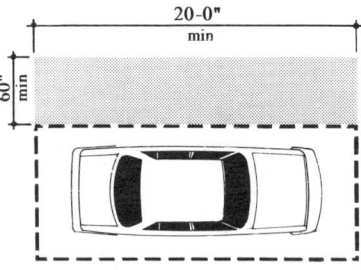

Fig. 20 **Loading Zone Access Aisle**

ADA ACCESSIBILITY DESIGN STANDARDS
FACILITY AREAS • Parking

vided that complies with Section C-5.1.

C-4.4.3 PARKING FACILITIES

1. **Independent Parking Facility**
Parking facilities not serving a particular facility shall locate accessible parking spaces on the shortest accessible route of travel to the parking facility's accessible pedestrian entrance.
2. **Facility Parking**
Buildings with an adjacent parking facility and multiple accessible entrances shall have dispersed accessible parking spaces located on the shortest accessible route to the nearest accessible entrance.

C-4.4.4 PARKING SPACES ^{CA: D-6.1.1}

1. **Width**
Accessible parking spaces shall not be less than 8 feet in width. *An 8-foot accessible space and 5-foot wide aisle does not allow space for a lift, a ramp, or the necessary space for a person in a wheelchair to exit a lift platform.*
2. **Vertical Clearance** ^{CA: D-6.1.2}
Van-accessible parking spaces and at least one access route from the entrance and the exit that services those parking spaces shall have a minimum vertical clearance of 8 feet 2 inches. *Disabled persons using high-top vans require a higher clearance in parking garages.*
3. **Ground Surface** ^{CA: D-6.1.1(5)}
Parking spaces and access aisles shall be level with surface slopes not exceeding 2 percent in all directions.
4. **Access Aisle** ^{CA: D-6.1.1(1)}
A common access aisle may serve two accessible parking spaces as shown in Figure 21.

ADA ACCESSIBILITY DESIGN STANDARDS
FACILITY AREAS • Parking

5. **Route of Travel**
   The parking access aisles shall be part of the accessible route to the facility entrance and comply with Section C-2.1. Vehicle overhangs shall not reduce the clear width of an accessible route.

6. **Van Accessible**
   CA: D-6.1.1(3)

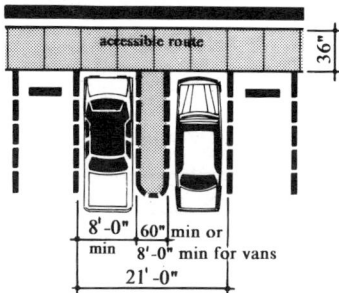

Fig. 21 **Parking Space Dimensions**

   The use of side-mounted lifts or ramps in vans for persons with disabilities require additional space. The "van accessible" parking space required by the ADA guidelines is an 8-foot wide parking space plus an 8-foot wide adjacent access aisle which is the minimum space in which to maneuver and exit from a side-mounted lift. A van/ lift/ wheelchair combination requires a parking space plus an aisle for a total width of 17 feet.

   Aisles
   Two van accessible spaces may share the use of the same 8-foot wide accessible aisle. Placing an access aisle at the end of a parking row may gain space that is normally unusable for parking purposes. (Fig. 22)

   Signs
   A sign should be provided to inform van users of the wider aisle even though the space is not restricted to van use.

ADA ACCESSIBILITY DESIGN STANDARDS
FACILITY AREAS • Parking

7. Universal Parking

The "Universal" parking design provides all accessible spaces with an 11-foot wide parking space and a 5-foot wide aisle. (Fig. 23) The wider space accommodates cars and vans and allows parking adjustment within the space where passengers with disabilities can enter or exit either side of the vehicle. However, in some instances, this may result in not entering or exiting within a marked access aisle. This design provides an alternative to the required percentage of wide aisles and extra signs.

Aisles

The accessible aisle should not have a ramp or a slope and should be level

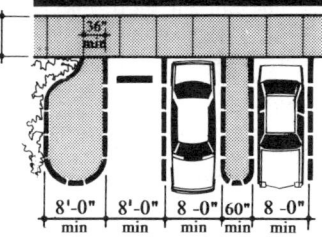

Fig. 22 **Van Accessible Aisle at End of Row**

with the parking space. Planters, curbs, or wheel stops shall not restrict the required dimensions of an access aisle. A person using a lift or ramp must have an aisle with no ramp or slope. The access aisle must be connected to an access route that leads to an accessible entrance. The access aisle must blend with the accessible route or have a curb ramp complying with Section C-5.1 that has the ramp opening located within the aisle but not within the parking space boundary.

C-4.4.5 SIGNS CA: D-6.1.3

Signs shall be placed in unobscured locations, shall designate

ADA ACCESSIBILITY DESIGN STANDARDS
FACILITY AREAS • Showers • Bathrooms

the reserved parking spaces, and display the symbol of accessibility as shown in Section C-3.3.3. Van accessible spaces shall have an additional sign mounted below the International Symbol of Accessibility which states "Van-Accessible". *The sign should be mounted at the front of a parking space high enough to be seen from the drivers seat. Universal parking does not require additional signs because these spaces accommodate all types of vehicles for the disabled.*

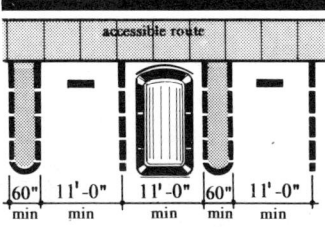

Fig. 23 **Universal Parking Design**

C-4.5 SHOWERS • BATHROOMS

C-4.5.1 APPLICATION ^{CA: D-3.13, D-6.2}

Accessible bathrooms, bathing facilities, shower rooms, and their fixtures and controls required by Sections C-1 shall be on an accessible route and comply with Section C-4.5.

C-4.5.2 WHEELCHAIR TURNING SPACE
CA: D-2.8.2.2, D-2.8.2.4

Accessible bathrooms shall provide an unobstructed wheelchair turning space that complies with Section C-2.3.1(5). This space may overlap the accessible route and the clear floor space at fixtures and controls.

ADA ACCESSIBILITY DESIGN STANDARDS
FACILITY AREAS • Showers • Bathrooms

C-4.5.3 DOORS

Accessible bathroom doors shall not swing into clear floor spaces required for fixtures and shall comply with the requirements of Section C-5.2.

C-4.5.4 SHOWERS • BATHTUBS CA: D-6.2.2, D-6.2.3

When provided, at least one accessible bathtub shall comply with Section C-6.2 or at least one accessible shower shall comply with Section C-4.6.

C-4.5.5 URINALS CA: D-6.3.7(1)

When provided, at least one urinal shall comply with Section C-6.9.

C-4.5.6 WATER CLOSETS CA: D-6.3.1, D-6.3.4(4)

Water closets in accessible stalls shall comply with Section C-6.10. When not in stalls, at least one water closet shall comply with Section C-6.10.

C-4.5.7 TOILET STALLS CA: D-6.3.4, D-6.3.5

When provided, at least one toilet stall shall be a standard stall complying with Section C-4.9. When more than five stalls are provided, at least one 36-inch wide stall shall be provided. This stall shall have parallel grab bars complying with Figure 29(d), Section C-6.5, and have an outward-swinging self-closing door. This stall shall be in addition to the standard stall defined in Section C-4.9.5.

C-4.5.8 LAVATORIES • MIRRORS CA: D-6.3.7(2,3), D-6.3.1

When provided, a minimum of one lavatory and one mirror

ADA ACCESSIBILITY DESIGN STANDARDS
FACILITY AREAS • Showers • Bathrooms

shall comply with Section C-6.6.

C-4.5.9 MEDICINE CABINETS

When provided, a minimum of one medicine cabinet shall have a usable shelf no higher than 44 inches above the accessible floor space that complies with Section C-2.3.2. *Accessible shelves, drawers, and floor-mounted cabinets are very useful alternatives to a medicine cabinet.*

C-4.5.10 CONTROLS • DISPENSERS CA: D-6.3.7

When provided, at least one of each type of control, dispenser, receptacle, and other equipment shall comply with Section C-6.3 and be located on an accessible route.

C-4.5.11 SHOWER STALL DESIGN CA: D-6.2.3

Two toilet room plans with a roll-in shower are shown in Figure 24. The shower stall fits within standard bathtub dimensions. Shower floor space can be utilized as a maneuvering space when the shower floor does not have a lip, thereby

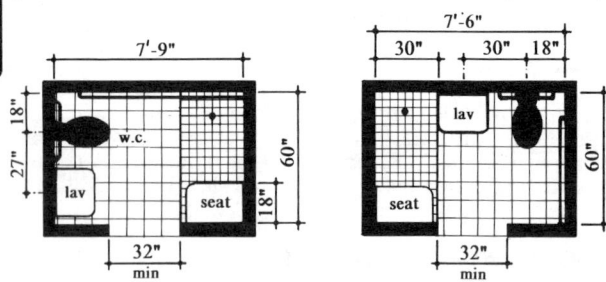

Fig. 24(a)   **Roll-in Shower Toilet Rooms**   Fig. 24(b)

ADA ACCESSIBILITY DESIGN STANDARDS
FACILITY AREAS • Shower Stalls

demanding less floor space than an accessible room with a bathtub. An alternate roll-in shower stall shown in Figure 72(b) places the plumbing on one wall and allows adequate clear space for a "T-turn".

C-4.6 SHOWER STALLS

C-4.6.1 APPLICATION ^{CA: D-6.2.3}

Accessible shower stalls shall comply with Section C-4.6.

C-4.6.2 SIZE ^{CA: D-6.2.3(1)}

Shower stall size and clear floor space shall comply with Figures 26(a,b) except as specified in Section C-7.2.4(3) for roll-in-showers. The shower enclosure in Figure 26(a) shall be 36 inches by 36 inches. Figure 26(b) shows a shower stall that fits into the same size space as a bathtub. Roll-in-showers required by Section C-7.2.4(3) shall comply with Figures 72(a or b).

C-4.6.3 SEATS ^{CA: D-6.2.3(5)}

A 36 by 36-inch shower stall shall have a seat the full depth of the stall as illustrated in Figure 25, placed between 17 and 19 inches above the finished floor, and located on the wall opposite the controls. Fixed seating shall be foldable and located on the wall adjacent to the

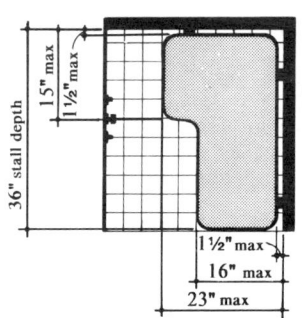

Fig. 25 **Shower Seat Design**

ADA ACCESSIBILITY DESIGN STANDARDS
FACILITY AREAS • Shower Stalls

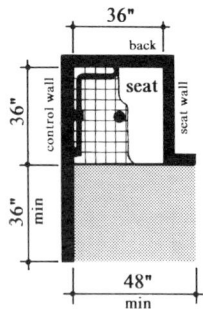 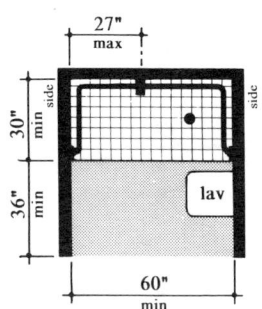

(a) **36" x 36" Enclosure** (b) **30" x 60" Enclosure**
Fig. 26 **Shower Enclosure Dimensions**

controls in 30 by 60-inch shower stalls as shown in Figure 72. The shower seat attachments and structural strength shall comply with Section C-6.5.4. *The walls also provide back support for those sitting in the shower.*

C-4.6.4 CURBS CA: D-6.2.3(2)

A 36 by 36-inch shower stall curb shall not exceed 1/2 inch in height. A 30 by 60-inch shower stall shall have no curb. *This provides additional bathroom maneuvering space and increases usability for wheelchair users.*

C-4.6.5 SHOWER ENCLOSURES CA: D-6.2.3(4)

When provided, shower stall enclosures shall not interfere with a person's transfer from a wheelchair onto the shower seat or obstruct the controls.

ADA ACCESSIBILITY DESIGN STANDARDS
FACILITY AREAS • Shower Stalls

C-4.6.6 FAUCETS ^{CA: D-6.2.3(8)}

Faucets and other controls shall be located according to the illustrations in Figure 27 and meet the specifications of Section C-6.3. The shower head, faucet, and other controls shall be installed on the side wall opposite the seat in a 36 by 36-inch shower stall.

Fig. 27 **Shower Grab Bars**

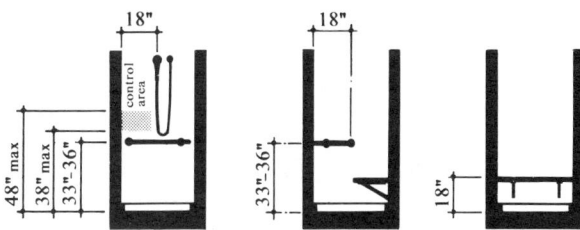

Fig. 27(a) **36" x 36" Enclosure**

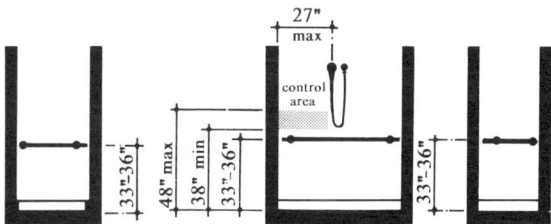

Fig. 27(b) **30" x 60" Enclosure**

ADA ACCESSIBILITY DESIGN STANDARDS
FACILITY AREAS • Storage

C-4.6.7 SHOWER HEAD ^{CA: D-6.2.3(8)}

A shower head used as both a fixed and a hand-held shower head shall be provided and have a hose no less than 5 feet long. A fixed shower head located 48 inches above the shower floor may be used in place of a hand-held shower in facilities where vandalism may likely occur.

C-4.6.8 GRAB BARS ^{CA: D-6.2.3(7)}

Shower grab bars shall be provided in shower enclosures as shown in Figure 27 and comply with Section C-6.5. *All grab bars and walls in 36 by 36-inch shower enclosures are within easy reach and thereby provide additional safety to those who have difficulty maintaining balance.*

C-4.7 STORAGE

C-4.7.1 APPLICATION ^{CA: D-3.14}

Accessible fixed storage, such as cabinets, closets, drawers and shelves required by Section C-1 shall comply with the requirements in Section C-4.7.

C-4.7.2 HARDWARE

Accessible storage facilities shall have hardware that complies with Section C-6.3.2. Acceptable hardware includes touch latches and U-shaped pulls.

C-4.7.3 FLOOR SPACE

Accessible storage facilities shall have a 30 by 48-inch clear floor space allowing a forward or parallel approach by

ADA ACCESSIBILITY DESIGN STANDARDS
FACILITY AREAS • Storage

wheelchair users and comply with Section C-2.3.

C-4.7.4 REACH RANGE

Accessible storage spaces shall be within at least one reach range as defined in Sections C-2.3.3 and as shown in Figures 14 and 15. The reach range for closet rods and shelves for a side approach shall not exceed 54 inches above the finished floor. The height and depth of closet rods and shelves shall comply with Figure 28 when their distance exceeds 10 inches from the wheelchair.

Fig. 28 **Storage**

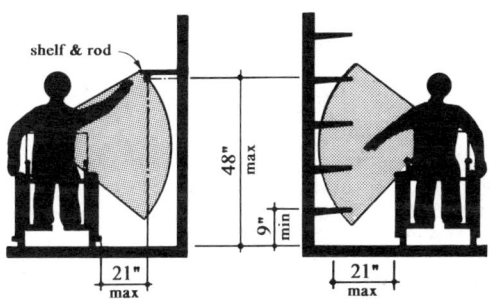

Fig 28(a) **Closet Rod**   Fig. 28(b) **Shelves**

ADA ACCESSIBILITY DESIGN STANDARDS
FACILITY AREAS • Toilet Rooms

C-4.8 TOILET ROOMS

C-4.8.1 APPLICATION CA: D-3.15, D-6.3

Accessible toilet facilities required by Section C-1 and accessible fixtures and controls required by Sections C-4.8.4 through C-4.8.7 shall be on an accessible route and comply with Section C-4.8.

C-4.8.2 DOORS CA: D-6.3.3

Accessible toilet room doors shall meet the requirements of Section C-5.2 and not swing into the clear floor space of any fixture.

C-4.8.3 TOILET STALLS CA: D-6.3.5

When provided, at least one stall shall be a standard stall and comply with the requirements of Section C-4.9. When more than five stalls are provided, at least one stall shall be 36 inches wide. This stall shall have an outward-swinging self-closing door and parallel grab bars that comply with Figure 29(d) and Section C-6.5. This stall shall be in addition to the stall complying with Section C-4.9.5.

C-4.8.4 WATER CLOSETS CA: D-6.3.1, D-6.3.4(4)

Water closets in stalls shall comply with Section C-6.10 requirements. At least one water closet shall comply with Section C-6.10 when there are no stalls.

C-4.8.5 URINALS CA: D-6.3.7(1)

When provided, a minimum of one urinal shall comply with

ADA ACCESSIBILITY DESIGN STANDARDS
FACILITY AREAS • Toilet Rooms

Section C-6.9 requirements.

C-4.8.6 LAVATORIES • MIRRORS
CA: D-6.3.1, D-6.3.7(2), D-6.3.7(3)

When provided, a minimum of one lavatory and one mirror shall be provided and comply with Section C-6.6 requirements.

C-4.8.7 CONTROLS • DISPENSERS CA: D-6.3.7(5,6)

When provided, one of each control, dispenser, receptacle, or other equipment shall be on an accessible route and comply with Section C-6.3 requirements.

C-4.8.8 TURNING SPACE CA: D-6.3.4(3), D-6.3.5(1)

An accessible toilet room shall have a clear wheelchair turning space that complies with Section C-2.3.1(5). The turning space may overlap the accessible route and any clear floor space within the toilet room.

C-4.8.9 UNISEX TOILET ROOMS CA: D-6.3.1, D-6.3.5.2

Small facilities may have only one single-user restroom. Where strict compliance is technically infeasible in alterations, "unisex" or "family" accessible toilet rooms are permitted. This type of provision allows wheelchair users accessibility and also accommodates any attendant. These facilities have proven very useful and advantageous when used in addition to accessible multi-stalls in new restroom facilities such as shopping centers, convention centers, and large auditoriums.

1. **Clear Floor Space**
    The minimum clear floor space dimensions for accessible

"unisex" toilet rooms are shown in Figure 69. The clear floor space required for users to transfer from a wheelchair onto the water closet is indicated by the floor limits shown. The 48 by 60-inch dimension conforms to the required space for the two most used transfers, the diagonal or side approach as shown in Figures 68(a,b). A lavatory placed directly to the side of a water closet precludes any side approach transfer as shown in Figure 68(b). Therefore, a 42-inch unobstructed space adjacent to and from the center line of the toilet must be provided to accommodate the side transfer.

2. **Fixture Placement**

    Considerations for fixture placement are (1) the maneuvering space at the door, (2) a T-turn or circle turning space and (3) the clear space at the lavatory. The toilet room door shall have a privacy latch or other accessible means to ensure privacy during use.

3. **Advantages**

    a) Accessible "unisex" toilet rooms are an alternative where accessibility requirements are technically infeasible in building alterations.

    b) Accessible single-user restrooms are desirable since they can accommodate a wide variety of users. However, they cannot be used in place of providing the accessible multi-stall toilet rooms required in new construction.

    c) Provisions allowing side transfers in accessible single-user toilet rooms will accommodate the majority of wheelchair users.

ADA ACCESSIBILITY DESIGN STANDARDS
FACILITY AREAS • Toilet Stalls

C-4.9 TOILET STALLS

C-4.9.1 APPLICATION   CA: D-6.3.5

Accessible toilet stalls shall be located on an accessible route and comply with the regulations of Section C-4.9. Accessible water closets in stalls shall meet the requirements of Section C-6.10.

C-4.9.2 STALL DOOR   CA: D-6.3.5(2)

Toilet stall doors and hardware shall comply with Section C-5.2. The clear space inside the stall between the door and any obstruction may be decreased to a 42-inch minimum when approached from the latch side of the door. *Installation of a closer, spring hinge, or an inside door pull bar near the hinge side allows easier door closing for persons with disabilities.*

C-4.9.3 GRAB BARS   CA: D-6.3.6

Grab bars shall comply with Section C-6.5 for the bar length and placement as shown in Figures 29(a-d). Any means of installation is allowed providing that the gripping surface is properly placed as shown in Figure 29, and the bars do not obstruct the required clear floor space.

C-4.9.4 TOE SPACE

Toe space allowance in a standard stall shall be at least 9 inches above the floor at the front and at one side partition. The toe space provision is not required in stall depths greater than 5 feet.

ADA ACCESSIBILITY DESIGN STANDARDS
FACILITY AREAS • Toilet Stalls

C-4.9.5 TOILET STALL DESIGN   CA: D-6.3.4(4), D-6.3.5

The standard toilet stall shall comply with the design and measurements shown in Figure 29(a). Design arrangements may be reversed allowing a left-hand or right-hand approach. Additional stalls shall be provided in compliance with the requirements of Section C-4.8.3 and C-4.8.4 where applicable. *The standard 5-foot wide stall shown in Figure 29(a) provides the clear space necessary for a wheelchair user to perform a diagonal or side transfer to the water closet.*

1. Water Closets

Wall-mounted water closets are required in stalls with depths between 56 and 59 inches. A floor-mounted water closet may be used with a stall depth of 59 inches or more.

Fig. 29 **Toilet Stalls**

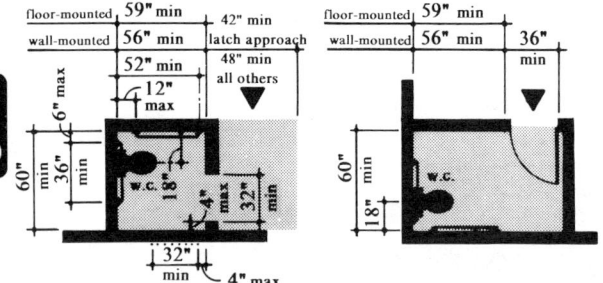

Fig. 29(a-1) **Standard Stall**   Fig. 29(a-2) **Standard Stall (end)**

ADA ACCESSIBILITY DESIGN STANDARDS
FACILITY AREAS • Toilet Stalls

Fig. 29 **Toilet Stalls** (cont.)

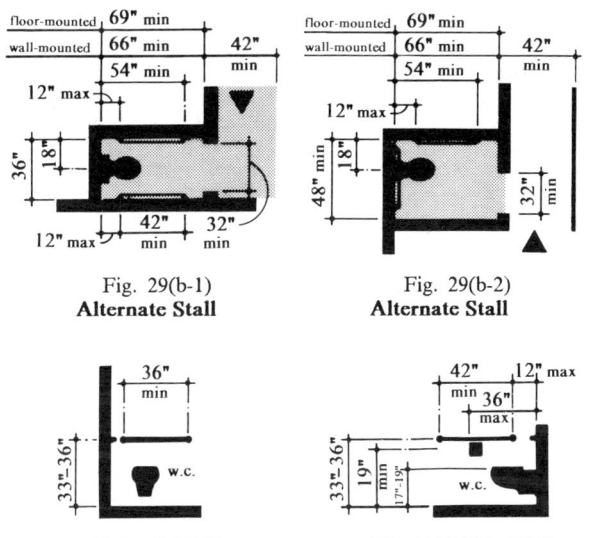

Fig. 29(b-1)
Alternate Stall

Fig. 29(b-2)
Alternate Stall

Fig. 29(c) **Back Wall Standard Stall**

Fig. 29(d) **Side Wall Standard Stall**

2. **Alternate Stalls**
   Alternate stall 1 or 2 shown in Figure 29(b) may be provided in place of the standard stall where
   (a) the plumbing code regulations do not allow combining existing stalls to obtain the necessary space, or

ADA ACCESSIBILITY DESIGN STANDARDS
FACILITY AREAS • Toilet Stalls

    (b)   it is technically infeasible to provide a standard stall in a building alteration.

An alternate 36-inch or 48-inch wide stall can be used only in alterations.

3. Grab Bars

Accessibility to two parallel grab bars in a 36-inch wide alternate stall is more useful to persons using a walker, crutches, or a cane than the standard 60-inch wide stall. The use of the grab bars are necessary to manage a standing position. Therefore, it is required to provide both the standard stall and the 36-inch wide stall with parallel grab bars in new construction where six or more toilet stalls are provided. A 36-inch wide stall is required for proper use of grab bars. Additional width creates too much space between bars, and less width places the bars too close to the toilet. Since this width is intended for persons with mobility walking aids, the length of the stall may be conventional, but the door must swing outward to provide the necessary usable space.

C 4.9

ADA ACCESSIBILITY DESIGN STANDARDS
FACILITY ELEMENTS • Curb Ramps

C-5 FACILITY ELEMENTS

C-5.1 CURB RAMPS

C-5.1.1 APPLICATION CA: D-4.4

Curb ramps shall be provided on all accessible routes that cross a curb and shall comply with Section C-5.1.

C-5.1.2 SURFACE CA: D-4.4.1(3)

Curb ramp surfaces shall comply with Section C-5.4.

C-5.1.3 SLOPE CA: D-4.4.1(1)

Curb ramp slopes shall comply with Section C-5.6.2. The transition from a ramp to a walk, gutter, or street shall be flush with no abrupt changes. Adjoining road surfaces, gutters, and accessible routes shall not exceed a slope of 1:20. The means to measure a slope is shown in Figure 30.

C-5.1.4 WIDTH CA: D-4.4.1(2)

A curb ramp shall have a 36-inch minimum width exclusive of flared sides.

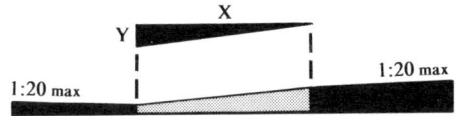

Fig. 30 **Curb Ramp Slope Measurement**

ADA ACCESSIBILITY DESIGN STANDARDS
FACILITY ELEMENTS • Curb Ramps

C-5.1.5 SIDES ^{CA: D-4.4.1(4)}

A curb ramp shall have flared sides when not protected by handrails or guardrails and where pedestrians have to walk across the ramp. The maximum slope of flared sides shall be 1:10. (Fig. 31) Returned curbs may be used where pedestrians do not normally cross the ramp. (Fig. 33)

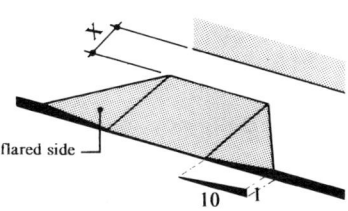

If "x" is less than 48", the side slopes shall not exceed 1:12.

Fig. 31 **Flared Sides**

C-5.1.6 BUILT-UP RAMP

Built-up curb ramps shall not project into vehicular traffic lanes. (Fig. 32)

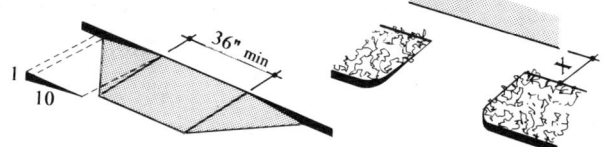

Fig. 32 **Built-up Curb Ramp**   Fig. 33 **Returned Curb**

C-5.1.7 WARNINGS ^{CA: D-3.9, D-4.4.1(6), D-5.2.3}

A curb ramp shall have a detectable warning strip that extends the full curb ramp width and depth and complies with Section C-3.2.

ADA ACCESSIBILITY DESIGN STANDARDS
FACILITY ELEMENTS • Curb Ramps

Fig. 34 Curb Ramps at Marked Crossings

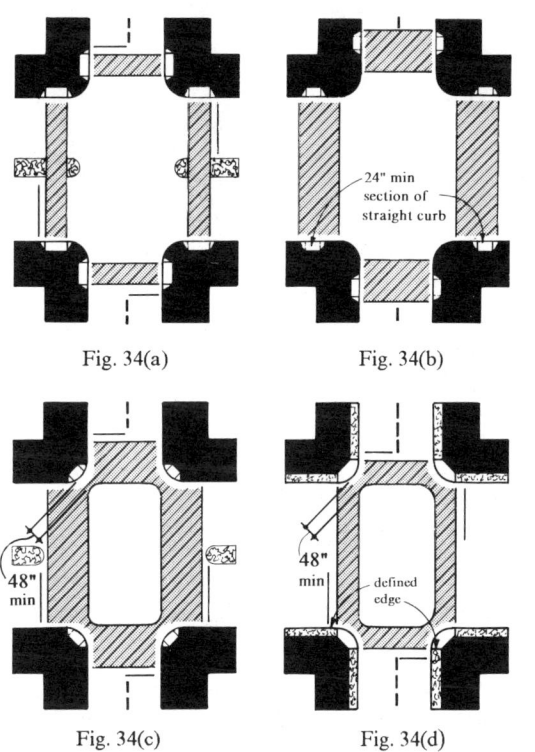

Fig. 34(a)

Fig. 34(b)

Fig. 34(c)

Fig. 34(d)

ADA ACCESSIBILITY DESIGN STANDARDS
FACILITY ELEMENTS • Doors

C-5.1.8 PLACEMENT CA: D-4.4.1(7)

Curb ramps shall be placed to protect and prevent blockage from parked vehicles.

1. **Corner Curb Ramps**
   Corner ramps with flared sides shall have at least a 24-inch long straight curb located on each side of the curb ramp within the marked crosswalk as shown in Figure 34(b). A minimum 48-inch clear space shall be provided in front of the corner curb ramp, at street level, and within the marked crosswalk as shown in Figures 34(c,d). Returned curbs or definite edges of corner ramps shall be parallel with pedestrian traffic. (Fig. 34d)

2. **Crosswalks**
   Curb ramps, exclusive of flared sides, shall be completely contained within the crosswalk markings. (Fig. 34)

3. **Islands**
   Crosswalks through raised islands shall be cut level with the street or have at least a 4-foot long and level walkway on the island and curb ramps at each end. (Figs. 30a,c)

C-5.2 DOORS

C-5.2.1 APPLICATION CA: D-3.16, D-7.1.1

Accessible doors required by Section C-1 shall comply with the requirements in Section C-5.2.

C-5.2.2 DOUBLE-LEAF DOORWAYS CA: D-7.1.2(3)

At least one door leaf shall be active and comply with the requirements of Sections C-5.2.9 and C-5.2.10 in a doorway that has two independently operated door leafs.

ADA ACCESSIBILITY DESIGN STANDARDS
FACILITY ELEMENTS • Doors

C-5.2.3 AUTOMATIC • POWER ASSISTED
CA: D-7.1.2(5)

Automatic doors shall comply with ANSI/BHMA A156.10-1985. Slow opening, low-powered, automatic doors shall comply with ANSI A156.19-1984. Doors shall take at least three seconds to open before back checking and not require more than a 15-pound force to stop the door movement. The door-opening force of a power-assisted door shall comply with Section C-5.2.12. Its closing shall conform with ANSI A156.19-1984. *Slow opening automatic doors are more convenient in busy doorways when they can be reactivated before their closing cycle is completed. Automatic sliding doors are especially convenient to persons in wheelchairs and the visually impaired. Guardrails are not necessary at automatic sliding doors allowing easier accessibility.*

C-5.2.4 REVOLVING DOORS • TURNSTILES
CA: D-7.1.2(4), D-7.1.8

An adjacent access door or gate shall be provided next to a revolving door or turnstile which serves as the only means of passage on an accessible route.

C-5.2.5 GATES

Gates shall meet all applicable specifications of Section C-5.2.

C-5.2.6 DOORS IN SERIES CA: D-7.1.4(3)

Multiple doors shall swing the same direction or away from the space between doors. (Fig. 35) The space between two doors in a series shall have at least a 48-inch clear space and be free of door swings.

ADA ACCESSIBILITY DESIGN STANDARDS
FACILITY ELEMENTS • Doors

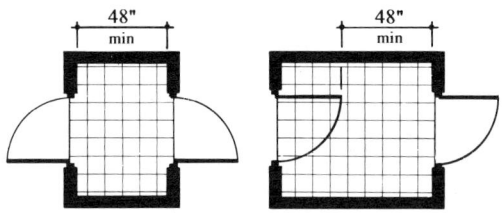

Fig. 35 **Two Hinged Doors in Series**

C-5.2.7 HARDWARE CA: D-7.1.3

The maximum height for hardware on accessible passage doors is 48 inches above the finished floor. Accessible door operating devices such as handles, pulls, locks, or latches shall be shaped for an easy one hand grip that does not require a tight grasp, pinch, or twist of the wrist to operate. Acceptable handle designs include the push-type, lever-operated, or U-shaped handle. The operating hardware of fully opened sliding doors shall be exposed and usable from both sides. *Walkers, wheelchairs, canes, and other devices used by persons with disabilities are often used to push or maneuver doors. Kickplates installed on doors with closers may reduce the required maintenance caused from such use. To be effective, the kickplate should be centered on the door, cover the door width within 2 inches of each side, and extend from the bottom edge up to a height of 16 inches.*

C-5.2.8 THRESHOLDS CA: D-7.1.5

Exterior sliding door thresholds shall not exceed 3/4 inch in height. All other door thresholds shall not exceed 1/2 inch in

ADA ACCESSIBILITY DESIGN STANDARDS
FACILITY ELEMENTS • Doors

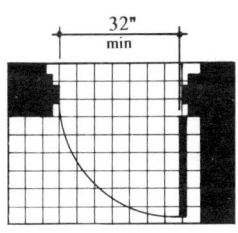

Fig. 36(a) **Hinged Door**

height. Raised thresholds and floor level changes shall be beveled at accessible doorways with a slope no greater than 1:2 (Fig. 47). *Persons in wheelchairs with low stamina or those with restricted arm movement may have difficulty in maneuvering over thresholds and surface height changes at doorways, particularly in conjunction with operating doors.*

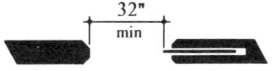

Fig. 36(b) **Pocket Door**

Fig. 36(c) **Accordion Door**

Fig. 36 **Doorway Clearance**

C-5.2.9 CLEARANCES[CA: D-7.1.2(1,2)]

A doorway's clear opening shall not be less than 32 inches measured from the face of the door to the opposite door stop with the door opened at 90 degrees. (Figs. 36, 38d-f) Openings with greater than a 2-foot depth shall comply with Section C-2.3.1. (Fig. 37) Door openings may be reduced to a 20-inch minimum when used to access a space, such as a closet, rather than pass through the door.

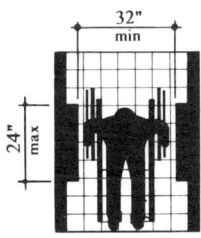

Fig. 37 **Maximum Opening Depth**

ADA ACCESSIBILITY DESIGN STANDARDS
FACILITY ELEMENTS • Doors

C-5.2.10 CLEAR SPACE CA: D-7.1.4(1,2)

Figures 38(a-c) illustrates the minimum clear floor space required at doors not automatic or power-assisted. The required clear floor space shall be level and clear. Entry doors that are at least 44 inches wide which access acute in-patient care hospital bedrooms are exempt from the requirement to provide additional space at the latch side of the door.

C-5.2.11 CLOSER

The sweep period of door closers shall be adjusted so the door will take at least 3 seconds to move to a point three inches from the latch when in an open position of 70 degrees. *Delay action closers allow*

Fig. 38 **Maneuvering Clearance**

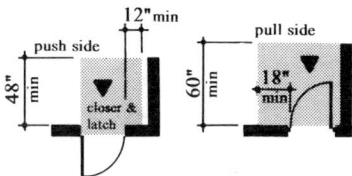

Fig. 38 (a) **Front Approach**

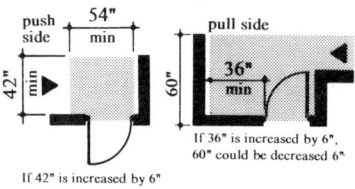

If 42" is increased by 6" or more, the door must have a latch & closer

Fig. 38 (b) **Hinge Side Approach**

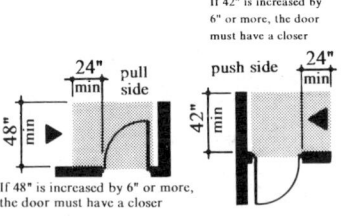

If 48" is increased by 6" or more, the door must have a closer

Fig 38 (c) **Latch Side Approach**

170

ADA ACCESSIBILITY DESIGN STANDARDS
FACILITY ELEMENTS • Doors

a person with disabilities additional time to maneuver through doorways and is particularly useful on frequently used doors.

Pocket, sliding, and Folding Doors
Note: All doors in alcoves shall comply with a front approach clearance.

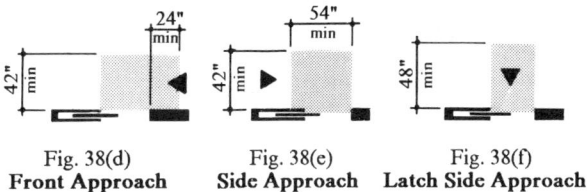

Fig. 38(d)
Front Approach

Fig. 38(e)
Side Approach

Fig. 38(f)
Latch Side Approach

C-5.2.12 OPENING FORCE ^{CA: D-7.1.6}

The maximum push or pull force to operate a door shall be:

- **Interior hinged door** - 5-lb. force
- **Sliding or folding door** - 5-lb. force
- **Fire door** - minimal force permissible by the appropriate governing authority

These forces do not include the force necessary to disengage devices that hold a door closed. *Most persons with disabilities are able to exert a 5-pound force to push or pull a door from a stationary position. Persons with severe disabilities may not be able to exert as much as a 3-pound force. However, for a door to close properly, the door closer must have a certain minimum closing force. The push or pull force to open doors are measured with a push-pull scale under the following conditions:*

ADA ACCESSIBILITY DESIGN STANDARDS
FACILITY ELEMENTS • Elevators

1. *Application of force.*
   Gradual force application where the force does not exceed the door resistance. Air pressure differentials, which may be present in high-rise buildings, may require specification modification to meet the functional intent.
2. *Hinged doors.*
   A perpendicular force applied to a door 30 inches from the door hinge or a force applied at the door opener, whichever is farthest from the hinge.
3. *Sliding or folding doors.*
   Force applied parallel to the door at the latch or pull.

C-5.3 ELEVATORS

C-5.3.1 APPLICATION CA: B-4.5, D-3.3.3, D-4.2

Accessible elevators shall be located on accessible routes and comply with Section C-5.3 and the Safety Code for Elevators and Escalators, ASME A17.1-1990. Freight elevators are not required to meet Section C-5.3 regulations except when they combine their use with transporting passengers.

C-5.3.2 ILLUMINATION CA: D-4.2.1(4)

A minimum 5-footcandle illumination level is required at car controls, platforms, landing sills, and thresholds.

C-5.3.3 FLOOR DESIGNATION CA: D-4.2.5

Raised and Braille building floor designations shall be located on both jambs of all elevator hoistway entrances. The characters shall be 2 inches high with their center line at 60 inches above the finished floor and shall comply with the

ADA ACCESSIBILITY DESIGN STANDARDS
FACILITY ELEMENTS • Elevators

requirements of Section C-3.3.8. Permanently applied character plates affixed to the jambs are acceptable. (Fig. 39-"C")

Note: Lines 1 and 2 represent two horizontal line zones which activate an automatic elevator reopening device when a vertical object passes through one or both of these zones.

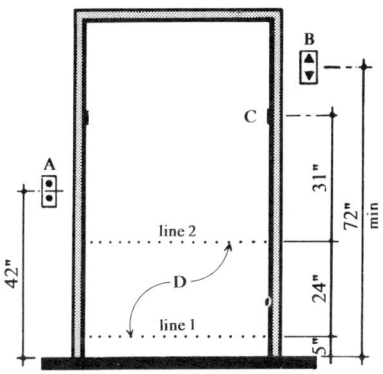

Fig. 39 **Hoistway and Elevator Entrance**

C-5.3.4 CALL BUTTONS ^{CA: D-4.2.3}

Call buttons shall indicate when each call is registered or acknowledged with a visual signal.

1. Buttons
Buttons shall be raised or flush to the finish surface with the "up" call button being the top button. A call button's smallest dimension shall be 3/4 inch.

ADA ACCESSIBILITY DESIGN STANDARDS
FACILITY ELEMENTS • Elevators

2. Placement
Lobby and hall elevator call buttons shall be centered at 42 inches above the floor. (Fig. 39-"A") Any mounted object placed below call buttons shall not protrude more than 4 inches into the corridor, lobby, or hallway.

C-5.3.5 HALL LANTERNS CA: D-4.2.4

Each hoistway entrance shall have a visible and audible signal to indicate which car is answering the call.

1. Visible Signals
Visible signals shall have the following features:
a) Lantern signals shall be visible from the vicinity of the hall call buttons.
b) Hall lanterns center line shall be located a minimum of 72 inches above the finished floor. (Fig. 39-B)
c) The smallest dimension of the visual elements shall be no less than 2.5 inches.
d) Interior car signals are acceptable if they meet the requirements of C-5.3.5(a-c).

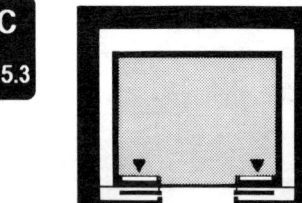

Fig. 40
**Panel Location Choice
Center Door Opening**

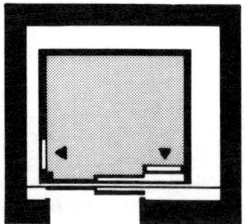

Fig. 41
**Panel Location Choice
Side Door Opening**

ADA ACCESSIBILITY DESIGN STANDARDS
FACILITY ELEMENTS • Elevators

2. Audible Signals
Audible signals shall sound once for the "up" direction and sound twice for the "down" direction. A verbal annunciator which says "up" or "down" may be used.

C-5.3.6 CONTROL PANEL ^{CA: D-4.2.3}

Elevator control panels shall comply with the following:

1. Placement ^{CA: D-4.2.3(3)}
Cars with center opening doors shall have the controls on the front wall.(Fig. 40) Cars with side opening doors shall have the controls on a side or front wall next to the door. (Fig. 41) The maximum height for floor indicator buttons is 54 inches above the finished floor for a side approach and 48 inches for a front approach. (Fig. 43)

2. Buttons ^{CA: D-4.2.3(2,3)}
Floor buttons shall have a visual indicator that registers with each call signal and then extinguishes when answered. All control buttons shall be raised or flush and the smallest dimension not less than 3/4 inch. Control buttons shall be designated by:

Numbers- Arabic characters

Letters- Braille and raised standard alphabet characters

Symbols- ASME A17.1-1990 standard symbols (Fig. 42)

3. Characters and Symbols
^{CA: D-4.2.3(1)}

Characters and symbols shall comply with Section C-3.3.8. Raised designations shall be placed directly to the left of each call button for which

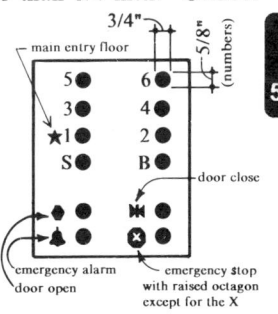

Fig. 42 **Control Panel**

ADA ACCESSIBILITY DESIGN STANDARDS
FACILITY ELEMENTS • Elevators

they apply. (Fig. 42) A raised star signifies the main entry floor call button. An acceptable means to provide the raised control designations is by permanently attached plates.

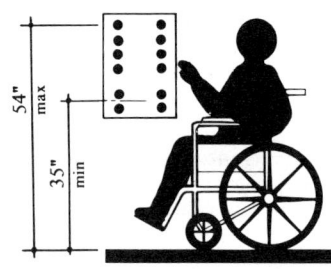

Fig. 43 **Control Panel Height**

4. **Emergency Control**
Emergency controls shall be grouped at the bottom of the panel.(Fig. 42) Their center lines must be at least 35 inches above the finished floor. (Fig. 43)

5. **Standardization**
One control panel design used throughout the elevator industry would better meet the needs of persons with visual impairments with the placement of the highest operating control within 48 inches of the floor.

C-5.3.7 LOCATION INDICATOR ^{CA: D-4.2.1(5)}

A visual indicator that shows where the elevator car is located in the hoistway shall be placed above the control panel or over the door. Numerals shall illuminate and an audible signal shall sound as the car passes or stops at the corresponding floor. Numerals shall be no less than 1/2 inch high. Audible signals shall be at least 20 decibels with a frequency no higher than 1500 hertz. The audible signal may be substituted with an automatic verbal floor number announcement as the car passes or stops at each floor. *Instead of having an audible signal in continuous operation, a button may be pro-*

ADA ACCESSIBILITY DESIGN STANDARDS
FACILITY ELEMENTS • Elevators

vided that manually activates the audible signal.

C-5.3.8 CAR FLOOR SPACE CA: D-4.2.1(2), D-4.2.2

The elevator car floor area shall provide adequate space for wheelchair users to enter, maneuver within reach of the controls, and exit the car. The clearance between the edge of the hoistway landing and the car platform sill shall not exceed 1.25 inches. Minimum dimensions for door openings and inside measurements are shown in Figure 44.

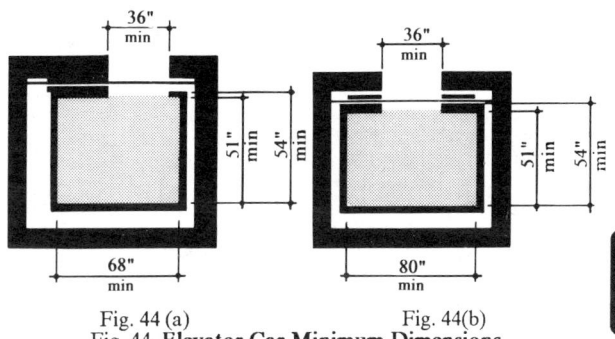

Fig. 44 (a)   Fig. 44(b)
Fig. 44 **Elevator Car Minimum Dimensions**

C-5.3.9 FLOOR SURFACES

Floor surfaces shall comply with Section C-5.4.

C-5.3.10 OPERATION CA: D-4.2.1(3)

Elevators shall operate automatically. Cars shall be equipped with a self-leveling feature and stop within a tolerance of

ADA ACCESSIBILITY DESIGN STANDARDS
FACILITY ELEMENTS • Elevators

1/2-inch under-rated loading to zero-loading conditions at each floor landing. This self-leveling feature shall correct the over-travel or under-travel and be automatic and independent of the operating device.

C-5.3.11 DOOR AND SIGNAL TIMING CA: D-4.2.2(1)

The equation $T = D / (1.5 \text{ ft./s})$ calculates the minimum acceptable time from when the car is signaled to when the elevator door starts to close. T is total time in seconds and D is distance in feet from a point in the lobby 60 inches directly in front of the farthest call button controlling the car to the center line of the hoistway door. (Fig. 45) For elevators with interior signals, T begins when the signal sounds and the lantern is visible from the vicinity of the corridor call buttons. An acceptable notification time is less than 5 seconds. *The location of call buttons, advance time for warning signals, and the door-holding period allows for some variation in meeting the time requirement.*

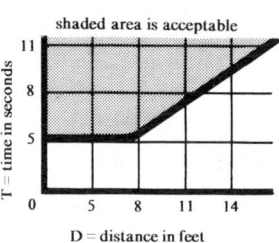

Fig. 45
Timing Equation

C-5.3.12 DOOR REOPENING DEVICE CA: D-4.2.2(3)

Elevator doors shall automatically open and close and provide a reopening device which stops and reopens the door automatically when the door is obstructed. The device must be able to complete these operations without requiring an obstruction contact within the door's opening activation zones

ADA ACCESSIBILITY DESIGN STANDARDS
FACILITY ELEMENTS • Elevators

located 5 inches and 29 inches above the finished floor. (Fig. 39-"D") The automatic protective door device shall remain effective for no less than 20 seconds and then close in accordance with the requirements of ASME A17.1-1990. *Sufficient force exerted against any point on the door edge should be able to stop the door movement.*

C-5.3.13 DOOR DELAY CA: D-4.2.2(2)

An elevator door shall remain fully open at least three seconds in response to a car call.

C-5.3.14 EMERGENCY COMMUNICATION CA: D-4.2.6

An emergency two-way communication system used between an elevator car and another location shall comply with ASME A17.1-1990. This intercommunication system does not require voice communication. Raised symbols or letters complying with Section C-3.3 shall be adjacent to and identify the intercommunication system mechanism. The system's highest operable part shall be no higher than 48 inches above the car floor. Cords to handsets shall be no shorter than 29 inches from the panel to the handset. The door hardware on a closed compartment that houses an intercommunication system must conform to Section C-6.3.

Persons that have difficulty reaching or grasping may not be able to use handsets or work small handles on compartment doors. An ideal situation calls for both a voice and visual display intercommunication emergency system to accommodate both the hearing impaired and visually impaired with an acknowledged response to their call for rescue.

ADA ACCESSIBILITY DESIGN STANDARDS
FACILITY ELEMENTS · Floor · Ground Surfaces

C-5.4 FLOOR · GROUND SURFACES

C-5.4.1 APPLICATION

Floor and ground surfaces shall be stable, firm, and slip-resistant in accessible areas and comply with Section C-5.4.

C-5.4.2 SURFACE CONDITIONS

Wheelchairs have difficulty on soft, loose, wet, and irregular surfaces. Cross slopes on ground and floor surfaces can cause difficulty in the straight and forward control of a wheelchair.

C-5.4.3 STATIC COEFFICIENT

Persons with mobility impairments are sensitive to slipping or tripping hazards. Some slippage is necessary for walking and especially for persons with restricted gaits. A completely "non-slip" surface could not be managed by persons with restricted gaits. A 0.6 static coefficient of friction is recommended for accessible routes and 0.8 for ramps. The coefficient of friction varies considerably due to varying conditions where compliance is difficult to measure. Many common flooring materials are labeled with information on the static coefficient of friction. As this concern becomes more predominant, it is likely there will be more improved uniformity with measurements and specifications.

C-5.4.4 LEVEL CHANGE[CA:D-7.1.5]

No edge treatment is required for a 1/4-inch or less vertical change. (Fig. 46) A level change between 1/4 and 1/2 inch requires beveled edges with

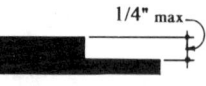

Fig. 46 **Level change**

ADA ACCESSIBILITY DESIGN STANDARDS
FACILITY ELEMENTS • Floor • Ground Surfaces

no greater than a 1:2 slope. (Fig. 47) A level change greater than 1/2 inch requires a ramp that complies with Sections C-5.1 or C-5.6.

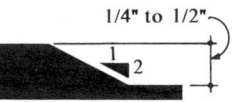

Fig. 47 **Beveled Edge**

C-5.4.5 CARPET

Carpet used in accessible areas shall have a firm back and pad, or no pad; have textures loops, level loops or pile, level cut, or a combination thereof; and be securely attached to the floor surface. The maximum pile thickness shall not exceed 1/2 inch. (Fig. 48) Exposed carpet edges shall be fastened to the floor and finished with trim that complies with Section C-5.4.4. *Minimum movement, preferably none, is recommended between the floor, pad, and carpet in order to prevent warping and humps in the floor. Wheelchair users and persons with ambulatory disabilities have difficulty maneuvering on thick carpet or soft pad.*

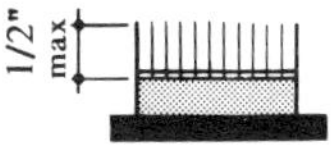

Fig. 48 **Carpet**

C-5.4.6 GRATINGS

A walking surface grate shall not have greater than 1/2-inch wide spaces in one direction. (Fig. 49) The long dimension of elongated openings in grates shall be perpendicular to the primary travel path. (Fig. 50)

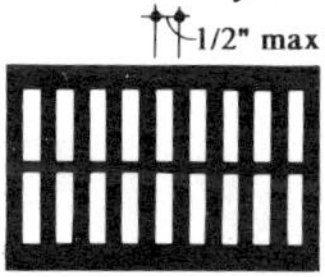

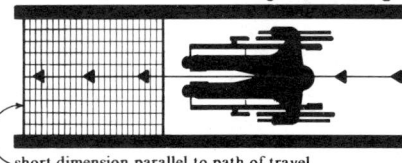

Fig. 49 **Grating**

short dimension parallel to path of travel

Fig. 50 **Grating Orientation**

ADA ACCESSIBILITY DESIGN STANDARDS
FACILITY ELEMENTS • Platform Lifts • Ramps

C-5.5 PLATFORM LIFTS

C-5.5.1 APPLICATION ^{CA: D-4.2.10}

Platform lifts (wheelchair lifts) permitted by Section C-1 shall comply with this Section and Sections C-2.3.2, C-5.4, C-6.3, and the "Safety Code for Elevators and Escalators" of ASME A17.1, Section XX, 1990. *Inclined and vertical platform lifts and stairway chairlifts are available for vertical transportation of persons with disabilities over a short distance. All lifts are not always appropriate for both wheelchair and semi-ambulatory users. Therefore, considerations should be given in the selection of lifts.*

C-5.5.2 OPERATION

Platform lifts shall accommodate persons in allowing unassisted entries, operations, and exits in compliance with Section C-5.5.1.

C-5.6 RAMPS

C-5.6.1 APPLICATION ^{CA: D-3.3.5, D-4.3}

A ramp is any portion of an accessible route greater than a 1:20 slope. Ramps shall comply with Section C-5.6. *Wheelchair users require ramps to connect different levels for access where vertical lifts are not available. Stairs are often preferred by persons with walking aids that have difficulty with ramps.*

ADA ACCESSIBILITY DESIGN STANDARDS
FACILITY ELEMENTS • Ramps

C-5.6.2 SLOPE • RISE ^{CA: D-4.3.2, D-4.3.3}

Ramp slopes shall have the least slope possible. Newly constructed ramps shall be 1:12 maximum with a maximum rise of 30 inches for any continuous run. (Fig. 51) When space limits the use of a 1:12 slope or less on existing sites, buildings, and facilities, the slope and rise may conform to the slope and rise of Section C-1.2.11. *A ramp slope and length relates to a person's usability. A slope between 1:16 and 1:20 is preferred. Persons with arm impairments or low stamina may have difficulty with wheelchairs on inclines. A 1:16 slope can be managed by wheelchair users and ambulatory persons, but not many can manage a slope of 1:12 for 30 feet.*

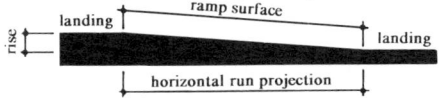

1:12 to <1:16 Slope • Max. Rise 30 inches • Max. Horizontal Run 30 feet
1:16 to <1:20 Slope • Max. Rise 30 inches • Max. Horizontal Run 40 feet

Fig. 51 **Single Ramp and Dimensions**

C-5.6.3 SURFACES ^{CA: D-4.3.2}

Ramp surfaces shall comply with Section C-5.4 and any cross slopes shall be no greater than 1:50.

C-5.6.4 LANDINGS ^{CA: D-4.3.3}

Level landings shall be provided at the top and bottom of each ramp run. Landings shall
a) have at least a 60-inch clear length,
b) be at least as wide as the ramp run leading to the landing,
c) shall comply with Section C-5.2.10 for doorways, and
d) be at least 60 by 60 inches where the ramp changes direc-

ADA ACCESSIBILITY DESIGN STANDARDS
FACILITY ELEMENTS • Ramps

tion. *Level landings are essential in preventing wheelchairs from tipping backwards or bottoming out when approaching a ramp and to maintain a continuous slope that complies with these guidelines.*

C-5.6.5 CLEAR WIDTH CA: D-4.3.1

Ramps shall have at least a 36-inch clear width.

C-5.6.6 EDGE PROTECTION

People shall be provided with protection on ramps and landings that have drop-offs with curbs, walls, railings, or other equivalent safeguards. Curbs shall be a minimum of 2 inches high. (Fig. 52)

C-5.6.7 EXTERIOR RAMPS

Exterior ramps and approaches shall be designed and constructed to prevent water from accumulating on the surface.

C-5.6.8 HANDRAILS CA: D-4.3.4

Handrails shall be placed on each side of ramps that have a horizontal projection greater than 6 feet or a rise greater than 6 inches. Handrails are not required on curb ramps or adjacent to assembly area seating. Ramp handrails shall have the following features and shall comply with Section C-6.5.
1. Handrails shall run along both sides.
2. Handrails shall have a continuous gripping surface.
3. The inside rail shall be continuous on switchback or dogleg ramps.
4. Handrails shall not rotate within their fasteners.
5. Handrails shall extend a minimum of 12 inches beyond the top and the bottom of a ramp and shall be parallel

ADA ACCESSIBILITY DESIGN STANDARDS
FACILITY ELEMENTS • Ramps

Fig. 52 **Edge Protection and Handrail Extensions**

Section   Side Elevation

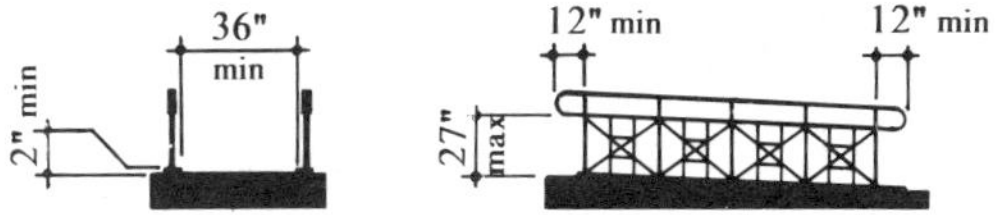

Fig. 52a **Curb**

Fig. 52b **Wall**

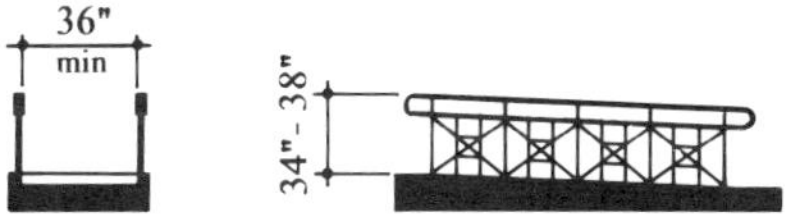

Fig. 52c **Vertical Guard Rail**

Fig. 52d **Railing with Extended Platform**

ADA ACCESSIBILITY DESIGN STANDARDS
FACILITY ELEMENTS • Stairs

with the floor or ground surface when the handrail is not continuous. (Fig. 52)

6. Handrails shall have rounded ends, or the ends shall be returned smoothly to a wall, post, or floor.
7. A 1.5-inch clear space shall be provided between the wall and the handrail.
8. The handrail grip surface shall be mounted between 34 and 38 inches above the ramp surface.

These guidelines are requirements for adults. A second set of handrails should be provided and placed at an appropriate height in facilities where children are the principal users.

C-5.7 STAIRS

C-5.7.1 APPLICATION CA: D-7.2

Accessible stairs required by Section C-1 shall comply with Section C-5.7. *Stairs must comply that join different levels and are not connected by an elevator, ramp, or other accessible vertical means.*

C-5.7.2 RISER • TREAD CA: D-7.2.1

Stairway steps shall have a uniform riser height and a uniform tread run with an 11-inch minimum run from riser to riser. (Fig. 53) No risers shall be open.

C-5.7.3 NOSING CA: D-7.2.1

The riser slope or the underside of the nosing shall not be less than 60 degrees from the horizontal. Nosing shall not project more than 1.5 inches with a maximum 1/2-inch curvature radius at the leading edge of the tread. (Figs. 53 and 54)

ADA ACCESSIBILITY DESIGN STANDARDS
FACILITY ELEMENTS • Stairs

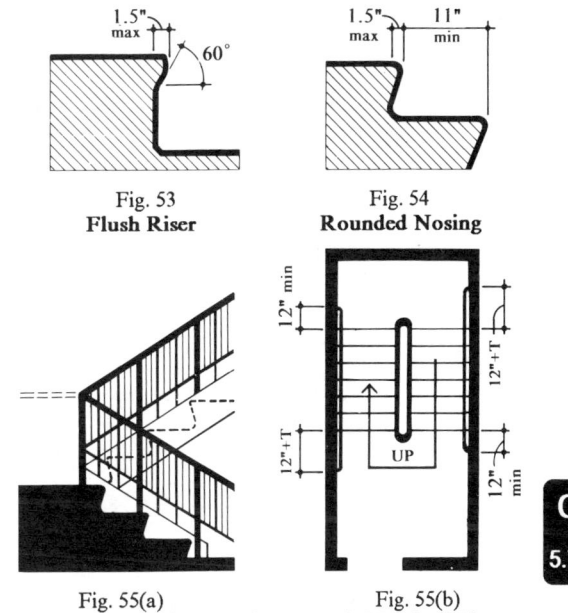

Fig. 53
Flush Riser

Fig. 54
Rounded Nosing

Fig. 55(a)
Elevation of Center Handrail

Fig. 55(b)
Stair Handrail Plan

Fig. 55 **Stair Handrails**

C-5.7.4 HANDRAILS ^{CA: D-7.2.3}

Handrails shall be placed on both sides of a stairway, comply with Section C-6.5, and have the following features:
1. Handrails shall be stable and not rotate.

ADA ACCESSIBILITY DESIGN STANDARDS
FACILITY ELEMENTS • Stairs

2. Handrails shall have an unobstructed and continuous gripping surface free from any construction elements.
3. A 1.5-inch clear space shall exist between a handrail and a wall.
4. Stairways shall have a continuous handrail along both sides of a stairway and on the inside of a switchback or dogleg stairway. (Figs. 55a,b)
5. The highest handrail gripping surface shall be positioned between 34 and 38 inches above the stair nosing.
6. Handrail ends shall be rounded or returned smoothly to the floor, wall, or post.
7. Non-continuous handrails shall extend at least 12 inches beyond the top riser and be parallel with the floor surface at the top of a stairway. (Fig 56a) At the bottom of a stairway, a handrail shall continue to slope for a distance of one tread run past the bottom riser and then continue parallel with the floor surface at least 12 inches. (Fig. 56b) Handrail extensions shall comply with Section C-2.2.

Fig. 56 **Handrail Extensions**

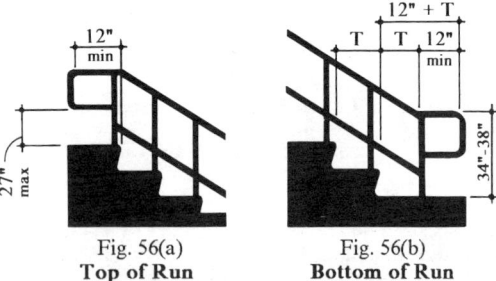

Fig. 56(a)
Top of Run

Fig. 56(b)
Bottom of Run

ADA ACCESSIBILITY DESIGN STANDARDS
FACILITY ELEMENTS • Windows

C-5.7.5 EXTERIOR STAIRWAYS

An exterior stairway shall be designed where water does not accumulate on the walking surface of the stair treads and the stairway approaches.

C-5.8 WINDOWS

C-5.8.1 OPERATION

Windows operated in accessible spaces by pushing, pulling, or lifting to open or close should not require more than a 5-pound force.

C-5.8.2 HARDWARE

Window hardware should comply with Section C-6.3.

C-6 FACILITY FIXTURES

C-6.1 AUTOMATED TELLER MACHINES

C-6.1.1 APPLICATION ^{CA: D-8.1.1}

Accessible automated teller machines required by Section C-1.3.20 shall comply with Section C-6.1.

C-6.1.2 CONTROLS

User activation controls shall comply with the requirements of Section C-6.3.

C-6.1.3 CLEAR SPACE ^{CA: D-8.1.2}

Free standing or built-in automated teller machines shall comply with Sections C-6.3.3 and C-6.3.4 when there are no clear spaces under them. A parallel approach allowing both a forward and side reach to the unit shall be provided for a person in a wheelchair to access the controls and dispensers.

C-6.1.4 VISION IMPAIRMENTS ^{CA: D-8.1.5}

Persons with vision impairments shall have accessible instructions on the machine's use. An ATM shall be independently usable by those persons.

ADA ACCESSIBILITY DESIGN STANDARDS
FACILITY FIXTURES • Bathtubs

C-6.2 BATHTUBS

C-6.2.1 APPLICATION CA: D-6.2.2

Bathtubs required to be accessible shall comply with Section C-6.2.

C-6.2.2 FAUCETS CA: D-6.2.2(5)

Faucets and other controls in compliance with Section C-6.3.2 shall be placed as shown in Figure 57.

C-6.2.3 SHOWER HEAD CA: D-6.2.3(8)

A shower head shall be provided that serves as both a fixed and hand-held shower head. The shower hose shall be no shorter than 60 inches.

C-6.2.4 SEATS CA: D-6.2.2(3)

A seat in the bathtub or at the head of a bathtub as shown in Figures 57 and 58 shall be installed securely, not move during use, and the structural strength and attachments shall comply with Section C-6.5.4.

C-6.2.5 ENCLOSURES CA: D-6.2.2(2)

When provided, bathtub enclosures shall not have tracks mounted on their rims. The enclosure shall not interfere with a person's transfer from a wheelchair onto a bathtub seat or into a bathtub. The enclosure shall not obstruct the operation of the bathtub controls.

ADA ACCESSIBILITY DESIGN STANDARDS
FACILITY FIXTURES • Bathtubs

C-6.2.6 GRAB BARS ^{CA: D-6.2.2(4)}

Grab bars shall be provided as shown in Figures 57 and 58 and comply with the requirements of Section C-6.5.

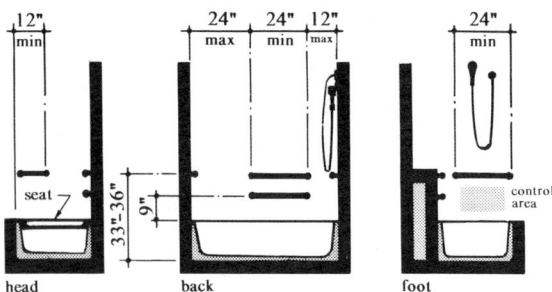

Fig. 57(a) **Bathtub with Seat in Tub**

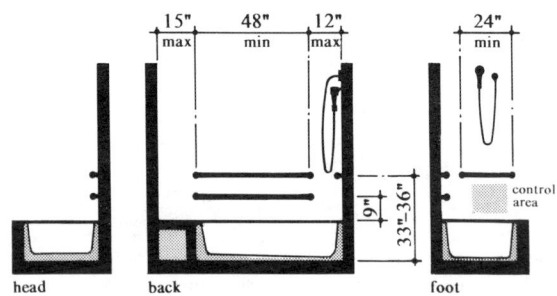

Fig. 57(b) **Bathtub with Seat at Head of Tub**
Fig. 57 **Bathtub Grab Bars**

ADA ACCESSIBILITY DESIGN STANDARDS
FACILITY FIXTURES • Equipment • Controls

C-6.2.7 CLEAR FLOOR SPACE ^{CA: D-6.2.2(6)}

Clear floor space in front of bathtubs shall be as shown in Figure 58.

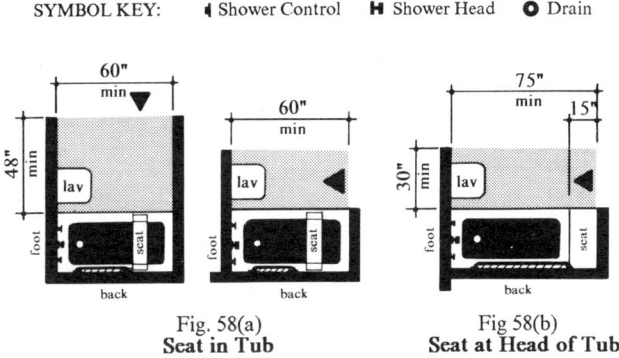

Fig. 58(a) **Seat in Tub**

Fig 58(b) **Seat at Head of Tub**

Fig. 58 **Bathtub Clear Floor Space**

C-6.3 EQUIPMENT · CONTROLS

C-6.3.1 APPLICATION ^{CA: D-8.2}

Accessible operating devices and hardware required by Section C-1 shall comply with Section C-6.3.

C-6.3.2 OPERATION

The force needed to initiate and operate controls and devices shall not require more than a 5-pound force, shall be work-

ADA ACCESSIBILITY DESIGN STANDARDS
FACILITY FIXTURES • Equipment • Controls

able with one hand, and not demand a tight grasp, pinch, or twist of the wrist.

C-6.3.3 CLEAR SPACE

A clear floor space shall be provided for wheelchair users complying with Section C-2.3.2 allowing a forward or parallel approach to containers, receptacles, and other operable equipment and controls.

C-6.3.4 HEIGHT

The highest operable part of equipment, containers, receptacles, and controls shall be placed within one or more of the reach ranges specified in Section C-2.3.3. The minimum height above the floor for electrical and communication system receptacles is 15 inches. Maximum height requirements do not apply where the electrical and communication system receptacles are not normally intended for the building occupants use and when the use of special equipment dictates otherwise.

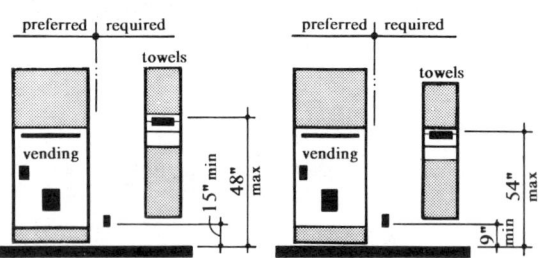

Fig. 59(a) **Forward Reach** Fig. 59(b) **Side Reach**
Fig. 59 **Reach Limitations**

ADA ACCESSIBILITY DESIGN STANDARDS
FACILITY FIXTURES • Drinking Facilities

Accessibility installation heights for recommended and mandatory controls for typical equipment are shown in Figure 59. Electrical receptacles that serve permanent individual appliances are not required to be within the specified reach range when not intended for regular use by building occupants.

C-6.4 DRINKING FACILITIES

C-6.4.1 APPLICATION CA: D-8.3

Accessible drinking fountains and water coolers required by Section C-1 shall comply with Section C-6.4. *Two drinking fountains should be installed to serve both those with disabilities and those with difficulty in bending over. The fountains may be installed side by side or on a single post.*

C-6.4.2 SPOUTS

1. **Location**
   Drinking fountain and water cooler spouts shall be at the front of the unit with a trajectory water flow parallel with the front of the unit.
2. **Height**
   The spout outlet shall not exceed 36 inches above the floor or ground surface. (Fig. 60)

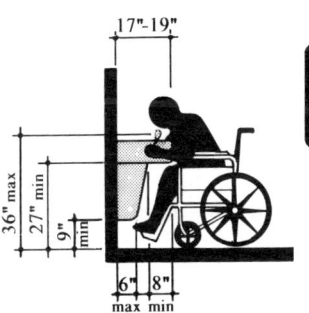

Fig. 60 **Spout Height and Knee Clearance**

195

ADA ACCESSIBILITY DESIGN STANDARDS
FACILITY FIXTURES • Drinking Facilities

3. Position
A spout must be position- ed where the water flow is within 3 inches of the front edge of a round or oval fountain bowl.

4. Water Flow
The water flow shall be at least 4 inches high to allow the insertion of a glass or cup under the water flow.

C-6.4.3 CONTROLS ^{CA: D-8.2}

Drinking unit controls shall be located on the front or side near the front edge and comply with Section C-6.3.2.

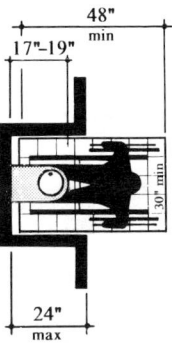

Fig. 61
Clear Floor Space

C-6.4.4 CLEAR SPACE

1. Approach
Cantilevered drinking units mounted on a post or wall shall allow a person in a wheelchair to approach the unit facing forward and provide a minimum clear floor space of 30 by 48 inches. (Fig. 61)

2. Floor Space
A 30 by 48-inch clear floor space shall be provided for wheelchair users to make a parallel approach at free-standing or built-in units that do not have a clear knee-space beneath them. (Figs. 62a,b) The clear floor space shall comply with Section C-2.3.

3. Knee Space
The knee-space between the bottom of the apron and the floor or ground on cantilevered drinking units shall be at

ADA ACCESSIBILITY DESIGN STANDARDS
FACILITY FIXTURES • Drinking Facilities

least 27 inches high, 30 inches wide, and 17 to 19 inches deep. (Figs. 60 and 61)

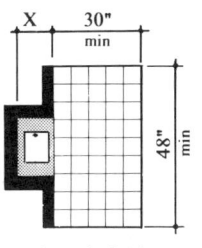
Fig. 62(a)
Free-standing Unit

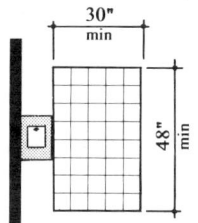
Fig. 62(b)
Built-in Unit

Fig. 62 **Parallel Approach to Drinking Units**

C-6.5 HANDRAILS • GRAB BARS • SEATS

C-6.5.1 APPLICATION CA: D-6.2.3(7), D-6.3.6, D-7.2.3

All handrails, grab bars, and the tub and shower seats required to be accessible by Sections C-1, C-4.6, C-4.9, C-5.6, C-5.7, C-6.2 or C-6.10 shall comply with the requirements of Section C-6.5. Grab bars shall not rotate or move within their fittings. *Persons with disabilities often depend on handrails and grab bars as leverage in lifting themselves and for support to retain balance.*

C-6.5.2 SIZE • SPACING CA: D-7.2.3(4)

1. Grip Size

A handrail or grab bar gripping surface shall be between

ADA ACCESSIBILITY DESIGN STANDARDS
FACILITY FIXTURES • Handrails • Grab Bars • Seats

1.25 and 1.5 inches in diameter or an equivalent gripping surface shape. *Handrails may have alternate shapes as long as they provide an opposing grip similar to a circular section of 1.25 to 1.5 inches.*

2. **Safety Clearance**
Grab bars and wall mounted handrails shall have a clear 1.5-inch space between the wall and the gripping surface as shown in Figure 63. *The 1.5-inch grab bar safety clearance allows an adequate grip space and prevents arms from slipping through the space between the wall and rail.*

3. **Recess Allowance**
Recessed space for handrails shall not exceed 3-inches in depth and be less than 18 inches in height above the top of the rail as shown in Figure 63(e).

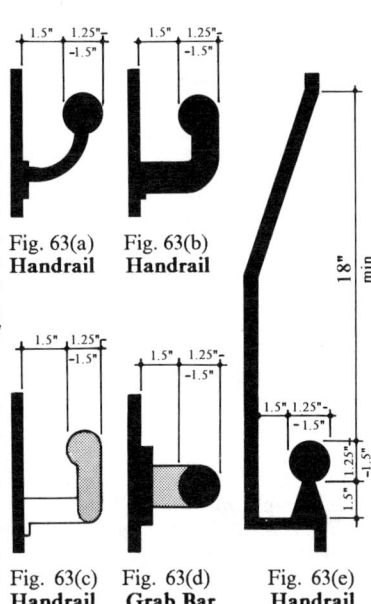

Fig. 63(a) **Handrail**
Fig. 63(b) **Handrail**
Fig. 63(c) **Handrail**
Fig. 63(d) **Grab Bar**
Fig. 63(e) **Handrail**

Fig. 63 **Rail and Bar Size and Spacing**

ADA ACCESSIBILITY DESIGN STANDARDS
FACILITY FIXTURES • Handrails • Grab Bars • Seats

C-6.5.3 SURFACES CA: D-7.2.3(4)

Handrails, grab bars, adjacent walls, or other adjacent surfaces shall be free of sharp or abrasive elements. Edges shall have a minimum radius of 1/8 inch.

C-6.5.4 STRUCTURAL STRENGTH CA: D-2.8.4.5(2)

The structural strength of handrails, grab bars, tub and shower seats, fasteners, and mounting devices shall meet the following requirements:

1. **Shear Force**
   The shear force on a mounting device from a 250-pound force shall be less than the allowable lateral load of the mounting device or support structure, whichever is the smaller allowable load.
2. **Tensile Force**
   The maximum moment of tensile force in a fastener by a 250-pound direct tension force shall be less than the allowable withdrawal load between the fastener and the supporting structure.
3. **Shear Stress**
   Shear stress induced by a 250-pound force on a bar or seat shall be less than the allowable shear stress of the bar or seat materials. If the connection between the support bracket and bar or seat is considered to be fully restrained, the combined total of direct and torsional shear stress shall not exceed the allowable shear stress.
4. **Bending Stress**
   The maximum bending moment from a 250-pound force on a bar or seat shall be less than the allowable material stress of the bar or seat.

ADA ACCESSIBILITY DESIGN STANDARDS
FACILITY FIXTURES • Lavatories • Mirrors

C-6.6 LAVATORIES • MIRRORS

C-6.6.1 APPLICATION CA: D-2.8.4.5(1), D-2.8.2.5

Lavatory fixtures, vanities, and built-in lavatories shall comply with Section C-6.6.

C-6.6.2 HEIGHT

A lavatory rim or counter surface shall not exceed 34 inches above the finished floor.

C-6.6.3 FAUCETS

Acceptable designs in faucets include push, electronic, and lever mechanisms. Faucets with self-closing valves shall remain open for no less than 10 seconds. Faucets shall comply with Section C-6.3.2.

C-6.6.4 KNEE SPACE

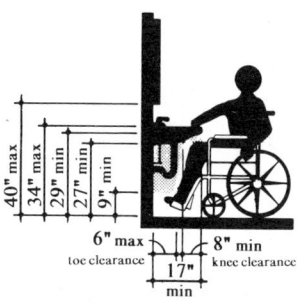

Fig. 64 **Lavatory Clearances**

Lavatory, knee, and toe spaces shall comply with the requirements in Figure 64. The minimum distance between the finish floor and the apron shall be 29 inches. Pipes beneath lavatories shall be configured or insulated to protect against contact from persons using the fixture. No sharp or abrasive surfaces shall be present under lavatories.

ADA ACCESSIBILITY DESIGN STANDARDS
FACILITY FIXTURES • Fixed Tables • Seating

C-6.6.5 FLOOR SPACE CA: D-6.3.7(2)

A lavatory shall have a 30 by 48-inch clear floor space that allows a forward approach, adjoins or overlaps an accessible route, extends no more than 19 inches beneath the lavatory, and complies with Section C-2.3 and Figure 65.

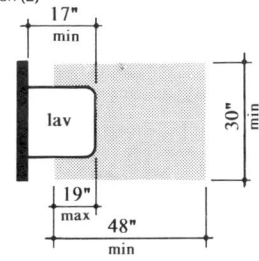

C-6.6.6 MIRRORS
CA: D-6.3.7(3)

Fig. 65 **Accessible Floor Space**

The lower reflective edge of mirrors shall not exceed more than 40 inches above the finished floor. (Fig. 64) *The top edge of a mirror must be at least 74 inches high for use by both ambulatory and wheelchair users. One full length mirror is preferred since it would accommodate all persons including children.*

C-6.7 FIXED TABLES • SEATING

C-6.7.1 APPLICATION CA: D-8.4.1

Fixed or built-in tables or seating required by Section C-1 shall comply with Section C-6.7.

C-6.7.2 FLOOR SPACE

When provided, the clear floor space for wheelchairs at fixed tables, counters, and seating areas shall comply with Section C-2.3.2 and shall not overlap the table knee space more than 19 inches. (Fig. 66)

ADA ACCESSIBILITY DESIGN STANDARDS
FACILITY FIXTURES • Fixed Tables • Seating

C-6.7.3 KNEE SPACE

Knee spaces at least 27 inches high, 30 inches wide, and 19 inches deep shall be provided when wheelchair seating is provided at tables or counters. (Fig. 66b)

Fig. 66 **Wheelchair Seating**

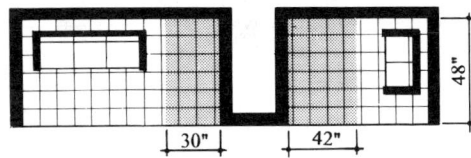

Fig. 66(a) **Seating Areas**

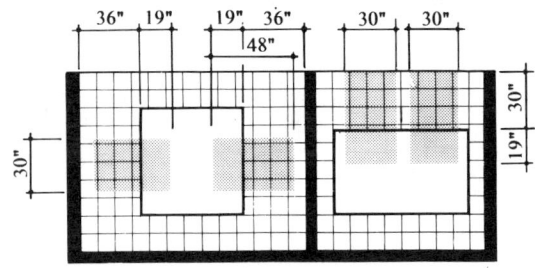

Fig. 66(b) **Seating at Tables**

C-6.7.4 WORKTABLE HEIGHT CA: D-8.4.2

Accessible table and counter tops shall be between 28 and 34 inches above the finished floor. *Different types of work re-*

ADA ACCESSIBILITY DESIGN STANDARDS
FACILITY FIXTURES • Fixed Tables • Seating

quires different table heights for comfort and optimum performance. The principle of a high/low working surface applies to both standing and seated persons. However, varying heights for seated persons is limited by the knee clearance below the working surface. The following table shows convenient work surface heights for seated persons. Where some people stand and others sit at the same counter, a compromise on the height must be made to achieve comfort and optimal performance for those persons. Table C-6A shows the standard convenient table and counter heights for seated persons.

TABLE C-6A		
WORK SURFACE[1] HEIGHT RANGE		
	Manual	**Light detailed**
Seated in wheelchair:		
Removeable armrests	26" - 30"	29" - 34"
Fixed armrests[2]	32"[3] - 32"[3]	32"[3] - 34"
Seated in 16" high chair:	26" - 27"	28" - 31"

Work surface height range above is based on the average short to the average tall person.

Dimensions are based on:
[1] A 1.5-inch work-surface thickness and 1.5-inch clearance beneath the work surface.
[2] Wheelchair positioned under the work surface.
[3] Limited to the armrest height.

ADA ACCESSIBILITY DESIGN STANDARDS
FACILITY FIXTURES • Sinks

C-6.8 SINKS

C-6.8.1 APPLICATION

Accessible sinks required by Section C-1 shall comply with Section C-6.8.

C-6.8.2 HEIGHT

The maximum height for sinks mounted with a counter or rim shall be 34 inches above the finished floor.

C-6.8.3 BOWL DEPTH

Sink bowls shall be no greater than 6.5 inches in depth.

C-6.8.4 FAUCETS

Faucets shall comply with Section C-6.3.2. Acceptable faucet designs include electronically controlled, push or touch-type, and lever-operated devices.

C-6.8.5 KNEE SPACE

An accessible sink shall have a minimum knee clearance of 30 inches wide, 27 inches high, and 19 inches deep underneath the sink. There shall be no sharp or abrasive surfaces beneath sinks. Exposed hot water pipes and drains shall be insulated or configured to protect against physical contact.

C-6.8.6 FLOOR SPACE

Sinks shall have a 30 by 48-inch clear floor space complying with Section C-2.3 and allow a forward approach. The space

ADA ACCESSIBILITY DESIGN STANDARDS
FACILITY FIXTURES • Urinals

shall not extend more than 19 inches underneath the sink as shown in Figure 65 and shall be on an accessible route.

C-6.9 URINALS

C-6.9.1 APPLICATION [CA: D-6.3.7(1)]

Urinals shall comply with Section C-6.9.

C-6.9.2 TYPE

Urinals required to be accessible shall be stall-type or wall-hung with an elongated rim no more than 17 inches above the finished floor.

C-6.9.3 FLUSH DEVICE

The flush control mechanism shall be operated manually or automatically, located no higher than 44 inches above the finished floor, and comply with Section C-6.3.

C-6.9.4 SHIELDS

Urinal shields may be provided with a clear 29-inch space between shields and must not extend beyond the urinal rim.

C-6.9.5 CLEAR SPACE

The front of urinals shall have a clear 30 by 48-inch floor space to allow a forward approach by wheelchair users. The clear floor space shall comply with Sections C-2.3.2 and C-2.3.3 and adjoin or overlap an accessible route.

ADA ACCESSIBILITY DESIGN STANDARDS
FACILITY FIXTURES • Water Closets

C-6.10 WATER CLOSETS

C-6.10.1 APPLICATION CA: D-6.3.1, D-6.3.4(4), D-6.3.5
Accessible water closets shall comply with Section C-6.10.

C-6.10.2 HEIGHT

Water closet heights shall be between 17 and 19 inches measured from the floor to the top of the toilet seat as shown in Figure 67. Toilet seats shall not automatically return to a lifted position. *Preference in a toilet seat height may vary considerably among persons with disabilities. Ambulatory disabled persons may prefer higher seats where persons in wheelchairs may prefer lower seats. A reasonable compromise would be a toilet seat 18 inches above the floor. Standard toilet fixtures can be adapted with filler rings and thick seats to meet these requirements.*

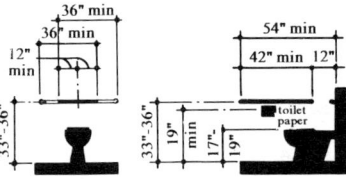

Fig. 67(a) **Back Wall**   Fig. 67(b) **Side Wall**
Fig. 67 **Water Closet and Grab Bars**

C-6.10.3 FLUSH DEVICE

Flush control devices shall be automatic or hand operated and comply with Section C-6.3.2. The control shall be no higher than 44 inches above the floor and shall be mounted on the wide side of the toilet. *Water closet plumbing fittings can be located to the side of the toilet, behind walls, or in*

ADA ACCESSIBILITY DESIGN STANDARDS
FACILITY FIXTURES · Water Closets

back when a toilet seat lid is provided for protection when leaning back against the fittings. Tank type toilets have a standard left side flush control mount. A right-side mount usually requires a special order. Grab bars behind the toilet may be shifted toward the wide side of the toilet area or split if the administrative authorities require the flush control to be in a location that conflicts with the grab bar.

C-6.10.4 PAPER DISPENSERS CA: D-6.3.7(5)

Toilet paper dispensers shall be installed within reach and shall not control the delivery or restrict continuous paper flow. (Fig. 67)

C-6.10.5 GRAB BARS CA: D-6.3.6

Water closet grab bars not located in stalls shall comply with Section C-6.5 and Figure 67. Grab bars shall be at least 36

Fig. 68 **Water Closet Transfers**

1.
- Positioned on toilet
- Positions wheelchair for transfer
- Sets brake
- Takes transfer position

2.
- Transfers
- Replaces armrest
- Swings footrest into position
- Releases brake

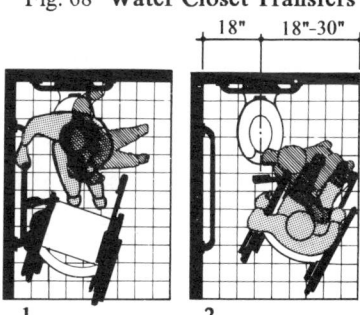

Fig. 68(a) **Diagonal Approach**

ADA ACCESSIBILITY DESIGN STANDARDS
FACILITY FIXTURES • Water Closets

inches in length when located behind the water closet. *Some wheelchair users transfer from the front of the toilet and others use a 90-degree transfer from their wheelchair. The most commonly used transfers are the diagonal or side approach shown in Figures 68(a,b). Most persons able to use a front or 90-degree transfer can also use the diagonal or side approach.*

C-6.10.6 FLOOR SPACE
CA: D-6.3.4(2)

Water closets not in stalls shall comply with the clear floor space requirements shown in Figure 69. A left-hand or right-hand approach may be provided.

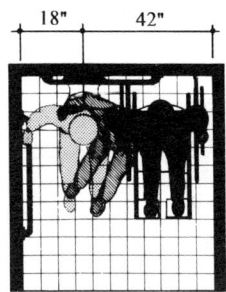

Fig. 68(b) **Side Approach**

1. Positioned on toilet
2. Takes transfer position
3. Transfers
4. Replace Armrest
5. Releases brake

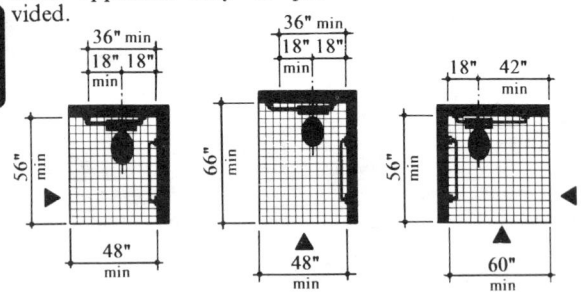

Fig. 69 **Clear Floor Space**

ADA ACCESSIBILITY DESIGN STANDARDS
SPECIFIC OCCUPANCIES • Libraries

C-7 SPECIFIC OCCUPANCIES

C-7.1 LIBRARIES

C-7.1.1 APPLICATION CA: D-2.4.1

Public libraries shall comply with the requirements of Section C-1 through C-6. The design of all library public areas shall comply with Section C-7.1.

C-7.1.2 STACKS CA: D-2.4.1(1)

The minimum clear aisle width between stacks shall comply with Section C-2.1 with a preferred 42-inch minimum clear aisle width where possible. The stack shelf heights are unrestricted. (Fig. 70)

C-7.1.3 READING AREAS
CA: D-2.4.2

A minimum of 5 percent or at least one of each element of fixed seating, tables, and study carrels shall comply with Section C-2.3 and C-6.7. Clearance space between fixed accessible tables and between study carrels shall comply with Section C-2.1.

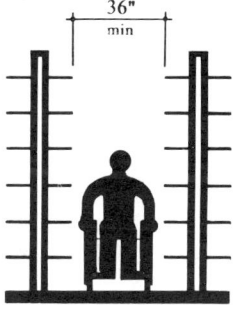

Fig. 70 **Stacks**

ADA ACCESSIBILITY DESIGN STANDARDS
SPECIFIC OCCUPANCIES • Lodging

C-7.1.4 FILES • DISPLAYS CA: D-2.4.1(3)

The minimum clear aisle space at card catalog files and magazine display racks shall comply with Figure 71. The maximum reach height shall comply with Section C-2.3.3 although a 48-inch height is preferred. Either direction of approach is allowed.

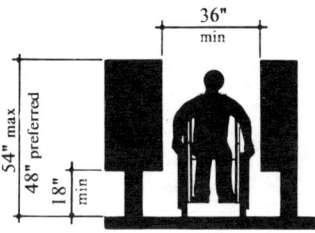

Fig. 71 **Card Catalog**

C-7.1.5 CHECK-OUT AREAS

A minimum of one lane at each checkout area shall comply with Section C-7.4.2. Traffic control, turnstiles, or book security gates shall comply with Section C-5.2.

C-7.2 LODGING

Transient lodging includes facilities used, all or in part, for sleeping accommodations when not classified as a medical care facility.

C-7.2.1 APPLICATION CA: D-2.8

1. **Lodging Facilities**
   Accessible transient lodging shall comply with the applicable requirements of Sections C-1 through C-6 except as specified in Section C-7.2.
2. **Rooms • Units** CA: D-2.8.1.1
   Transient lodging rooms and units required to be accessi-

ADA ACCESSIBILITY DESIGN STANDARDS
SPECIFIC OCCUPANCIES • Lodging

ble by Section C-7.2.4 shall comply with the minimum requirements of Section C-7.2.2.

3. Passageways CA: D-2.8.2.1, D-2.8.3.4(2)
Doors and doorways used for passage into and within sleeping units or other covered spaces shall comply with Section C-5.2.9.

4. Visual Alarms CA: D-2.8.1.5, D-3.8
Auxiliary visual alarms required in sleeping rooms by Section C-7.2.3(2) shall be provided and comply with Section C-3.1.4.

5. Telephones
Volume controls complying with Section C-3.4.8 shall be installed in accessible permanent telephones and comply with Section C-7.2.3(1).

6. General Public Areas
All public and common use areas are required to be designed and constructed in compliance with Section C. Sections C-7.2.1 through C-7.2.4 do not apply to commercial facilities occupied by the owner as a residence and having 5 or less rooms for rent.

C-7.2.2 MINIMUM REQUIREMENTS

Accessible units, sleeping rooms, or suites shall be on an accessible route that complies with Section C-2.1 and have the following accessible elements and spaces:

1. Accessible Route
All accessible spaces and elements within a unit, sleeping room, or suite shall be on an accessible route complying with Section C-2.1. An elevator is not required to serve multi-story units as long as the accessible living spaces and their elements are on an accessible level, provide double occupancy, and comply with Section C-7.2.2.

ADA ACCESSIBILITY DESIGN STANDARDS
SPECIFIC OCCUPANCIES • Lodging

2. **Accessible Spaces**
   The following spaces provided as part of an accessible sleeping accommodation unit shall be accessible and located on an accessible route:
   a) Living area
   b) Dining area
   c) One sleeping area
   d) Patio, terrace, or balcony
      Exception: The requirements of Sections C-2.1.2 and C-5.2.8 do not apply when it is necessary to utilize a higher door threshold or change in level to protect a unit from wind or water damage. Equal facilities shall be provided where patios, terraces, or balconies are not on an accessible level such as providing accessibility by a raised deck or ramp.
   e) One full bathroom containing a water closet, lavatory, and a bathtub or shower.
   f) One half-bath when only half-baths are provided.
   g) Covered parking or parking spaces
3. **Maneuvering Space** CA: D-2.8.1.1(3)
   Accessible sleeping rooms shall have a minimum 36-inch clear width maneuvering space along both sides of a bed or between two beds when two beds are provided.
4. **Doorways**
   Passage doors and doorways in sleeping rooms, suites, or other covered spaces shall comply with Section C-5.2.
5. **Storage**
   At least one of each fixed or built-in storage facility types provided shall contain storage space complying with Section C-4.7. Additional storage may be provided which is not required to meet the minimum design regulations.
6. **Accessible Controls**
   All controls in accessible units, sleeping rooms, and suites

shall comply with Section C-6.3.

7. Visual Alarms CA: D-2.8.1.5, D-3.8
Accessible sleeping room accommodations shall be provided for persons with hearing impairments as required by Section C-7.2.1(4) and comply with Section C-7.2.3(2).

8. Kitchens • Wet Bars CA: D-2.8.1.4, D-2.8.3.4(3-5)
Accessory elements and spaces of accessible sleeping units shall be accessible when provided. Cabinets, counters, sinks, and appliances shall be accessible and usable with the working surface no higher than 34 inches above the floor. Required clear floor space complying with Sections C-2.3.2 and C-2.3.3 shall be provided to allow a front or parallel approach for the full use and operation of cabinets and appliances. No less than 50 percent of shelf space including appliances shall be within the reach range requirements of Sections C-2.3.3. Operating mechanisms shall comply with Section C-6.3.

C-7.2.3 COMMUNICATION DEVICES CA: D-2.8.1.5

1. Telephones
Volume controlled telephones complying with Section C-7.2.1(5) shall have an accessible electrical outlet within 48 inches for the use of a text telephone.

2. Visual Alarms CA: D-2.8.1.5, D-3.8
Visual notification devices shall be provided in units, sleeping rooms, and suites to alert room occupants of incoming telephone calls and a door knock or doorbell. Auxiliary alarms shall be provided in units where visual alarms are installed. Notification devices shall not be connected to an auxiliary visual signal-alarm appliance.

3. Equivalent Facilitation
Equivalent facilitation in compliance with Section C-7.2 shall include accessible electrical outlets, an outlet connec-

ADA ACCESSIBILITY DESIGN STANDARDS
SPECIFIC OCCUPANCIES • Lodging

tion to the facility's central alarm system, and telephone wiring for the use of portable visual alarms and communication devices provided by the facility.

C-7.2.4 COMMERCIAL FACILITIES • DORMITORIES
CA: D 2.8.1.1, D-2.8.1.2

This section refers to hotels, motels, inns, boarding houses, dormitories, resorts, and other similar places of transient lodging.

1. Sleeping Accommodations

Accessible sleeping rooms or suites and hearing impairment elements required by Section C-7.2.1 that comply with the minimum requirements of Section C-7.2.2 shall be provided as shown in Table C-7A.

2. Accommodation Choice CA: D-2.8.1.1(2)

Each type or class of room shall be offered to persons with

TABLE C-7A	
Number of Rooms	**Accessible Rooms and Accessible Elements**
1 to 100	1 for each 1-25 rooms
101 to 200	4, +1 for each 1-50 rooms
201 to 500	6, +1 for each 1-100 rooms
501 to 1000	2% of total rooms
1001 and over	20, +1 for each 100 over 1000

ADA ACCESSIBILITY DESIGN STANDARDS
SPECIFIC OCCUPANCIES • Lodging

disabilities equivalent to those offered to other patrons. Sleeping units required to be accessible shall be dispersed among the various classes of units available to other patrons. Room classification may be based on room size, cost, number of beds, and amenities provided. It is deemed an equivalent facilitation when a facility limits their accessible rooms to multiple occupancy types and provides an accessible room at a single-occupancy rate to an individual with disabilities that requests a single-occupancy room.

3. Roll-in-Shower
Hotels which have more than 50 sleeping rooms or suites shall provide additional accessible sleeping rooms or suites that include a roll-in shower complying with Table C-7B and the requirements of Sections C-7.2.2, C-4.6, and Figures 72(a,b).

4. Alterations
An alteration to a facility, or portion thereof, shall provide accessible sleeping units as required by Sections C-7.2.4 and comply with the minimum requirements of Sections C-7.2.2 and the communication device requirements of Section C-7.2.3.

TABLE C-7B	
Total Rooms	**Rooms with Roll-in Showers**
1 to 50	0
51 to 100	1
101 and over	1, + 1 additional each 1-100

ADA ACCESSIBILITY DESIGN STANDARDS
SPECIFIC OCCUPANCIES • Lodging

Fig. 72 **Roll-in Shower with Folding Seat**

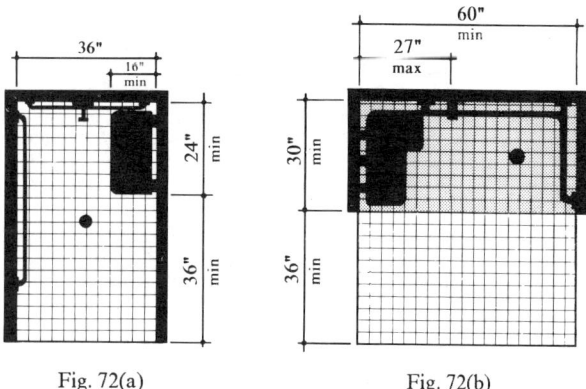

Fig. 72(a)   Fig. 72(b)

C-7.2.5 SOCIAL SERVICE LODGING CA: D-2.8

1. Application
This section covers transient lodging other than private commercial establishments which include homeless shelters, halfway houses, group homes, and other similar establishments.

2. New construction
2.1 Common Areas
Public and common areas shall be designed and constructed in compliance with the requirements of Section C. At least one of each type of amenity in each occupant common area shall be accessible. The amenity shall be on an accessible route to each accessible

ADA ACCESSIBILITY DESIGN STANDARDS
SPECIFIC OCCUPANCIES • Lodging

unit or sleeping accommodation within the facility. The amenities may be washers, dryers, and other similar equipment. Accessible amenities are not required on inaccessible floors of buildings without an elevator as allowed by Section C-1.1.5 when each type of amenity is provided in common areas on accessible floors.

2.2 Sleeping Rooms
Accessible sleeping rooms shall comply with the minimum requirements of Section C-7.2.2 and be provided in number according to Table C-7A. Additional sleeping rooms that comply with Section C-7.2.3 shall be provided in number according to Table C-7A. Facilities that have multi-bedrooms or spaces shall comply with the maneuvering space of Section C-7.2.2(3) and in number according to Table C-7A.

3. Alterations
3.1 Social Service Transient Lodging
Alterations in social service transient lodging facilities, other than homeless shelters, shall comply with the new construction requirements of Section C-7.2.5(2) and sleeping room requirements of Section C-7.2.4(4).

3.2 Homeless Shelters
These requirements apply when the following elements are altered:

a. One Location
The following requirements of (b) through (f) can be met by providing accessible spaces and elements on one accessible floor.

b. Accessible Route
At least one accessible route shall connect the following accessible spaces of (c), (d), (e), and (f). The route must comply with Section C-2.1.2 for any change in floor levels, shall have a minimum

ADA ACCESSIBILITY DESIGN STANDARDS
SPECIFIC OCCUPANCIES • Lodging

36-inch clear width, a turning space complying with Section C-2.3.1, and a passing space complying with Section C-2.1.3.

c. Common Areas
One or more common areas shall be provided where persons with mobility impairments can approach, enter, and exit a common area. The access doors shall have a 32-inch minimum clear door width.

d. Public Entrance
At least one public entrance shall have a minimum 32-inch clear door width where persons with mobility impairments can approach, enter, and exit a public entrance.

e. Sleeping Space
Sleeping spaces shall be provided in accordance with Section C-7.2.4. Access doors to the sleeping area shall have a 32-inch minimum clear width. Spaces around the beds shall comply with Section C-7.2.2.

f. Toilet Room
A minimum of one toilet room for each gender or one unisex toilet room shall have at least:
1) a door with a privacy latch,
2) an access door with a 32-inch minimum clear width,
3) one water closet complying with Section C-6.10,
4) one lavatory complying with Section C-6.6,
5) when provided, one tub complying with Section C-6.2 or one shower complying with Section C-4.6, and
6) a minimum turning space complying with Section C-2.3.1.

ADA ACCESSIBILITY DESIGN STANDARDS
SPECIFIC OCCUPANCIES • Medical Care Facilities

C-7.3 MEDICAL CARE FACILITIES

C-7.3.1 APPLICATION CA: D-2.6.1

1. Facility Defined
Medical care facilities applicable to this section are those where:
a) people receive physical or medical treatment or care,
b) people needing emergency assistance, and
c) the period of stay can exceed 24 hours.

2. Design • Construction
In addition to the requirements of Sections C-1 through C-6, medical care facilities and buildings shall be designed and constructed accessible in compliance with Section C-7.3 as follows:

2.1 Hospitals
At least 10 percent of patient bed/toilet rooms plus the public and common use areas in general hospitals, psychiatric facilities, and detoxification facilities.

2.2 Mobility Rehabilitation Facilities
All patient bed/toilet rooms and all public and common use areas in hospitals and rehabilitation facilities specializing in mobility treatment including units within large facilities.

2.3 Long Term Care Facilities
At least 50 percent of patient bed/toilet rooms plus the public and common use areas in nursing homes and other long-term care facilities.

2.4 Multi-bedroom Alteration
A percentage of the patient bedrooms added or altered within a planned renovation of a distinct medical facility area, such as an entire wing, shall comply with

ADA ACCESSIBILITY DESIGN STANDARDS
SPECIFIC OCCUPANCIES • Medical Care Facilities

Section C-7.3.2. The percentage of accessible rooms required and provided shall be consistent for facilities in Section C-7.3.1 until the number of the accessible patient bedrooms equal the overall number required in new construction. Each added or altered toilet/bathroom required to be accessible as part of a patient bedroom shall comply with Section C-7.3.3.

The following is an example based on the same hospital:

Type	Alterations/Additions	Accessibility %
Obstetrics unit	40 patient bedrooms	10%- 4 bedrooms
Mobility unit	55 patient bedrooms	100%-55 bedrooms
Accessible unit	55 patient bedrooms	100%-55 bathrooms

2.5 Single Bedroom Alteration

An individual patient bedroom alteration or addition that is not a part of an entire alteration area shall comply with Section C-7.3.2 unless:
a) The number of accessible patient bedrooms provided in the facility area containing the altered patient bedrooms equal the percentage of accessible patient bedrooms for that specific facility area if the requirement of Section C-7.3.1 were applied; or
b) The number of accessible patient bedrooms shall equal the number required in new construction for that facility. Where accessible patient bedrooms are added or altered, their toilet/bath rooms shall also be accessible and comply with Section C-7.3.3.

C-7.3.2 PATIENT BEDROOMS   CA: D-2.6.6.1

Accessible patient bedrooms shall be provided in compliance with Sections C-1 through C-6 and comply with the following:

ADA ACCESSIBILITY DESIGN STANDARDS
SPECIFIC OCCUPANCIES • Medical Care Facilities

1. **Floor Space**
   Each bedroom shall provide at least a 36-inch clear floor space along each side of the bed, and both spaces shall adjoin an accessible route complying with Section C-2.1.3.
2. **Maneuvering Space**
   Each bedroom shall provide a minimum maneuvering space that complies with Section C-2.3.1(5). This space is preferable between beds in rooms that have two beds.
3. **Door**
   Each bedroom shall have a door that complies with Section C-5.2. Acute-care in-patient hospital bedroom entry doors that are at least 44 inches wide shall be exempt from the maneuvering space requirement of Section C-5.2.10 at the latch side of the door.

C-7.3.3 PATIENT TOILET ROOM CA: D-2.6.6.3

Each accessible patient bedroom shall have an accessible toilet/bath room that complies with Section C-4.5 or C-4.8 when toilet/bath rooms are provided as part of the patient bedroom. The toilet/bath room shall be on an accessible route.

C-7.3.4 FACILITY ENTRANCES CA: D-2.6.2

At least one accessible entrance complying with Section C-4.3 shall provide a passenger loading zone that complies with Section C-4.4.2. and provide a roof overhang or canopy for weather protection.

ADA ACCESSIBILITY DESIGN STANDARDS
SPECIFIC OCCUPANCIES • Mercantile

C-7.4 MERCANTILE

C-7.4.1 APPLICATION CA: D-2.3.2.2

All public business transaction areas in a facility shall be designed in compliance with the requirements of Sections C-1 through C-6 and comply with Section C-7.4.

C-7.4.2 SALES • SERVICE COUNTERS

Section C-7.4.2 refers to counters without aisles that can be approached from more than one direction.

1. **Accessible Portion**
   A portion of each type of counter that has a cash register and is used for sales, goods distribution, or services to the public in a retail establishment shall have a portion accessible to persons in wheelchairs.

2. **Minimum Size**
   The accessible counter space shall be no more than 36 inches above the finished floor, no less than 36 inches in length, located on an accessible route complying with Section C-2.1, and dispersed throughout the business area.

3. **Auxiliary Counter**
   An auxiliary counter that meets these requirements may be provided in alterations where it is technically infeasible to meet the standard accessibility requirements for counters.

4. **Service Counters**
   Service counters that may not have a cash register but where goods or services are sold or distributed, such as ticket registration or teller counters, shall provide either:
   a) a portion of the main counter no higher than 36 inches above the finished floor and no less than 36 inches in length; or

ADA ACCESSIBILITY DESIGN STANDARDS
SPECIFIC OCCUPANCIES • Mercantile

b) an auxiliary counter no higher than 36 inches near the main counter; or

c) an equivalent facilitation.

All accessible counters shall be on an accessible route complying with Section C-2.1.

5. Assistive Listening Devices

At least one permanent assistive listening device complying with Section C-4.1.6 is recommended at each location or at one of each series of locations where a physical barrier separates the personnel from the customers. Signs should be provided identifying those stations equipped with assistive listening devices.

C-7.4.3 CHECK-OUT AISLES ^{CA: D-2.3.2.2(3)}

Section C-7.4.3 concerns check-out aisles which must be entered at a defined point, pay for goods, and exit at another defined point. Accessible check-out aisles shall have a clear aisle width complying with Section C-2.3.1. The adjoining counter height shall not exceed 38 inches and a lip 40 inches above the finished floor. Accessibility signs shall be displayed along with the check-out aisle number or type of aisle sign that is posted above the accessible aisle. The accessibility sign shall comply with Section C-3.3.3

1. New Construction

In new construction, a selling area less than 5000 square feet requires a minimum of one accessible check-out aisle. Accessible check-out aisles shall be provided in conformance with Table C-7C:

2. Alterations

Altered facilities with a selling area less than 5000 square feet requires a minimum of one accessible check-out aisle. Selling areas of more than 5000 square feet require at least one accessible check-out aisle of each design until the ac-

ADA ACCESSIBILITY DESIGN STANDARDS
SPECIFIC OCCUPANCIES • Restaurants • Cafeterias

cessible aisles equal those required in new construction. Check-out aisles may include specific designs for different functions such as a permanent express lane versus a regular lane or different features as a moving belt versus no belt.

TABLE C-7C				
Check-out Aisles of Each Design or Type				
Total Aisles:	1-4	5-8	8-15	15-over
Accessible Aisles::	1	2	3	3, + 20% over 15

C-7.4.4 SECURITY BOLLARDS

Accessibility to wheelchair users shall not be prevented by any device used to prevent removal of shopping carts from a store. An alternate entry equally convenient to that provided for ambulatory customers is acceptable.

C-7.5 RESTAURANTS • CAFETERIAS

C-7.5.1 APPLICATION CA: D-2.2.3, D-8.4

Restaurants and cafeterias shall comply with the requirements of Sections C-1 through C-6 except as specified or modified in Section C-7.5.

1. Design

Design of new facilities shall distribute accessible fixed tables and counter space throughout the facility and where

ADA ACCESSIBILITY DESIGN STANDARDS
SPECIFIC OCCUPANCIES • Restaurants • Cafeterias

practicable in alterations.
2. **Accessible Percentage**
When provided and where table service is not available, at least 5 percent and never less than one fixed dining table or a portion of counter shall be made accessible and comply with Section C-6.7 as required by Section C-1.3.11. The required number of accessible fixed tables or counter space shall be proportionally distributed between smoking and non-smoking areas when provided as separate areas. *Small facilities that provide only a narrow dining counter with no service shall have a portion of the counter at the required accessible height.*

C-7.5.2 COUNTERS • BARS

Where customers receive and consume food or drink seated or standing at counters exceeding 34 inches in height, a portion of counters exceeding 60 inches in length shall be in compliance with Section C-6.7 or service shall be available at accessible tables within the same area.

C-7.5.3 DINING AREA

New construction requires that dining areas including raised, sunken, terraced, and outdoor seating areas be accessible. This is not required in alterations when the same service and decor are provided in a similar accessible space used by the general public and not restricted for use by only persons with disabilities. Vertical accessible means to a mezzanine is not required under the following conditions:
a) The mezzanine seating is less than 34 percent of the total seating area.
b) The mezzanine is not accessible by an elevator.
c) The accessible areas are not restricted to persons with

ADA ACCESSIBILITY DESIGN STANDARDS
SPECIFIC OCCUPANCIES • Restaurants • Cafeterias

disabilities.
d) The same service and decor provided in the mezzanine is available in the accessible space used by the general public.

C-7.5.4 AISLES

Accessible fixed tables shall have a 36-inch minimum clear aisle between parallel table edges or between a wall and a table edge.

C-7.5.5 FOOD SERVICE LINES CA: D-2.2.3.5

At least 50 percent of each type of self-service shelves must be within the specified reach ranges of Section C-2.3.3. Tray slides shall be no higher than 34 inches above the finished floor. (Fig. 73) Food service lines shall have at least a 36-inch clear width. A 42-inch clear width is preferred to enable a person to pass a person in a wheelchair.

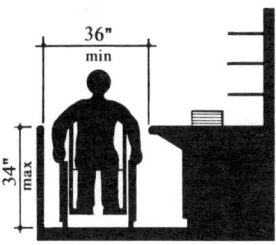

Fig. 73 **Food Service Lines**

C-7.5.6 SELF-SERVICE AREAS CA: D-2.2.3.4

Tableware, dishes, condiments, food and beverage dispensing devices, and self-service shelves shall be installed to comply with Section C-2.3. (Fig. 74)

ADA ACCESSIBILITY DESIGN STANDARDS
SPECIFIC OCCUPANCIES • Transportation

C-7.5.7 VENDING MACHINES • EQUIPMENT
CA: D-8.5

Vending machines and other equipment shall be located on an accessible route and comply with the space requirements of Section C-2.3.

C-7.5.8 PLATFORMS
CA: D-2.2.4.4

Raised platforms in assembly dining areas shall be accessible where a head table or speaker podium is located and shall comply with Sections C-5.5 or C-5.6. A curb or placement of tables shall exist along open platform edges.

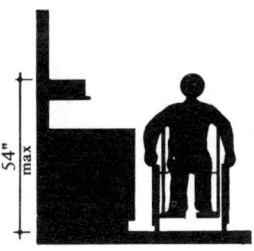

Fig. 74 **Self-Service Areas**

C-7.6 TRANSPORTATION

The NPRM reserved Section 10 for transportation facilities. A supplemental notice of proposed rule making, SNPRM, was issued in the Federal Register March 20, 1990. The proposal required the guidelines to be applicable to transportation facilities constructed or altered by public entities covered by the ADA, Title II. The Department of Transportation also proposed to adopt the Board's guidelines as the accessibility standards.

SECTION D

Americans with Disabilities Act Accessibility Guidelines
modified and adopted as Chapter 31 of the
California Building Code

CALIFORNIA BUILDING CODE

TITLE 24 · ACCESS CODE

SECTION D

D-1 GENERAL PROVISIONS

The state of California has set building code standards to conform with the Americans with Disabilities Act and the Fair Housing Amendments. The Office of the State Architect has presented the code standards to the State Building Standards Commission (SBSC) for adoption as an amendment of Part 2, Title 24, of the California Code of Regulations (CCR). These standards will take effect six months subsequent to the approval by the SBSC. The requirements provided herein are based on the code standards presented to the SBSC as of the date of this printing.

Information source:
Office of the State Architect
400 P Street, 5th Floor
Sacramento, California 95814
Phone: 916- 445-2163

D-1.1 PURPOSE

D-1.1.1 MINIMUM STANDARDS

The California Building Code provides minimum design and building standards to protect the general public by regulating and controlling the design, construction, quality of materials, occupancy use, location, and maintenance of all buildings

CALIFORNIA ACCESS CODE • TITLE 24
GENERAL PROVISIONS • Application

and structures within the scope of the California Building Code.

D-1.1.2 ACCESSIBILITY

The accessibility standards of the California Building Code provide accessibility to persons with disabilities assuring that barrier free design is incorporated in all buildings, facilities, site work, and other developments to which the code applies.

D-1.2 APPLICATION
ADA: B-4.1, C-1.1.1

Construction, alteration, repair, demolition, moving, and use of any building or structure within the authority of any California state agency shall be in compliance with the accessibility building standards. The access code does not apply to work located primarily in public ways, at public utility towers or poles, or mechanical equipment not specifically regulated by these building standards.

D-1.2.1 PUBLICLY FUNDED

1. Buildings, structures, sidewalks, curbs, and related facilities shall be accessible to persons with disabilities.
2. Buildings, structures, and facilities 50 percent or more occupied and which are rented or contracted for periods in excess of two years by any municipal county, state division of government, or by a special district shall be accessible. The California Building Code determines the occupancy percentage and usable floor area.
3. Existing buildings and facilities in which additions, alterations, or structural repairs are made shall be accessible.
4. Living accommodations shall be accessible.

CALIFORNIA ACCESS CODE • TITLE 24
GENERAL PROVISIONS • Priority Order • Fire Codes

5. One or two-unit family buildings, congregate residences, and related facilities shall conform to the provisions applicable to living accommodations.

D-1.2.2 PRIVATELY FUNDED

Public accommodations and commercial facilities shall be accessible to persons with disabilities as defined:
1. Buildings, structures, facilities, complexes, improved areas, or portions thereof used by the general public shall be accessible.
2. Public accommodations to which additions, alterations, or structural repairs are made shall be accessible including historic buildings.
3. Sanitary facilities made available for the public, clients, or employees shall be accessible to persons with disabilities.
4. Curbs and sidewalks intended for public use shall be accessible.

D-1.3 PRIORITY ORDER

The accessibility standards adopted by the State Building Standards Commission and amended to the California Building Code shall take precedence over any differences between these standards and the standard reference documents. Specific requirements shall govern over general requirements.

D-1.4 FIRE CODES

Nothing in these regulations shall diminish the requirements of the State Fire Marshall.

CALIFORNIA ACCESS CODE • TITLE 24
GENERAL PROVISIONS • OSA/AC • Administrative Agency

D-1.5 OSA/AC

The Office of the State Architect, Access Compliance, (OSA/AC) is the state agency that assures barrier-free design is incorporated in all buildings, facilities, site work, and other improvements to which this code applies; assures additions, alterations, and structural repairs in all buildings and facilities comply with the accessibility provisions for new buildings, except as otherwise specified herein; assures such improvements are in compliance with state law; and assures the improvements are accessible to and usable by persons with disabilities. These provisions also apply to temporary and emergency buildings and facilities and to any portable building used by a school district within the state.

The Office of the State Architect may incorporate standards at least as restrictive as those required by the federal government for barrier free design under Title III, Subpart D and Appendix A, and Title II, Section 35.151 both from the Americans with Disabilities Act of 1990 and the Fair Housing Amendments of 1988.

D-1.6 ADMINISTRATIVE AGENCY

The California Amendments to the Uniform Building Code provides a matrix adoption table in the index and reference guide for each chapter of the California Building Code. The tables list the state agencies, their scope of application, and statutory authority for enforcement unless other statutory authority is specifically cited under a specific matrix adoption table.

CALIFORNIA ACCESS CODE • TITLE 24
GENERAL PROVISIONS • Special Provisions

D-1.6.1 VESTING AUTHORITY [ADA: B-5]

These regulations shall be enforced by the appropriate state enforcing agency adopting such provisions but only to the extent of authority granted by the state legislature.

D-1.6.2 ENFORCEMENT [ADA: B-5]

The following are enforcing agencies:
1. The building department of every city, county, or city/county within its territorial area and where private funds are utilized.
2. Governing bodies when funds of counties, municipalities, or other political subdivisions are utilized except as otherwise provided in 3 below.
3. Director of General Services when funds of counties, municipalities, or other political subdivisions are utilized for the construction of elementary schools, secondary schools, or community colleges and where state funds are used for projects.

D-1.7 SPECIAL PROVISIONS

D-1.7.1 APPEALS

An appeal action ratification for persons with disabilities, in reference to these regulations, shall be subject to ratification through an appeals process from the findings and determinations rendered by the local enforcing agency.

D-1.7.2 VALIDITY

If any phrase, clause, sentence, subsection, section, or chapter of the California Building Code is held to be unconstitutional, contrary to statute, exceeding the authority of the state as stipulated by statutes, or otherwise inoperative, such decision shall not affect the validity of the remaining portion of the code.

CALIFORNIA ACCESS CODE • TITLE 24
GROUP OCCUPANCIES • General

D-2 GROUP OCCUPANCIES

D-2.1 GENERAL

Various facilities are classified by the character of its use or occupancy. Buildings or portions of buildings for all occupancy classifications of Section D-2 shall be accessible to persons with disabilities except as modified or enhanced in Section D, but never to the exclusion of the requirement. Multi-story buildings must provide a ramp or elevator for accessibility. Each part of a building is comprised of a distinct occupancy in buildings with multiple occupancy uses.

Exceptions:
1. Building floors or portions of floors not customarily occupied are exempt such as elevator pits and machinery catwalks and pits. ADA C-1.1.7
2. Privately funded buildings that do not require a ramp or elevator above or below the first floor are:
    a) Multi-story office buildings and passenger vehicle service stations less than three stories high or less than 3000 square feet per story. This exception does not include buildings with a professional health care office.
    b) When a reasonable portion of all facilities and accommodations used by the public are readily accessible and usable by persons with disabilities in other types of multi-story buildings that have less than three stories or less than 3000 square feet per story and do not house a shopping center or a professional health care office.

D-2.2 GROUP A OCCUPANCY

ASSEMBLY FACILITIES

Group A occupancy falls within five divisions. A building, facility, or portion thereof used for assembly purposes having the following:

DIVISION 1: Occupant load of 1000 or more with a legitimate stage.

DIVISION 2: Occupant load of less than 1000 with a legitimate stage.

DIVISION 2.1: Occupant load of 300 or more without a legitimate stage including educational use not classified under Group E or Group B, Division 2 occupancy.

DIVISION 3: Occupant load less than 300 without a legitimate stage including educational use not classified under Group E or Group B, Division 2 occupancy.

DIVISION 4: Buildings and structures not included in Division 1 through 3 such as stadiums, reviewing stands, and amusement parks.

All Group A Occupancies shall be accessible and comply with this Section.

CALIFORNIA ACCESS CODE • TITLE 24
GROUP OCCUPANCIES • Group A

D-2.2.1 AUDITORIUMS, THEATERS, ASSEMBLY HALLS, AND RELATED FACILITIES
ADA: B-3.7.7, C-1.2.5, C-1.3.10, C-4.1

Where seating is provided, seating spaces shall be provided for semi-ambulatory persons and persons in wheelchairs.

Exceptions in existing buildings and facilities occur when:
1. The enforcing agency determines that code compliance with the seating requirements would create an undue hardship. In such case, 1 percent of the total seating shall be accessible to wheelchair users and comply with Sections D-2.2.1.2(7,8).
2. A theater is subdivided with upper levels inaccessible to an elevator or ramp, and the enforcing agency determines full code compliance would create an undue hardship. The upper levels need not be accessible if all facilities are also provided on an accessible level and the activities are scheduled to assure that all functions available to the public are also available to persons with disabilities.

D-2.2.1.1 TICKET BOOTHS

Both the customer and the employee side of ticket booths and concession facilities shall be accessible to persons with disabilities

D-2.2.1.2 SEATING
ADA: B-3.3.1, C-1.3.10, C-1.3.11, C-4.1.2, C-4.1.3, C-4.1.5

1. Percentage
Wheelchair spaces in assembly areas shall comply with Section C-1.3.10 (2a-c) and Table C-1B except where California requires one space for a 4 to 26 seating capacity and two spaces for a 27 to 50 seating capacity.

CALIFORNIA ACCESS CODE • TITLE 24
GROUP OCCUPANCIES • Group A

2. **Semi-ambulant Seating** ADA: C-4.1.2(7)
Semi-ambulant individuals shall be provided with at least 1 percent of the total seating capacity and never less than two seats in addition to the spaces provided for wheelchair users. The seats shall provide at least a 24-inch clear leg space between the front of the seat and the back of the seat immediately in front or other nearest obstruction.

3. **Location** ADA: C-4.1.2(3)
Wheelchair locations shall comply with number 5 below, Sections C-4.1.2 through C-4.1.2(3), and Section C-4.1.2.(4) when the seating capacity is less than 300.

4. **Life Safety** ADA: C-4.1.2(6)
Life safety must be considered in determining location for persons with disabilities, and the seating shall comply with the fire and panic-safety requirements of the State Fire Marshal.

5. **Accommodation Choice** ADA: C-4.1.2(5)
Places of public amusement and resort, including theaters, stadiums, concert halls, and except hotels and motels, shall provide a variety of accessible seating and accommodations offering a choice of admission prices to persons with disabilities similar to those offered to the general public.

6. **Route of Travel** ADA: C-4.1.2(1)
Seating for persons with disabilities shall be on an accessible route of travel to the primary entrance and toilet facilities.

7. **Clear Floor Space** ADA: C-4.1.3
Each wheelchair location shall provide at least the minimum clear floor space which adjoins an egress aisle on at least one side as shown in Figures 19(a,b).

CALIFORNIA ACCESS CODE • TITLE 24
GROUP OCCUPANCIES • Group A

8. Floor Surface ADA: C-4.1.4

Ground and floor surfaces shall be level at wheelchair locations and comply with Sections C-5.4.4, C-5.4.,5 and C-5.4.6 and carpet edges with Section C-5.4.4.

D-2.2.1.3 PERFORMING AREAS
ADA: C-1.3.10, C-1.3.11, C-4.1.5

Stages, enclosed and unenclosed platforms, and orchestra pits shall be accessible to persons with disabilities. Performing areas shall comply with Section C-4.1.5.

Exceptions:
1. An enclosed or unenclosed platform or a depressed area 24 inches or less above or below an adjacent accessible level may be made accessible by a portable ramp with a slope not exceeding 1:12 when the enforcing agency finds this code compliance would create an unreasonable hardship.
2. Stages, enclosed and unenclosed platforms, and orchestra pits in existing buildings and facilities need not be accessible when the enforcing agency determines this code compliance would create an undue hardship.

D-2.2.1.4 PUBLIC AREAS

Public toilets and other public areas shall be accessible to persons with disabilities.

D-2.2.2 SPORT FACILITIES ADA: C-4.1.2, C-4.1.5

D-2.2.2.1 TICKET BOOTH

The customer side of ticket booths shall be accessible to persons with disabilities. The employee side is optional.

CALIFORNIA ACCESS CODE • TITLE 24
GROUP OCCUPANCIES • Group A

D-2.2.2.2 SPECTATOR SEATING
ADA: B-3.3.1, C-1.3.10, C-1.3.11

Stadiums, gymnasiums, bleachers, grandstands, athletic pavilions, and other miscellaneous sport related facilities shall comply with Sections D-2.2.1.2(1,5,6) and the allowed exceptions in Sections D-2.2.1(1,2).

D-2.2.2.3 PARTICIPATION AREAS

Activity participation areas shall be accessible to persons with disabilities including the following:
a) Gymnasium floors
b) General exercise rooms
c) Activity courts such as tennis, badminton, racquetball, basketball, and volleyball
d) Bowling lanes
e) Playing fields and tracks
f) Swimming pool deck areas and pool assistive devices for entry into the pool
g) Athletic team rooms and facilities

D-2.2.2.4 SANITARY • LOCKER ROOMS ADA: C-4.1.5

When provided, spectator, and participant sanitary and locker facilities shall comply with Sections D-6.2.

Exceptions:
1. Equivalent facilitation through the use of other means or materials may be provided when the enforcing agency determines that compliance with these regulations would create an undue hardship.
2. When the enforcing agency finds compliance to these regulations creates an undue hardship in an existing building and when all of the following minimum requirements are met.

CALIFORNIA ACCESS CODE • TITLE 24
GROUP OCCUPANCIES • Group A

a) One of each type of participation area is accessible and usable by persons with disabilities.
b) When one percent of the total seating capacity of 5000 or less is accessible to persons with disabilities. When the seating capacity exceeds 5000, one additional accessible seat shall be provided for each additional 2000 capacity.
c) Sanitary facilities, concessions, ticket booths, and club rooms are accessible to persons with disabilities.

D-2.2.2.5 CLUB ROOMS ADA: B-1.1.4

Club rooms shall be accessible to persons with disabilities.

D-2.2.3 DINING, BANQUET, AND BAR FACILITIES
ADA: C-7.5

Such facilities shall be accessible to persons with disabilities and comply with the following minimum regulations.

Exceptions:
1. When floors and levels in new and existing buildings are exempted by Section D-3.17.
2. When the enforcing agency determines compliance with these regulations would create an undue hardship in existing buildings and equivalent facilitation is provided.
3. When a legal or physical constraint in existing buildings do not allow compliance with these regulations or the provision for equivalent facilitation without creating an undue hardship.

D-2.2.3.1 FUNCTIONAL ACTIVITY

Each type of functional activity area shall be accessible to persons in wheelchairs.

CALIFORNIA ACCESS CODE • TITLE 24
GROUP OCCUPANCIES • Group A

D-2.2.3.2 ENTRANCES ^{ADA: C-1.3.4, C-4.3.1}

Facility primary entrances and exits shall be accessible to persons with disabilities as required by Section D-3.3.4.

D-2.2.3.3 SEATING ^{ADA: C-1.2.4, C-1.3.10, C-1.3.11, C-4.1.2}

Each functional area shall have one wheelchair seating space for each 20 seats provided, but never less than one seat, and shall comply with Section D-8.4. A minimum 36-inch clear width accessible aisle shall be provided to those seating areas. The accessible seating spaces shall be disbursed among the general seating area to allow a reasonable selection of seating and avoid a specific area being designated for persons with disabilities.

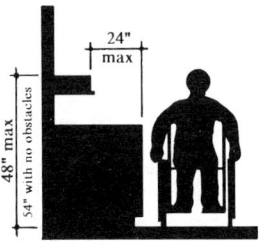

Fig. 75 **Self-Service Areas**

D-2.2.3.4 SELF-SERVICE AREAS ^{ADA: C-7.5.6}

Tableware, dishes, condiments, and food and beverage dispensing devices shall be accessible to persons with disabilities and shall comply with Section D-8.4. (Fig. 75)

D-2.2.3.5 FOOD SERVICE LINES ^{ADA: C-7.5.5}

Food service aisles shall comply with Section C-7.5.5 and Figure 73. California requires a "reasonable portion" of the shelves to be accessible rather than 50 percent required by the ADAAG.

CALIFORNIA ACCESS CODE • TITLE 24
GROUP OCCUPANCIES • Group A

D-2.2.3.6 FOOD PREPARATION AREAS

Accessibility to food preparation areas shall comply with the door regulations in Sections D-3.16 and the aisle regulations in Section D-8.4.3.

D-2.2.3.7 RESTROOMS ADA: B-1.1.4

Restrooms shall be accessible to persons with disabilities and comply with the regulations of Section D-6.3.

D-2.2.4 RELIGIOUS FACILITIES

Religious facilities shall be accessible to persons with disabilities as required by this section.

> **Exception**
> An exception is granted when the enforcing agency determines that compliance with a regulation under this section for an existing building creates an undue hardship.

D-2.2.4.1 SANCTUARY ADA: C-1.3.10, C-1.3.11, C-4.1

Sanctuary areas shall be accessible to persons with disabilities.

1. **Performing Areas** ADA: C-1.2.5, C-4.1.5
   Choir rooms and lofts, raised platforms, performing areas, and similar areas shall be accessible.
   Exception
   A choir loft in an existing building when the enforcing agency determines that compliance would create an undue hardship.

2. **Wheelchair Spaces**
   Wheelchair seating spaces shall comply with the requirements of Sections D-2.2.1.2(1,5,6) and the exceptions in Section D-2.2.1(1,2)

CALIFORNIA ACCESS CODE • TITLE 24
GROUP OCCUPANCIES • Group A

D-2.2.4.2 SANITARY FACILITIES

Sanitary facilities shall be accessible and comply with the requirements of Section D-6.2, when provided, and Section D-6.3.

D-2.2.4.3 CLASSROOMS • OFFICES

Classrooms and offices shall have entry doors that comply with the requirements of Section D-7.1.

D-2.2.4.4 ASSEMBLY AREAS ^{ADA: C-7.5.8}

Assembly areas having enclosed and unenclosed platforms shall be accessible to persons with disabilities. Stages shall also comply with these requirements.

D-2.2.4.5 ASSISTIVE-LISTENING SYSTEMS
^{ADA: B-3.2.2, C-1.3.10(3), C-4.1.6}

Assembly area conference and meeting rooms shall provide assistive-listening systems for persons with hearing impairments and comply as follows:

1. **Type** ^{ADA: C-4.1.6(2)}
   Types of assistive-listening systems include but are not limited to a radio frequency system, audio-induction loop, and infrared transmission.
2. **Placement** ^{ADA: C-4.1.6(1)}
   Systems limited to specific areas or seats shall be within a 50-foot viewing distance of the performing area.
3. **Personal Receivers**
   At least 4 percent of the total number of seats shall be provided but never less than two personal receivers.
4. **Portable Systems**
   When used, portable systems may serve more than one room. A permanent system is required in fixed seating

CALIFORNIA ACCESS CODE • TITLE 24
GROUP OCCUPANCIES • Group A

areas that accommodate 50 or more persons or have an audio-amplification system.

5. Signage
A sign shall be posted in a prominent place indicating the availability of an assistive-listening device that states "Assistive-listening System Available". The sign shall include the International Symbol of Accessibility for the hearing impaired as shown in Figure 17(d).

6. Usage Fee
Nothing in this section shall preclude a facility from charging its usual fee for the use of its audio visual equipment.

Exception:
Systems used exclusively for paging, background music, or a combination of both.

CALIFORNIA ACCESS CODE · TITLE 24
GROUP OCCUPANCIES · Group B

D-2.3 GROUP B OCCUPANCY

BUSINESS FACILITIES

Group B occupancy consists of four divisions of specific types of facilities.

DIVISION 1: Gasoline service stations and automotive service garages which only exchange parts or provide maintenance that requires no open flame.

DIVISION 2: Office buildings
Retail and wholesale stores
Drinking and dining establishments
Printing plants
Factories and workshops not using highly flammable or combustible materials
Sales room or the storage of combustible goods
Paint stores without bulk handling
Police and fire stations

DIVISION 3: Open parking garages
Helistops
Aircraft hangars with no repair maintenance or service except for exchange of parts

DIVISION 4: Factories and workshops using noncombustible and nonexplosive materials.
Storage and sales rooms containing only noncombustible and nonexplosive materials.
Power plants, pumping plants, ice plants, cold storage, and creameries.

CALIFORNIA ACCESS CODE • TITLE 24
GROUP OCCUPANCIES • Group B

Group B occupancies shall be accessible as required by Section D-2.3 and comply with the applicable minimum requirements of Section D-3.

D-2.3.1 OFFICE • SERVICE FACILITIES

Office buildings and personal and public service facilities shall comply with the requirements of Section D-2.3.
Exceptions:
1. When an enforcing agency determines compliance with these requirements would create an undue hardship in an existing building and when equivalent facilitation is provided.
2. The requirements of this section do not apply in existing buildings when legal or physical constraints do not allow compliance with these building standards or equivalent facilitation without creating an undue hardship.

D-2.3.2 SPECIFIC FACILITIES • AREAS

Facilities required to be accessible are places of employment and those used by the public which include, among others, the following categories:

D-2.3.2.1 OFFICE FACILITIES

All types of general and specialized business and professional offices including architectural, medical, dentistry, legal, insurance, real estate, counseling, accounting and other such offices. Specific areas within such facilities required to be accessible are
  a) Client and visitor areas, office areas, and related toilet rooms;
  b) Conference rooms, counseling rooms or cubicles, and other similar areas;

CALIFORNIA ACCESS CODE • TITLE 24
GROUP OCCUPANCIES • Group B

c) Employee work areas shall have at least a 36-inch wide clear access aisle except as modified in Section D-8.4.3; and
d) Professional medical and dental offices which must comply with Section D-2.6, Group I Occupancy.

D-2.3.2.2 RETAIL FACILITIES
ADA: C-1.2.6, C-1.3.12, C-1.3.16, C-4.2, C-7.4

All types of retail facilities including all general and special merchandise and equipment and other retail related businesses shall be accessible. Specific areas within such facilities required to be accessible are:

1. **General sales**, display, office areas, and related toilet rooms. Exceptions are:
    a) Specialized display areas utilizing 200 square feet or less, excluded from the general public, and not required to be accessible.
    b) Sale office facilities located on inaccessible levels, having a total of 5000 square feet or less, and which do not need to be made accessible.
2. **Employee sales stations** shall be located on accessible levels. The customer side of sales or checkout stations and employee work areas shall be made accessible.
3. **Check-out areas** ADA: C-7.4.3
    a) New construction
       - A 36-inch wide clear aisle shall be provided on the customer side of a checkstand.
       - When provided, at least one quick checkstand shall be accessible.
       - Regular checkstands shall comply with Table C-7C.
    b) New and existing construction
       - Provide a clear 36-inch wide check-out aisle

- Provide an adjoining counter with a maximum height of 38 inches with a lip no higher than 40 inches above the finished floor.
- Accessible checkstands shall always be open to customers with disabilities and identified by the International Symbol of Accessibility sign clearly visible to wheelchair users. The sign shall be white on blue background and state "This checkstand to be open at all times for customers with disabilities".

c) Existing buildings shall comply with the requirements of Section C-7.4.3(2).

4. Point-of-sale machines. Machines used for executing transactions with the customer shall comply with Section D-8.1.

5. Turnstiles shall comply with Section D-7.1.8.

6. Shopping cart barriers. Barriers for theft prevention, when provided, shall comply with the following:

a) Each public entrance and exit shall be accessible and usable by persons with disabilities.

b) Each barrier at public entrances or exits shall provide a clear 32-inch wide opening for the ingress and egress of persons with disabilities.

c) When provided, a clear unobstructed opening shall have at least a 44-inch long by 48-inch wide level area adjoining both sides of the opening or gate.

d) Interior and exterior pedestrian traffic barriers, such as posts, rails, and turnstiles, shall allow unobstructed travel through a clear 32-inch opening for persons with disabilities.

e) When used, gates shall:
- stay open and unobstructed during business hours,
- provide a 32-inch clear opening,
- open in the direction of travel,

CALIFORNIA ACCESS CODE • TITLE 24
GROUP OCCUPANCIES • Group B

- not require more than a 5-foot pound force,
- have the lowest edge within 3 inches of the floor,
- have at least a 60 by 60-inch wide level area in the direction of travel adjacent to the gate opening,
- have a level area opposite the gate swing that extends at least 42 inches long by 48 inches wide beyond the opening,
- not operate a publicly audible alarm system,
- have a smooth surface,
- be structurally adequate to be opened by a wheelchair footrest, and
- be designed to prevent vehicles and other obstructions from being placed in the path of travel that services the gate.

7. **Fitting and dressing rooms** ADA: C-1.3.12, C-4.2.1

    At least one of each type shall be accessible for both male and female customers with disabilities.

    a) Entry doors shall comply with Section D-7.1.
    b) Aisles leading to the door shall comply with Section D-8.4.3.
    c) The minimum clear space within a dressing room shall be 60 by 60 inches with no encroachment from a door swing.
    d) Accessible dressing rooms shall have a bench that complies with Sections C-4.2.4 through C-4.2.4(2) and C-6.5.4.
    e) The bottom of mirrors shall be no higher than 20 inches above the floor and comply with Section C-4.2.3.
    f) Clothing hooks shall be no higher than 48 inches above the floor.

D-2.3.2.3 SERVICE FACILITIES

All personal and public service facilities including household, rental, financial, publications, veterinarian, travel, public utility, public protection and detention, courtroom facilities, and other related service facilities shall be accessible to persons with disabilities and specifically in the following areas:
a) Client, customer, and visitor areas; office areas; and related toilet rooms shall be accessible.
b) Employee work areas shall have a 36-inch wide clear access except as modified in Section D-8.4.3.
c) Automated teller machines used for financial transactions shall comply with Section D-8.1.

D-2.3.2.4 PUBLIC USED FACILITIES AND AREAS

a) Office areas, meeting rooms, similar use areas, and their related toilet rooms shall be accessible.
b) Public tour areas in or about a facility shall be accessible in areas where the public is permitted to walk. Operational areas within a facility not being used by persons in wheelchairs are not required to be accessible. An exception to these accessibility provisions shall be granted when the enforcing agency determines compliance would create an undue hardship and when equivalent facilitation is provided.
c) Visitor overlook facilities, orientation areas, related sanitary facilities, and similar public used areas shall be accessible.
d) When provided, public parking spaces shall provide accessible spaces for persons with disabilities and comply with Section D-3.12.

CALIFORNIA ACCESS CODE • TITLE 24
GROUP OCCUPANCIES • Group B

D-2.3.2.5 PUBLIC SERVICE FACILITIES

Law enforcement, fire departments, and courtroom facilities shall be accessible in the following areas:
a) office areas, conference rooms, classrooms, dispatch rooms, and other similar areas as well as related sanitary facilities;
b) detention visitor rooms;
c) at least one detention cell with a supporting sanitary facility; and
d) courtroom areas including the jury box, witness stand, counsel tables, judge's chamber and bench, and public seating areas.

D-2.3.2.6 FACTORIES • WAREHOUSES

Factories and warehouses shall comply with the following requirements except in existing buildings where the enforcing agency determines compliance would create an undue hardship and when equivalent facilitation is provided. The following areas shall be accessible to persons with disabilities:
a) Factories principal floor areas, office areas, and sanitary facilities serving those areas.
b) Warehouse areas on the floor nearest grade; other areas served by an entry level, ramp, or elevator; office areas; and the sanitary facilities serving those areas.

D-2.3.2.7 ASSEMBLY AREAS ^{ADA: C-1.3.10, C-4.1}

Group B occupancies used for assembly purposes that have an occupant load less than 50 shall comply with the requirements for assembly areas of Section D-2.2.

CALIFORNIA ACCESS CODE • TITLE 24
GROUP OCCUPANCIES • Group B

D-2.3.2.8 DINING • BANQUET • BAR ADA: C-7.5

Floors and building levels relating to dining, banquet, and bar facilities in Group B occupancies shall comply with Section D-3.17, if applicable.

D-2.3.2.9 GENERAL ACCESSIBILITY STANDARDS

General accessibility standards include:
a) Circulation aisles and pedestrian walkways shall never have less than a clear 36-inch width.
b) Storage access doorways shall never have less than a 32-inch clear width. Storage facilities shall be accessible in number and dimensions complying with Section D-3.14.

CALIFORNIA ACCESS CODE • TITLE 24
GROUP OCCUPANCIES • Group E

D-2.4 GROUP E OCCUPANCY

EDUCATIONAL FACILITIES

Group E occupancies fall within three divisions.

DIVISION 1: Buildings for educational use through grade 12 that are used by 50 or more persons, more than 12 hours per week, or four hours on any day.

DIVISION 2: Buildings for educational use through grade 12 that are used by less than 50 persons, more than 12 hours per week, or four hours on any day.

DIVISION 3: A nonresidential building or a portion thereof used for day-care by more than six persons.

Residential building used for day-care of more than twelve persons.

Group E occupancies shall be accessible and comply with the requirements in Section D-2.4 with the following exceptions. In existing buildings, an exception shall be granted when the enforcing agency determines that (1) compliance would create an undue hardship and when equivalent facilitation is provided, or (2) due to physical constraints, regulation compliance or equivalent facilitation would create an undue hardship.

CALIFORNIA ACCESS CODE • TITLE 24
GROUP OCCUPANCIES • Group E

D-2.4.1 LIBRARIES [ADA: C-7.1]

Service desks, circulation counters, book stacks, periodicals, reading and reference areas, card files, and other general public use areas shall be made accessible to persons with disabilities.

1. Book Stacks [ADA: C-7.1.2]
Open book stacks may be of normal height, have at least 44-inch wide main aisles, and have no less than 36-inch wide side, range, and end aisles. Exceptions to the accessibility requirement in existing buildings are (1) multi-tiered or closed-book stacks not used by the public, and (2) an inaccessible mezzanine level containing no more than 15 percent of the total library shelving.

2. Book Shelves
Book shelving shall be no higher than 54 inches above the floor unless an assisting attendant is available.

3. Card Catalogs [ADA: C-7.1.4]
The reach range at card catalogs and magazine displays shall comply with Section D-3.4. A maximum height of 48 inches is preferred.

D-2.4.2 CUBICLES • STUDY CARRELS [ADA: C-7.1.3]

Teaching facilities, cubicles, study carrels, and similar provisions shall be at least 5 percent accessible to persons with disabilities, but never less than one facility of each type or group, shall comply with the space allowances and reach ranges of Sections D-3.4 and with the table and counter regulations of Section D-8.4. In addition, the minimum maneuvering space required between a table and wall or object is 48 inches rather than 36 inches as shown in Figure 66(b).

D-2.4.3 LABORATORY ROOMS

At least 5 percent of all work stations in laboratory rooms, but never less than one work station, shall be accessible and usable by persons with disabilities. An exemption to this requirement shall be granted when the enforcing agency determines compliance for special use rooms would create an undue hardship. Those rooms may be used for laboratory preparation, research, supply, and rooms containing specialized equipment not readily usable by persons with particular disabilities. A clear 32-inch wide access aisle shall be maintained into the rooms.

CALIFORNIA ACCESS CODE • TITLE 24
GROUP OCCUPANCIES • Group H

D-2.5 GROUP H OCCUPANCY

HAZARDOUS MATERIAL FACILITIES

Group H occupancy is used primarily for storage of hazardous materials.

DIVISION 1: Quantities of materials that have a high explosive hazard.

DIVISION 2: Quantities of materials that have a moderate explosive hazard or a hazard from accelerated burning.

DIVISION 3: Quantities of materials that present a high fire or physical hazard.

DIVISION 4: Repair garages not classified as Group B, Division 1.

DIVISION 5: Aircraft repair hangars not classified as Group B, Division 3, and heliports.

DIVISION 6: Semiconductor fabrication facilities, research, and development areas where hazardous production materials are used.

DIVISION 7: Quantities of health hazard materials.

DIVISION 8: Scientific experiment and research laboratories or similar areas with limited quantities of hazardous materials not classified as Group B, Division 2, occupancy.

CALIFORNIA ACCESS CODE • TITLE 24
GROUP OCCUPANCIES • Group H

D-2.5.1 APPLICATION

Group H occupancies shall be accessible as required by Section D-2.5. Accessible facilities are those used by the public as customers, clients, visitors, or which are potential places of employment. In existing Group H occupancies, an exception shall be granted if equivalent facilitation and protection are provided when an enforcing agency determines regulation compliance with Section D-2.5 would create an undue hardship. The requirements of Section D-2.5 shall not apply in existing occupancies when legal or physical constraints prevent compliance or equivalent facilitation without creating an undue hardship as determined by an enforcing agency.

D-2.5.2 ROUTE OF TRAVEL [ADA: C-2.1]

Primary entrances, corridors, stairs, ramps, doors, turnstiles, walkways, and hazards shall be made accessible in compliance with Sections D-3 through D-8.

D-2.5.3 FLOORS AND LEVELS [ADA: C-5.4]

Accessible floors and levels shall comply with the requirements specified in Section D-3.17.

D-2.5.4 EMPLOYEE WORK AREAS [ADA: C-1.1.6]

Employee areas shall have at least a clear 36-inch wide aisle and 32-inch wide door opening as specified in Section D-3.6.

D-2.5.5 SANITATION [ADA: C-4.8]

Accessible sanitation facilities in Group H occupancies shall be provided as specified in Section D-3.15 and the OSA/ACS requirements of the integrated Uniform Plumbing Code.

CALIFORNIA ACCESS CODE • TITLE 24
GROUP OCCUPANCIES • Group I

D-2.6 GROUP I OCCUPANCY

ADA: C-7.3

INSTITUTIONAL • FULL-TIME CARE FACILITIES

Group I occupancies are provided in three main divisions.

DIVISION 1.1: Accommodating more than five persons. Nurseries of children under six years of age. Hospitals, sanitariums, nursing homes, and aged homes with nonambulatory patients; protective social-care facilities or homes with nonambulatory guests; and similar buildings.

DIVISION 1.1A: Accommodating six or less persons. Hospitals, sanitariums, nurseries for full-time care of children under six years of age excluding infants, nursing homes, and aged homes that have nonambulatory patients; protective social-care facilities or homes with nonambulatory guests; and similar buildings.

DIVISION 1.2: Accommodating more than five persons. Health-care centers which provide outpatient medical care for ambulatory patients that may be incapable of unassisted self-preservation.

DIVISION 2.1: Accommodating less than five persons. Facilities for ambulatory patients and guests including nursing and aged homes, homes for children six years and older, protective social-care facilities or homes, and similar buildings as well as honor farms and conservation camps housing unrestrained inmates.

CALIFORNIA ACCESS CODE • TITLE 24
GROUP OCCUPANCIES • Group I

DIVISION 2.2A: Accommodating six or less persons. Facilities for ambulatory patients and guests including nursing homes and aged homes, homes for children six years of age or over, protective social-care facilities or homes, and similar buildings.

DIVISION 3: Mental hospitals or sanitariums, jails, prisons, reformatories, and buildings where inmate personal liberties are restrained. Exceptions are (1) where homes, institutions, or day-care facilities provide nonmedical board, room, and care for six or less ambulatory persons; (2) does not include buildings used as a private residence for a family group; and (3) the more restrictive requirements apply to facilities that house both ambulatory and nonambulatory persons.

D-2.6.1 APPLICATION   ADA: C-7.3

All Group I occupancies shall be accessible as required by Section D-2.6 and the applicable design and construction requirements of Sections D-3 through D-8. An exception shall be granted when equivalent facilitation is provided and when regulation compliance with Section D-2.6 would create an undue hardship in existing buildings as determined by the enforcing agency.

D-2.6.2 ENTRANCES   ADA: C-7.3.4

A minimum of one accessible entrance shall have a roof overhang or canopy for protection from the weather. Such entrances shall provide a passenger loading zone that complies with the requirements of Section C-4.4.2(1-3) and Section D-4.4. Exempt buildings are those clinics and other medical facilities not intended for patient stays exceeding 24 hours, located above the first story of a building, and do not have a dedicated first story exterior entrance.

D-2.6.3 OFFICE • SUITES

Buildings that house offices and suites of physicians, dentists, and other health care services shall be accessible and comply with the applicable requirements of Sections D-3 through D-8.

D-2.6.4 OFFICES • WAITING AREAS

Offices, waiting areas, and related sanitary facilities shall be accessible and comply with the applicable requirements of Section D-3 through D-8.

D-2.6.5 DIAGNOSTIC • TREATMENT AREAS

Diagnostic and treatment areas and at least one dressing room and sanitary facility in each unit or suite shall be made accessible, where applicable.

D-2.6.6 PATIENT ROOMS ADA: C-7.3.1

D-2.6.6.1 APPLICATION

Patient bedrooms and associated toilet facilities shall be accessible and meet the following requirements.

1. **Long Term Care Facilities** ADA: C-7.3.2
   Shall comply with Section C-7.3.1(2.3) in such facilities as skilled nursing facilities, intermediate facilities, bed and care, and nursing home facilities.

GROUP OCCUPANCIES • Group I

2. Hospitals
Shall comply with Section C-7.3.1(2.1).

3. Mobility Rehabilitation Facilities
Shall comply with Section C-7.3.1(2.2)

D-2.6.6.2 ACCESSIBLE PATIENT ROOMS

Accessible patient rooms shall meet the requirements of Sections C-7.3.2(1,2) and have an accessible door complying with Section D-7.1.

D-2.6.6.3 PATIENT TOILET ROOMS   ADA: C-7.3.3

Patient toilet rooms required to be accessible shall comply with Section D-6.3.

CALIFORNIA ACCESS CODE • TITLE 24
GROUP OCCUPANCIES • Group M

D-2.7 GROUP M OCCUPANCY

MAINTENANCE FACILITIES

Group M occupancies are classified in two divisions.

DIVISION 1: Private garages, carports, sheds, and agricultural buildings.

DIVISION 2: Fences over 6 feet high, tanks, and towers.

Group M, Division 1, occupancies required to be accessible by Section D-2.7 shall comply with the applicable requirements of Section D-3 through D-8.

D-2.7.1 PARKS • RECREATION AREAS

The following parks and recreational areas shall comply with Section D-2.7.

Exceptions
1. A variance shall be granted for existing buildings when equivalent facilitation is provided and when the regulation compliance would create an undue hardship as determined by the enforcing agency.
2. When the natural environment would be materially damaged in specific areas by accessibility compliance as determined by the enforcing agency. This exception is only to the extent that material damage would occur.
3. Automobile access shall not be provided nor paths of travel made accessible when compliance with these regulations create an undue hardship as determined

CALIFORNIA ACCESS CODE • TITLE 24
GROUP OCCUPANCIES • Group M

by the enforcing agency.

1. **Highway Rest Areas**
   Highway rest areas and similar facilities shall comply with the following specific requirements and other applicable requirements of Section D-3 through D-8.
   Permanent Facilities
   When provided, at least one of each kind of permanent functional areas or facilities shall be accessible to persons with disabilities. Those facilities include:
   - at least one parking space
   - information and display areas
   - a sanitary facility for each sex
   - at least one picnic table plus one table for each additional 20 tables, or portion thereof
   - drinking fountains

   Curb Ramps
   Curb ramps shall be provided at pedestrian ways where appropriate and shall comply with Section D-4.4.

2. **Parking Lots**
   Parking lots shall be provided with accessible parking spaces and with curb cuts leading to all adjacent walks, paths, or trails.

3. **Campsites**
   At least three campsites for each one hundred provided, and never less than two, shall be accessible by providing a level path or a ramp. Routes of travel shall have no more than a 1:12 slope to sanitary facilities. Permanent sanitary facilities serving campgrounds shall be accessible to wheelchair users.

4. **Beaches • Picnic Areas**
   Beaches, picnic areas, day-use areas, vista points, and other similar areas shall be accessible.

5. **Boat Docks**
   Boat docks, fishing piers, and similar facilities shall be

CALIFORNIA ACCESS CODE • TITLE 24
GROUP OCCUPANCIES • Group M

accessible.

6. **Sanitary Facilities**
   When provided, sanitary facilities shall be accessible at each public use area which is accessible to wheelchair occupants and accessed by automobile, walks, or other paths of travel.

7. **Trails**
   Trails, nature walk areas, or portions thereof shall have the proper gradients which permit their use by wheelchair occupants. Buildings and other functional areas shall be provided with hard surface paths or walks that serve them.

8. **Nature Trails**
   Educational and informational areas, nature trails, and other similar areas shall be accessible to the blind with the provision of rope guidelines, identification symbols, raised Arabic numerals, information signs, and other related guide and assistance provisions.

9. **Buildings**
   Support buildings and facilities such as visitor centers, museums, retail shops, restaurants, sanitary facilities, and other similar provisions shall comply with the applicable group occupancy use requirements of Section D.

CALIFORNIA ACCESS CODE • TITLE 24
GROUP OCCUPANCIES • Group R

D-2.8 GROUP R OCCUPANCY

RESIDENTIAL • LODGING FACILITIES

Lodging facilities, Group R occupancies, are categorized under two sections.

DIVISION 1: Hotel and apartment houses.
Congregate housing of more than ten persons.

DIVISION 2.1: Residential care for more than six nonambulatory elderly persons.

DIVISION 2.1A: Residential care for six or less nonambulatory elderly persons.

DIVISION 2.2: Residential care for more than six ambulatory elderly persons.

DIVISION 2.2A: Residential care for six or less ambulatory elderly persons.

SECTION 3: Dwellings and lodging houses.
Congregate residences of 10 persons or less.

Group R occupancies shall be made accessible or adaptable. Public use and common use areas serving adaptable guest or dwelling units shall be accessible and comply with the applicable design and construction requirements of Section D.

CALIFORNIA ACCESS CODE • TITLE 24
GROUP OCCUPANCIES • Group R

D-2.8.1 TRANSIENT LODGING [ADA: C-7.2]

Hotels, motels, inns, dormitories, resorts, homeless shelters, halfway houses, transient group homes, and other similar places of transient lodging shall be accessible to persons with disabilities in accordance with the provisions of the accessibility requirements of the California Building Code, except as herein provided.

D-2.8.1.1 GUEST ROOMS • SUITES

1. **General** [ADA: C-7.2.1(2), C-7.2.2, C-7.2.4, C-7.2.5(2.2)]

    Places of transient lodging shall incorporate the accessibility requirements of this code as modified by Section D-2.8 in at least one guest room or dormitory room together with their sanitary facilities and shall be in compliance with Table C-7A. All accessible sleeping rooms and suites required by Table C-7A shall comply with Section D-2.8.1.5 for hearing impaired guests.

2. **Choice of Accommodations** [ADA: C-7.2.4(2)]

    Accessible guest rooms and suites shall be dispersed among the various classes of sleeping accommodations to provide a range of options to persons with disabilities. Accommodation classifications may be based on room size, cost, number of beds, and amenities provided.

3. **Accessibility** [ADA: C-7.2.1(3), C-7.2.2(1,4), C-7.2.2(3)]

    Accessible sleeping rooms shall have a clear 36-inch wide maneuvering aisle on both sides of a bed. Where two beds are provided, only one 36-inch wide aisle is required between the beds.

CALIFORNIA ACCESS CODE • TITLE 24
GROUP OCCUPANCIES • Group R

D-2.8.1.2 DORMITORY ROOMS   ADA: C-7.2.4

Other dormitory rooms not specified herein shall comply with the adaptability requirements of Section D-2.8.3.4.

D-2.8.1.3 TOILET FACILITIES

Toilet facilities modified for hotel, motel, and dormitory accommodation shall comply with Section D-2.8.2.

D-2.8.1.4 KITCHENS   ADA: C-7.2.2(8)

When provided, accessible units shall provide accessible kitchens equal in number to those in Table C-7A and comply with the requirements of Sections D-2.8.3.4(3,4,5).

D-2.8.1.5 NOTIFICATION DEVICES
ADA: B-3.2.2, C-1.3.21, C-7.2.1(4), C-7.2.2.7, C-7.2.3(2)

In addition to those accessible units required by Section D-2.8.1.1(1), additional accessible sleeping accommodations shall be provided equal in number to those in Table C-7A and shall comply with Section D-5.1. Visual alarms shall comply with Section D-5.1.1. Permanent telephones shall have volume controls that comply with Section D-5.4. An accessible electric outlet shall be provided within 48 inches of the telephone to facilitate the use of a text telephone.

D-2.8.1.6 PUBLIC • COMMON AREAS   ADA: C-7.2.1(6)

Public and common use rooms and similar areas shall be made accessible to persons with disabilities subject to specific requirements contained in Section D including applicable design and construction requirements of Sections D-3 through D-8.

GROUP OCCUPANCIES • Group R

D-2.8.1.7 RECREATIONAL FACILITIES

When provided, recreational facilities shall comply with Sections D-2.2.2.3 and D-2.7.1.

D-2.8.2 TRANSIENT LODGING BATHROOMS
ADA: C-4.5, C-7.2.2(2e,2f)

Required accessible bathrooms in places of transient lodging shall comply with the following requirements.

D-2.8.2.1 ENTRANCE ADA: C-7.2.1(3)

Doors to accessible bathrooms shall not swing into any clear floor space of bathroom fixtures and shall comply with Section D-7.1.

D-2.8.2.2 BATHTUBS • SHOWERS ADA: C-4.5.4

When provided, at least one accessible bathtub shall comply with Section D-6.2.2(4) and Section 1506 of the California Plumbing Code (CPC); or, at least one accessible shower shall comply with Sections D-6.2.3 and D-6.2.4 and Section 1505 of the CPC. Hotel and motel bathrooms beyond those specified in Section D-2.8.1 need not comply with the accessibility requirements of the California Building, Electrical, and Plumbing Codes if the following is provided:
  a) Bathroom fixtures are located to allow a person occupying a 30 by 48-inch wheelchair space to use each fixture and the accommodations provided.
  b) All bathroom entrance doors shall have a clear 32-inch wide opening. The door shall be either a sliding door or hinged to swing in the direction of egress from the bathroom.

CALIFORNIA ACCESS CODE • TITLE 24
GROUP OCCUPANCIES • Group R

D-2.8.2.3 WATER CLOSETS [ADA: C-6.10]

When provided, toilet stalls shall comply with Section D-6.3.4 or D-6.3.5. The water closet shall comply with Section D-6.3 herein and Section 1502 of the CPC.

D-2.8.2.4 CLEAR FLOOR SPACE [ADA: C-2.3, C-4.5.2]

The bathroom must have a clear floor space measuring 30 by 60 inches with all fixtures and controls on an accessible route. The clear floor space at fixtures and controls, the turning space, and the accessible route of travel may overlap.

D-2.8.2.5 LAVATORY • MIRRORS [ADA: C-4.5.8]

When provided, lavatory and mirrors shall comply with Sections C-6.6.5 and C-6.6.6 herein and Section 1504 of the CPC.

D-2.8.2.6 CONTROLS • DISPENSERS [ADA: C-4.5.10]

When provided, at least one of each control, dispenser, receptacle, or other types of equipment provided shall be on an accessible route of travel and comply with Section D-6.3.7(5,6).

D-2.8.3 BUILDINGS • MULTI-UNIT COMPLEXES

D-2.8.3.1 PUBLICLY • PRIVATELY FUNDED

Buildings and complexes containing publicly and privately funded covered multi-family dwelling units shall be accessible as modified by this section. Individual dwelling units shall be adaptable as required by Section D-2.8.4. All units must be served by an accessible route of travel when the first floor containing dwelling units is a floor above grade. For sites with steep slopes or unusual characteristics refer to Table D-2A.

D-2.8.3.2 MULTI-STORY BUILDINGS

In multi-story buildings, living accommodations on the primary entrance floors and the floors above or below that are served by a ramp, elevator, or special lift shall comply with adaptable dwelling units in Section D-2.8.3.4 subject to the provisions of Table D-2A.

D-2.8.3.3 PUBLIC • COMMON USE AREAS

Public and common use rooms and similar areas shall be accessible to persons with disabilities as required in other portions of the accessibility code. Common use laundry rooms shall comply with Section D-2.8.3.4(8).

D-2.8.3.4 ADAPTABLE DWELLING UNITS

Each adaptable unit shall have the following features:
1. **Entrance** ADA: C-7.2.1(3)
   Every primary entrance and individual living accommodation shall have a door buzzer, bell, chime or equivalent fixture connected to permanent wiring and be located no higher than 48 inches above the floor.
2. **Doorways** ADA: C-5.2
   Doors and their openings shall comply with the requirements of Sections D-3.16, D-7.1, as modified by Section D-2.8.4(1), or in privately funded covered multi-family construction as permitted by Section D-2.8.4(1).
3. **Kitchens** ADA: C-7.2.2(8)
   Kitchens shall have a minimum 60-inch clear widthR

CALIFORNIA ACCESS CODE • TITLE 24
GROUP OCCUPANCIES • Group R

TABLE D-2A

ACCESSIBLE ENTRANCE REQUIREMENTS
Residential Non-Elevator Buildings

Exempt: Privately funded multi-story dwelling units, hotel, or motel

Adaptable Units Accessibility Requirement

All ground floor units must be adaptable, on an accessible route, and have an accessible entrance.

Exempt:

Single Building with a Common Lobby Entrance
1. Meets the "individual building" conditions of Test No. 1, or
2. Meets the "unusual characteristics" conditions of Test No. 3

All Other Sites
1. Meets the "individual building" conditions of Test No. 1, or
2. Meets the "site analysis" conditions of Test No. 2, or
3. Meets the "unusual characteristics" conditions of Test No. 3

Requirements for Test 1 and Test 2
1. An elevator used as an accessible route only to the ground level of a building is not considered an elevator building. The ground level units do apply to the California Access Code.
2. At least 20% of the total ground level units shall be adaptable unless the building is a single building with a common lobby entrance regardless of whether Test 1 or Test 2 applies.

TEST 1 - INDIVIDUAL BUILDING

An accessible entrance on an accessible route is not required when the finish grade of an undisturbed site exceeds 10% between the planned entrance and all vehicular and pedestrian arrival points are within 50 feet of the entrance. Distances are determined by:
- Measure a straight line from the planned entrance to each arrival point that is within 50 feet.
- Measure the closet arrival point when farther than 50 feet.
- Closest sidewalk approach is measured from the intersection of the entrance sidewalk and the public sidewalk.
- Measuring from the closest parking entry point to the entrance.

CALIFORNIA ACCESS CODE • TITLE 24
GROUP OCCUPANCIES • Group R

TEST 2 - SITE ANALYSIS

The requirement for an accessible entrance on an accessible route is determined for a site with multiple buildings or a single building with multiple entrances when the following conditions are met.
1. Calculate the percentage of buildable area on the undisturbed site having less than a 10% natural grade slope. The certified analysis shall be done by a topographic survey with two foot contour intervals.
2. The minimum percentage of accessible ground floor units shall equal the calculated percentage of the buildable site area to the total area of undisturbed terrain having a 10% slope or less.
3. In addition to the calculated percentage in number 2, all ground floor units or those served by a single entrance shall be made accessible if that entrance or the units are on an accessible route with a slope not exceeding 8.33% between the entrance(s) and the arrival point.

TEST 3 - UNUSUAL CHARACTERISTICS

A site located in a coastal high hazard area, federally designated floodplain, or other similar restricted area where the lowest level, or the lowest structural member of the lowest level, must be raised to a specified level above the base flood elevation and is categorized as having an unusual characteristic. Unusual characteristics of a site may cause a building entrance to be impractical when:
1. A difference in finished grade elevation exceeding 30 inches and 10% grade between the planned entrance and all vehicular or pedestrian arrival points are within 50 feet of the entrance.
2. A difference in finished grade elevation exceeding 30 inches and 10% grade between the planned entrance and the closest vehicular or pedestrian arrival point.

D

2.8

between cabinet fronts, counters, or walls in U-shaped kitchen areas. Other designs shall be at least 48 inches between surfaces. The base cabinet directly under the sink counter, toeboard, and shelving shall be removable without the use of special tools or knowledge in kitchens with less than a 60-inch clear width and where the sink or cook range is at the base of the "U". Finished flooring shall be installed on the floor beneath the removable cabinet. Kitchen sink faucet controls shall comply with the requirements of Section 1508, CPC, and Title 24, CCR.

4. Counters [ADA: C-7.2.2(8)]

A kitchen sink counter shall be provided in at least a 30-inch linear length with an additional 30-inch of linear work surface counter. Both counters shall be designed for repositioning to a minimum height of 28 inches. The sink and work surface may be a single integral unit or separate components. The base cabinets directly under the sink and counter work surface shall be removable allowing accessibility by a wheelchair occupant. When the counter is lowered, the exposed sides and back of the adjacent cabinets shall be constructed of a durable, non-absorbent material finish. Finished flooring shall be installed on the floor beneath the removable cabinets. Stone, cultured stone, and tile counter tops may be used without meeting the repositioning requirements.

5. Shelves

Lower shelves or drawer space shall be provided in the kitchen at a height of no more than 48 inches.

6. Bathrooms

Bathrooms shall be provided in compliance with the requirements of Section D-2.8.4.

CALIFORNIA ACCESS CODE • TITLE 24
GROUP OCCUPANCIES • Group R

7. Toilet Facilities
Toilet facilities shall comply with Section D-2.8.4 as modified for living accommodations.

8. Laundry Rooms
At least one of each type of appliance shall be provided in each laundry area of covered multi-family buildings or dwelling units when such appliances are provided. The laundry rooms are not required to have front-loading washers, but management shall provide assistive devices upon request to allow a resident to use a top loading washer when front loading washers are not provided.

D-2.8.4 DWELLING BATHROOMS ADA: C-4.8

Bathrooms in required adaptable publicly funded dwelling units and privately funded covered multi-family dwelling units shall comply with the requirements of the code as modified by the following additional provisions for adaptable use.

D-2.8.4.1 ROOM

All bathrooms for adaptable dwellings must provide the following minimum requirements.

1. Entrance ADA: C-7.2.2(4)
Bathroom entrance doorways shall have a clear 18-inch space to the side of the strike edge on the swing side of the door and meet other requirements of Section D-7.1 except as modified in paragraph 2 and 3 below.

2. Door Swing
The bathroom shall have an approximate 30 by 48-inch clear floor space, free of any door swing, that allows the use of the fixtures by a person in a wheelchair or person using mobility aids.

CALIFORNIA ACCESS CODE • TITLE 24
GROUP OCCUPANCIES • Group R

3. **Maneuvering Space** ADA: C-2.3.2, C-7.2.2(3)
   The room shall provide sufficient maneuvering space for a person in a wheelchair or other mobility aid to enter, close the door, use the fixtures, reopen the door, and exit. Doors may swing into the clear space provided at any fixture if adequate maneuvering space is provided. Maneuvering spaces may include a kneespace or toespace available below bathroom fixtures.
4. **Reinforced Walls**
   Reinforced walls for grab bars shall be provided in compliance with Section D-2.8.4.5(2).

D-2.8.4.2 SHOWER STALLS ADA: C-4.6

When provided, shower stalls shall comply with the requirements of Section D-6.2.3 except that folding seats are not required.

D-2.8.4.3 BATHTUBS ADA: C-6.2

The side of a bathtub or bathtub-shower combination shall have a minimum 30 by 48-inch space parallel in length for the maneuvering and transfer between the bathing facilities and a wheelchair. The required space may include the maneuverable area under a lavatory.

D-2.8.4.4 WATER CLOSETS ADA: C-6.10

The water closet shall comply with the requirements of Section 1502, CPC, and Title 24, CCR. Water closet seats shall be no less than 15 inches above the floor. The water closet may be located in a clear 36-inch wide space with a clear 48-inch space in front of the water closet. This space may include the maneuvering space under a lavatory but

CALIFORNIA ACCESS CODE • TITLE 24
GROUP OCCUPANCIES • Group R

must be arranged to prevent obstruction from a door swing and not impede access.

D-2.8.4.5 LAVATORIES • GRAB BARS [ADA: C-6.5, C-6.6]

Grab bars shall comply with Section C-6.5. Wall reinforcement for lavatories, accessories, and future grab bars shall conform to the following requirements:

1. **Installation**
   Lavatories and accessories shall be mounted or installed in compliance with Section D-2.8.4.5(2).
2. **Wall Reinforcement** [ADA: C-6.5.4]
   Reinforcement for the future installation of grab bars shall be installed around toilets, bathtubs, shower stalls, and shower seats when grab bars are provided. The reinforcement shall be of sufficient length to meet the requirements of the grab bar installation specified herein. The reinforced wall shall be capable of supporting at least a 250-pound point load in compliance with Section C-6.5.4.
3. **Toilet Area** [ADA: C-6.10.5]
   Grab bar reinforcement shall be installed on both side walls or one side wall and the back wall when a toilet is placed adjacent to a side wall. Floor mounted, foldaway, or similar grab bars shall be provided in lieu of wall grab bars when the toilet is not placed adjacent to a side wall. A room with just a sink and toilet shall comply with the requirement for reinforced walls for grab bars when it is the only toilet facility located on an accessible level of a multi-story dwelling unit. Grab bar reinforcement shall be at least 6 inches in height and 40 inches in length and shall be located between 32 and 38 inches above the finished floor. The side wall reinforcement shall be

aligned with the front of the tank and shall extend at least 26 inches in front of the water closet stool. (Fig. 94)

4. Bathtub Area ^{ADA: C-6.2.6}

Grab bar reinforcement shall be installed on each end wall of a bathtub between 32 and 38 inches above the finished floor, aligned with the front edge of the bathtub, and extended at least 24 inches towards the back wall of the bathtub. Bathtubs may be installed without adjacent walls when reinforcement areas are provided for the installation of floor-mounted grab bars. Grab bar reinforcement shall be installed on the back wall of the bathtub extending from a maximum of 6 inches above the bathtub rim to a minimum height of 38 inches above the floor. The grab bar reinforcement shall be a minimum of 6 inches in height, installed horizontally with each end a maximum of 6 inches from the end walls permitting the installation of a 48-inch grab bar. (Fig. 86)

5. Shower Stall Area ^{ADA: C-4.6.8}

Grab bar reinforcement shall be a nominal 6 inches in height and run continuous in the walls at 32 to 38 inches above the floor in adaptable showers. (Fig. 88) Glass-walled shower stalls may comply when floor-mounted grab bar reinforcement is installed that meets the load requirements of Section D-2.8.4.5(2).

CALIFORNIA ACCESS CODE • TITLE 24
MINIMUM REQUIREMENTS • Application • Alterations

D-3 MINIMUM REQUIREMENTS

D-3.1 APPLICATION ADA: B-4, C-1

When accessibility to persons with disabilities is required by Section D in buildings and facilities located in California, accessibility design and construction standards shall comply with the California Access Code, Title 24, CCR along with the California Amendments.

D-3.2 ALTERATIONS

D-3.2.1 APPLICATION ADA: B-3.7.3, B-4.4, C-1.2.1

An alteration, structural repair, or addition to an existing building or facility shall comply with the new construction requirements of Section D except as modified by Section D-3.2. These requirements apply only to the specific alteration project and shall comply with the requirements of Sections B-4.4.2(2-4) and includes providing accessibility to all of the following.
1. Primary entrance
2. Primary path of travel to the altered area
3. Sanitary facilities
4. Drinking fountains
5. Public telephones serving the altered area

D-3.2.2 LIMITATIONS ADA: C-1.2.1

Compliance shall be limited to the actual work of the

CALIFORNIA ACCESS CODE • TITLE 24
MINIMUM REQUIREMENTS • Alterations

alteration when:
1. Alterations meeting the accessibility requirements by removing barriers and altering one or more of
   a) one building entrance,
   b) one existing toilet facility,
   c) existing elevators,
   d) existing steps,
   e) existing handrails, and
   f) barrier removal alterations listed in Section B-3.7.8
2. a) The total alteration cost does not exceed a valuation threshold of $50,000 based on the January 1981 "ENR US 20 Cities" average construction cost index of 3372.02 <u>Engineering News Record</u> published by McGraw Hill Publishing Company, and
   b) the "valuation threshold" shall be updated annually to a current amount based on the index increase from the last figure used. For example, the 1991 valuation threshold is $70,729.56.

D-3.2.3 UNDUE HARDSHIP ADA: B-4.4.2(2)

An undue hardship exists when the cost of providing an accessible entrance, path-of-travel, sanitary facility, drinking fountain, and a public telephone serving the altered area is disproportionate by exceeding 20 percent of the altered area cost.

D-3.2.4 BUILDINGS WITHOUT ELEVATORS

Alteration projects in certain types of privately-funded multi-story buildings and facilities that do not have an elevator must provide accessibility to persons with disabilities subject to the twenty percent disproportionality provision when the alteration value exceeds the valuation threshold described in

Section D-3.2.2(2) in the following buildings and facilities.
  a) Offices of physicians and surgeons
  b) Shopping centers
  c) Office buildings and passenger vehicle service stations which are three or more stories and 3000 square feet or more per floor.
  d) Other types of buildings three or more stories, having more than 3000 square feet per floor, and when a reasonable portion of the services sought and used by the public is available on the accessible level (Also see general exception in Section D-2.1.2)

D-3.2.5 EXCEPTIONS

1. Cosmetic changes, heating, ventilation, air conditioning, re-roofing, and electrical work not affecting the items regulated for accessibility in Section D.
2. The enforcing agency determines that compliance with these regulations would create an undue hardship.

D-3.3 ROUTE OF TRAVEL
ADA: C-1.3.1, C-1.2.1(4), C-2.1

A building or portion of a building required to be accessible or adaptable for persons with disabilities shall provide an accessible route of travel to the maximum extent possible as required by Sections C-1.3.1.(1,2) and C-2.1.5. An accessible route of travel shall not pass through kitchens, restrooms, storage rooms or closets, or other spaces similarly used except within an individual dwelling unit.

D-3.3.1 APPLICABLE AREAS • ELEMENTS

The following areas and elements are applicable to a route of

CALIFORNIA ACCESS CODE • TITLE 24
MINIMUM REQUIREMENTS • Route of Travel

travel:
   a) Aisles
   b) Corridors
   c) Doorways
   d) Elevators and lifts
   e) Entrances
   f) Ramps
   g) Stairways
   h) Walkways

D-3.3.2 CORRIDORS   ^{ADA: C-1.2.1.4, C-1.3.1, C-2.1}

Corridors within an accessible route of travel shall comply with Section D-4.1. Every corridor serving as a required exit for an occupant load of 10 or more persons shall not be interrupted by intervening rooms except reception rooms, lobbies, and foyers that were constructed as required for corridors. Exit corridors include exterior exit balconies and covered or enclosed exit pedestrian passageways. A space that is divided by partitions, counters, rails, or similar space dividers not exceeding 5 feet 9 inches above the finished floor is not considered a corridor.

D-3.3.3 ELEVATORS   ^{ADA: C-1.1.5, C-1.2.9, C-1.3.7, C-5.3}

The design, installation, construction, operation, alteration, and repair of elevators, dumbwaiters, escalators, moving walks, and their hoistways shall comply with Section D-4.2.

D-3.3.4 ENTRANCES • EXITS   ^{ADA: C-1.3.4, C-1.3.8, C-4.3}

All primary entrances and exterior ground floor exit doors shall be accessible. In buildings or portions of buildings required to be accessible, an accessible means of egress shall be provided in number as required for exits in Sections D-3.16

CALIFORNIA ACCESS CODE • TITLE 24
MINIMUM REQUIREMENTS • Route of Travel

and D-7.1. The primary entrance and all other entrances within 6 inches of grade shall be accessible to persons with disabilities and comply with the accessibility design standards of Sections D-3 through D-8. The International Symbol of Accessibility shall be posted at accessible entrances and comply with Sections D-3.10 and D-5.3 All gates shall meet the accessibility requirement for doors in Sections D-3.16 and D-7.1. Elevators or escalators shall not be used as a required exit.

Exceptions:
1. **Exits**
   a) Exterior ground floor exits serving smokeproof enclosures, stairwells, or stairs only.
   b) Not-required emergency exits that are more than 24 inches above grade unless required by Section D-3.5. The door shall have a warning sign of inaccessibility that complies with Section D-5.3.
2. **Undue Hardship**
   a) An exception shall be granted when the enforcing agency determines that compliance would create an undue hardship and when equivalent facilitation is provided with at least one accessible entrance.
   b) Existing buildings where legal or physical constraints do not allow compliance with the accessibility building standards or equivalent facilitation without creating an undue hardship.

D-3.3.5 RAMPS   ADA: C-1.2.11, C-5.6

Ramps within an accessible route of travel or used as exits shall comply with Section D-4.3. Ramped aisles in assembly rooms must comply with the aisle requirements of the California Building Code, Section 3315.

CALIFORNIA ACCESS CODE • TITLE 24
MINIMUM REQUIREMENTS • Route of Travel

D-3.3.6 EXTERIOR ROUTES ADA: C-1.2.1(4), C-1.3.1

Site development and grading shall allow accessibility to persons with disabilities to all ground floor exterior entrances and exits, shall connect to normal paths of travel, and shall incorporate pedestrian ramps, curb ramps, or other similar accessibility elements. Multiple buildings and facilities within a site shall be connected by the most accessible direct route between the accessible site entrances, the accessible building entrances, and the accessible site facilities. Exterior stairs shall comply with Section D-7.2.

D-3.3.7 MULTIPLE ROUTES ADA: C-2.1

All routes of travel shall be accessible to persons with disabilities when more than one route is provided. Only one accessible elevator is required to provide accessible vertical travel. When more than one elevator is provided, they shall all be accessible.

D-3.3.8 SIGNS ADA: C-1.2.3, C-1.3.2, C-3.3

The International Symbol of Accessibility sign shall be displayed at every primary public entrance and every major junction along or leading to an accessible route of travel. The signs shall direct persons to accessible entrances and facilities and comply with Section D-5.3.1.

D-3.3.9 PROTRUDING OBJECTS ADA: C-1.3.1(3), C-2.2

Objects projecting from walls into walkways, halls, corridors, passageways, or aisles shall comply with Section C-2.2.

CALIFORNIA ACCESS CODE • TITLE 24
MINIMUM REQUIREMENTS • Wheelchair Space

D-3.3.10 EXCEPTIONS

An exception shall be granted when the enforcing agency determines that compliance would create an undue hardship because of topography, natural barriers, and other similar barriers and when equivalent facilitation is provided by other means. An exception shall be granted in existing buildings where legal or physical constraints do not allow compliance with the accessibility building standards or equivalent facilitation without creating an undue hardship.

D-3.4 WHEELCHAIR SPACE

ADA: C-1.3.10.1, C-2.1.3, C-2.3, C-4.1.2, C-4.1.3, C-4.1.5, C-4.2.5

All accessible buildings and facilities shall provide accessible wheelchair spaces, minimum passing allowances, and minimum reach ranges for persons with disabilities complying with Section C-2.3. In addition, the California Access Code requires a minimum 60 inches in length and 60 inches in width for two passing wheelchairs. (Fig. 9)

D-3.5 RESCUE ASSISTANCE AREAS

ADA: C-1.3.9, C-2.1.6

Areas of Rescue Assistance required by Sections C-1.3.8 and C-1.3.9 shall comply with Section C-2.1.6 except as allowed by Section C-1.2.1(8). An area of rescue assistance may be located in the elevator lobby within a building of any height or occupancy when such building is constructed in compliance with the California Building Code Sections 1807 or 1907 and Section C-2.1.6 herein.

D-3.6 EMPLOYEE AREAS

ADA: C-1.1.6

General employee areas shall conform to all the requirements of the OSA/AC in the California Building, Plumbing, and Electrical Codes. Specific work stations only need to comply with the requirements of Section D-3.16 and have a clear 32-inch wide entryway. A non-occupied employee service area described in Section C-1.1.7 is exempt from providing accessibility to persons with disabilities.

D-3.7 HISTORIC PRESERVATION

ADA: C-1.4

Qualified historical buildings shall comply with the California State Historical Building Code, Part 8, Title 24, CCR.

D-3.8 ALARMS

ADA: C-1.3.21, C-3.1, C-7.2.1(4), C-7.2.2(7), C-7.2.3(2)

When required, emergency warning systems shall activate a means to warn the hearing impaired, be part of the fire-protective signaling system, and comply with Section D-5.1. When emergency warning systems are provided, areas of the public accommodation types and similar uses of those listed in Table A-A shall include both audible and visual alarms. Sleeping units for persons with hearing impairments shall have a visual alarm connected to the building emergency alarm system equal in number to that required in Table C-7A.

CALIFORNIA ACCESS CODE • TITLE 24
MINIMUM REQUIREMENTS • Detectable Warnings • Signs

D-3.9 DETECTABLE WARNINGS

ADA: C-1.3.22, C-3.2, C-5.1.7

The pedestrian access at transit boarding platforms, curb ramps, and hazardous vehicular areas shall be identified with a detectable warning strip and comply with the requirements of Section D-5.2.

D-3.10 SIGNS

ADA: C-1.2.3, C-1.3.2, C-3.3, C-4.4.5

The International Symbol of Accessibility shall be the standard used to identify facilities that are accessible and usable by persons with disabilities. Signs shall comply with the requirements of Section D-5.3. Signs are not required within an adaptable dwelling unit, an accessible patient room, or an accessible guest room.

D-3.10.1 ENTRANCES

All accessible entrances shall be identified by at least one standard sign. When required, additional directional signs visible to persons along approaching pedestrian walkways shall be provided.

D-3.10.2 INFORMATION

Buildings altered to provide accessible sanitary facilities or a public elevator shall post this accessibility information in the building lobby or preferably the building directory.

D-3.10.3 TRAFFIC CONTROL DEVICES

Pedestrian traffic control buttons shall be identified with a

CALIFORNIA ACCESS CODE • TITLE 24
MINIMUM REQUIREMENTS • Telephones • Parking

colored textured horizontal band encircling the pole and shall comply with Section D-5.3.7.

D-3.11 TELEPHONES ADA: C-1.3.18, C-3.4

When provided, public telephones accessible to persons with disabilities shall comply with Section D-5.4.

D-3.12 PARKING

D-3.12.1 APPLICATION ADA: C-1.3.3, C-4.4

Accessible parking facilities shall be provided for guests, clients, or employees with disabilities and comply with Sections D-6.1, C-4.4.3, and in number to Table C-1A. The parking spaces shall be located on the shortest accessible route-of-travel to an accessible entrance.

Exception
The parking requirements herein do not apply to existing facilities where local ordinance compliance precludes complying with the requirements herein or providing equivalent facilitation unless a change of occupancy occurs.

D-3.12.2 HEALTH CARE FACILITIES ADA: C-1.3.3(6)

Medical care facilities and other services provided for persons with mobility impairments shall comply with the parking requirements of Section D-6.1 in accordance with Table C-1A except as follows:

CALIFORNIA ACCESS CODE • TITLE 24
MINIMUM REQUIREMENTS • Shower • Storage

1. **Outpatient facility**
   Ten percent of the total patient parking spaces in outpatient facilities shall meet the requirements of Section D-6.1.
2. **Facilities treating mobility impairments**
   Twenty percent of the patient parking spaces of facilities that specialize in the treatment or provide services to those with mobility impairments shall meet the requirements of Section D-6.1.

D-3.12.3 PASSENGER LOADING ZONES
ADA: C-1.3.3(1), C-4.4.2

When provided, at least one passenger drop-off and loading zone shall comply with Section C-4.4.2.

D-3.12.4 VALET PARKING
ADA: C-1.3.3.2

Valet parking facilities shall comply with Sections D-6.1 and D-3.12.3.

D-3.13 SHOWER • BATHROOMS
ADA: C-1.3.14, C-4.5, C-4.6

Facilities required to be accessible to persons with disabilities that provide shower or bathing facilities shall comply with the requirements of Sections D-6.2.

D-3.14 STORAGE
ADA: C-1.3.15, C-4.7

Fixed storage facilities required to be accessible shall comply with Section C-4.7.

CALIFORNIA ACCESS CODE • TITLE 24
MINIMUM REQUIREMENTS • Toilet Rooms • Doors

D-3.15 TOILET ROOMS
ADA: C-1.3.13, C-4.8, C-7.3.3

Toilet rooms serving buildings, facilities, or a portion thereof required to be accessible to persons with disabilities shall comply with the California Plumbing Code, Group R occupancy requirements, and Section D-6.3 except as may be exempted in other portions of the CCR.

Exceptions:

An exception shall be granted in existing buildings or facilities when the enforcing agency determines compliance with any building standard under this section would create an undue hardship and when equivalent facilitation is provided that meets the following conditions:

1. The sanitary facilities are within a reasonable distance of the accessible area and are accessible and useable by persons with disabilities, then all sanitary facilities are not required to comply.
2. Equivalent facilitation would require either a lateral or front transfer toilet stall as shown in Figure 88 and provide at least a 30-inch unobstructed door opening.

D-3.16 DOORS
ADA: C-1.2.13, C-1.3.5, C-2.1.4, C-5.2

Doors and door landings located within an accessible route of travel, every exit door serving an area having an occupant load of 10 or more, and doors serving hazardous rooms or areas must be made accessible in compliance with Section D-7.1. Building and structures used for human occupancy must have at least one exterior exit door that complies with Section D-7.1. All exit doors shall comply with Sections D-7.1.4 through D-7.1.8 regardless of the occupant load.

CALIFORNIA ACCESS CODE • TITLE 24
MINIMUM REQUIREMENTS • Floors • Levels

D-3.17 FLOORS • LEVELS
ADA: C-1.3.1(4), C-2.1.2, C-5.4

Floor surfaces shall comply with Section C-5.4. Accessible floors of buildings and facilities shall have a common level throughout a given story and be connected by an accessible vertical means of travel.

Exceptions:
1. When specifically exempted in other portions of this code.
2. An exception shall be granted when the enforcing agency determines that compliance would create an undue hardship and when equivalent facilitation is provided in existing buildings excluding dining, banquet, and bar facilities.
3. Existing buildings where legal or physical constraints do not allow compliance with accessibility standards or equivalent facilitation without creating an undue hardship.
4. An exception shall be granted when the enforcing agency determines that compliance would create an undue hardship provided at least 75 percent of the dining, banquet, and bar facilities of an existing or new building are located on a common level or connected by an accessible elevator, ramp, or lift.

CALIFORNIA ACCESS CODE • TITLE 24
ROUTE OF TRAVEL • Corridors

D-4 ROUTE OF TRAVEL

ADA: C-1.2.1(4), C-1.3.1, C-2.1

D-4.1 CORRIDORS

ADA: C-2.1.3, C-2.3.1

All corridors shall comply with Section D-4.1.

1. **Width**
   Corridors shall be at least 44 inches wide except as specified herein. (Fig. 76) Occupant loads up to 49 shall be served by corridors at least 36 inches wide. Special requirements for Groups E and I occupancies can be located in the California Building Code, Sections 3318 and 3320.

2. **Length**
   Corridors exceeding 200 feet in length shall have at least one of the following:
   a) minimum 60-inch clear width,
   b) a minimum 60-inch by 60-inch wheelchair turning space or passing alcove located at a central location,
   c) minimum 44-inch wide

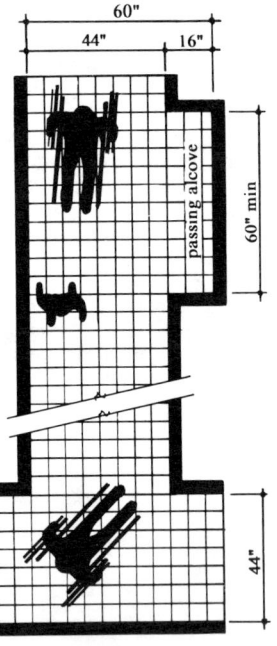

Fig. 76 **Corridors over 200 ft**

intervening cross or tee corridor located in a central location

d) an openable door at a central location

Exceptions
1. An exception shall be granted when the enforcing agency determines compliance would create an undue hardship and when equivalent facilitation is provided.
2. Existing buildings where legal or physical constraints do not allow compliance with the accessibility building standards or equivalent facilitation without creating an undue hardship.

D-4.2 ELEVATORS

ADA: B-4.5, C-1.1.5, C-1.2.9, C-1.3.7, C-5.3

Passenger elevators shall be located near the major path of travel and shall remain accessible and usable at all times when the building is occupied.

D-4.2.1 ELEVATOR CARS

All elevators required to be accessible in buildings having two or more stories shall provide adequate space for a wheelchair.

Exceptions:
1. An exception shall be granted when the enforcing agency determines that compliance would create an undue hardship and when equivalent facilitation is provided to allow a person in a wheelchair to enter and operate the elevator.
2. Existing buildings where legal or physical constraints do not allow compliance with the accessibility building standards or equivalent facilitation without creating an undue hardship.

Passenger elevators shall be near a major path of travel and be accessible and usable when the building is occupied.

CALIFORNIA ACCESS CODE • TITLE 24
ROUTE OF TRAVEL • Elevators

1. **Maximum in Hoistway**
   Three elevator cars in a building may be located in one hoistway enclosure. Four elevator cars in a building shall be located in at least two hoistway enclosures. When there are more than four elevators, no more than four cars shall be located in one hoistway enclosure.
2. **Size** ADA: C-5.3.8
   Elevator cars shall comply with Section C-5.3.8 and Figure 44.
3. **Level Position** ADA: C-5.3.10
   An elevator shall comply with Section C-5.3.10 and be self-leveling with the landing.
4. **Illumination** ADA: C-5.3.2
   Minimum illumination at the car controls, threshold, and landing shall have a minimum of 5 foot-candles when the elevator doors are open.
5. **Position Indicator** ADA: C-5.3.7
   Car position indicators shall comply with Section C-5.3.7.
6. **Handrails**
   A handrail shall be provided on one wall of the car, preferably the rear wall. The rail shall be smooth, have a 1.5 inch clearance from the wall, and a nominal height of 32 inches above the floor. Nominal being ± 1 inch.

D-4.2.2 DOORS ADA: C-5.3.8

Elevators shall have horizontal automatic sliding car doors and hoistway doors with at least a 36-inch clear width. The width may be reduced to 32 inches if a wheelchair occupant is able to enter and operate the elevator and when approved by the building official.

1. **Car Signal • Activation Time** ADA: C-5.3.11
   The minimum acceptable time shall comply with Section

CALIFORNIA ACCESS CODE • TITLE 24
ROUTE OF TRAVEL • Elevators

2. **Delay Time** ADA: C-5.3.13
   Five seconds is the minimum acceptable time which elevator doors must remain fully open.
3. **Reopening Device** ADA: C-5.3.12
   An elevator car door and adjacent hoistway door shall comply with Section C-5.3.12 and ANSI 117.1-78.

D-4.2.3 CONTROLS ADA: C-5.3.4, C-5.3.6

Control buttons shall be illuminated, have square shoulders, raised 1/8-inch $\pm$ 1/32-inch above the surrounding surface, have no dimension less than 3/4-inch, and be activated by a mechanical motion that is detectable. At least a 3/8-inch clear space or other suitable separation means shall be provided between rows of control buttons.

1. **Identification**
   Control buttons shall be identified by a 5/8-inch minimum standard alphabet character, an Arabic number, or a symbol to the left of the button. A Braille symbol shall be located directly below the character, number, or symbol. Raised characters shall be white on a black background. Raised symbols shall include door open, door close, stop, alarm, and telephone among others. A raised star shall be located to the left and identify the main floor button. (Fig. 42).
2. **Call Buttons**
   Elevator call buttons shall be raised 1/8-inch ($\pm$ 1/32 inch) above the surrounding surface and shall meet the requirements of Section C-5.3.4.
3. **Floor Buttons** ADA: C-5.3.6(2)
   The elevator floor buttons shall comply with Section C-5.3.6(4), except for photoelectric tube by-pass switches, and shall be placed no higher than 48 inches above the floor for a front approach and 54 inches for a side

approach. Where possible, a 48-inch maximum height is preferred for all floor buttons. Only one set of controls need to comply with the height requirement where multiple controls exist. Floor buttons shall have visual indicators that register with each call signal and then extinguish when answered.

4. Illumination
See Section D-4.2.1(4).

D-4.2.4 LANTERNS   ADA: C-5.3.5

Elevator lanterns shall comply with Section C-5.3.5. In addition, visible signals must show the direction of travel and arrow shapes are preferred. Lanterns located on a car door jamb shall comply with the in-car lantern regulations.

D-4.2.5 JAMB SYMBOLS   ADA: C-5.3.3

Passenger elevators shall have each floor landing identified on both hoistway door jambs by raised Arabic numerals at least 2 inches high and raised Braille symbols conforming to Section D-5.3.1 and placed approximately 5 feet above the floor where they are visible from the elevator interior.

D-4.2.6 INTERCOMMUNICATION   ADA: C-5.3.14

An emergency telephone handset shall be provided and located within 48 inches above the floor with no less than a 29-inch cord. Door hardware of closed telephone compartments shall be type 8 lock or latch and comply with Section D-7.1.3. Voice communication is not required for emergency intercommunication.

CALIFORNIA ACCESS CODE • TITLE 24
ROUTE OF TRAVEL • Elevators

D-4.2.7 LOBBY ENCLOSURES

Elevator lobbies shall have at least one exit that requires no special knowledge, effort, or use of tools. Elevators, dumbwaiters, and escalator shaft walls and partitions shall not be less than the fire-resistive construction required by Part IV of the California Building Code.

D-4.2.8 SMOKE-DETECTION

Elevators having a vertical traveling distance of 25 feet or more shall have an approved smoke detector for elevator recall in entrance areas, lobbies, and machine rooms. The detector may serve to close the elevator lobby and hoistway doors allowed in the CBC, Section 5106. When activated in those areas, the elevator door is prevented from opening and the car is returned to the main floor. The door shall then be under manual control. If the main floor smoke-detector is activated, the car shall return to an alternate and approved location by the Fire Chief and the building official.

D-4.2.9 STANDBY POWER

At least one elevator in each bank shall provide standby power when required by the CBC, Section 1807. Standby power shall be capable of operating a full-load elevator at a speed at least 150 feet per minute and transferable manually to other elevators in each bank. Standby-power shall be provided by an approved self-contained generator that automatically activates when there is a loss of power to the building. The room housing the generator shall be at least one-hour fire-resistant. The fuel supply shall adequately operate the equipment for at least six hours.

Exceptions:
1. Only one elevator may have standby-power when that ele-

vator serves all floors, and all areas of the building are within 300 feet of the elevator.
2. Standby power shall be capable of operating one elevator at all times in any bank or group of banks having a common lobby.

D-4.2.10 WHEELCHAIR LIFTS ADA: C-1.3.7(3), C-1.2.10, C-5.5

Wheelchair lifts may be provided in lieu of passenger elevators when the distance between landings, structural design, and safeguards are approved by federal, state, and local administrative authorities. When provided, wheelchair lifts shall be designed and constructed for unassisted entry, operation, and exit by persons using wheelchairs and shall comply with Sections C-2.3.2, D-3.16, D-8.2 and ASME A17.1 Safety Code for Elevators and Escalators, Section XX, 1990.

1. **Route of Travel**
   Wheelchair lifts may be part of an accessible route of travel under the following conditions:
   a. to a performing area in an assembly occupancy,
   b. to access occupiable spaces and rooms housing five or less persons which are not open to the general public,
   c. to comply with the wheelchair viewing position line-of-sight and dispersion requirements, and
   d. to provide access where existing constraints prevent the use of an elevator or ramp.

   Exceptions:
   1) An exception shall be granted when the enforcing agency determines the hoistway opening compliance would create an undue hardship and equivalent facilitation is provided.
   2) Existing buildings where physical constraints do not allow compliance with the accessibility building standards or equivalent facilitation without creating an

dards or equivalent facilitation without creating an undue hardship.
3) As part of an accessible route of travel for an addition or alteration, a wheelchair lift installation is not limited to the conditions in Sections D-4.2.10 (1a-1d).

2. Landings
Each floor served by a wheelchair lift shall provide a level and clear floor area to allow safe accessibility to and from the lift platform. Landings shall be part of the path of travel. In new construction, the minimum landing size shall be at least 60 by 60 inches. Other dimensions may be substituted if a person using a 30 by 48-inch wheelchair can enter and operate the lift safely.

3. Assembly
The lift assembly shall be securely supported to
a) maintain the platform in a level position,
b) prevent loosening or displacement of parts, and
c) provide protection from water intrusion.

4. Platform
The lift platform shall accommodate large motorized wheelchairs, comply with Section D-3.17, and have at least the rated capacity required by ASME A17.1, Section XX, 1990.

5. Safety
The platform shall have a solid, smooth enclosure required by ASME 17.1 in order to provide a reasonable degree of safety to the user and others exposed to the lift except when meeting the provisions of Section D-4.2.10.5. The following safety devices shall be installed:
- **Landing Gate**
  The top landing shall have a door or gate 42 inches high that is equipped both electrically and mechanically to prevent platform operation unless properly closed.

CALIFORNIA ACCESS CODE • TITLE 24
ROUTE OF TRAVEL • Elevators

- **Controls**
  Each landing shall have "call/send" controls complying with Section D-8.2.
- **Safety Pan Cover**
  When a lift enclosure is not provided because it serves only two landings, the underside of the lift shall be equipped with a safety pan cover that automatically shuts the lifting device off when an obstruction interferes with the downward travel. The bottom landing entrance shall have a 42-inch high solid gate. The vertical wall from the lower landing to the top landing sill shall be smooth.

6. **Pit**
   A pit may be provided to allow the platform to stop flush with the bottom landing level.

7. **Landing Enclosure**
   The bottom landing level shall have a runway enclosure extending at least 42 inches above the highest landing level for protection when a pit exists.

8. **Ramp**
   In lieu of a pit, a non-skid ramp may be provided not exceeding a 1:12 slope at the bottom level landing. If the ramp does not exceed a 15-inch horizontal run, then a maximum rise of 2.5 inches may be used but shall never exceed a 2:12 slope.

9. **Operation**
   The speed of the platform shall not exceed 20 feet per minute. A constant pressure type, push-bar control designed for easy operation by a person with a disability shall be provided or an alternate control equally usable.

10. **Hydraulic Lift**
    Hydraulic or an electric-hydraulic type shall have re-leveling switches to keep the platform level with the landings.

CALIFORNIA ACCESS CODE • TITLE 24
ROUTE OF TRAVEL • Ramps

D-4.3 RAMPS
ADA: C-1.2.11, C-2.1.2, C-5.6

All ramps used as exits and any path of travel having a slope greater than 1:20 shall comply with Section D-4.3. Ramps shall have the least possible slope.

D-4.3.1 PRIMARY ENTRANCE ADA: C-5.6.5

Pedestrian ramps serving primary entrances to a building shall have the following minimum width:

Clear Width	Occupancy Load
60 inches	300 or more
36 inches	50 or less/Group R
48 inches	all other

D-4.3.2 SLOPE ADA: C-2.1.2(1), C-5.6.2, C-5.6.3

All ramps in areas accessible to persons with disabilities on a path of travel or serving exits shall have a 1:12 slope with cross slopes no greater than 1:50.

D-4.3.3 LANDINGS ADA: C-5.6.4

1. **Location**
   Ramps shall have landings at the top and the bottom. Intermediate landings shall be placed at each change of direction and at each interval not exceeding a 30-inch vertical rise. Landings are not part of the maximum horizontal distance. (Fig. 77a-c)
2. **Size**
   - Top landing shall be at least 60 by 60 inches.
   - The bottom and intermediate landings shall be at least as wide as the ramp.

CALIFORNIA ACCESS CODE · TITLE 24
ROUTE OF TRAVEL · Ramps

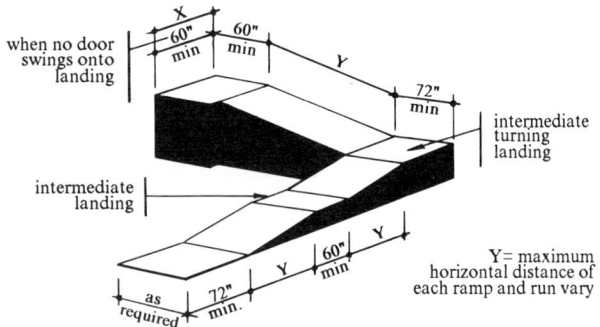

Fig. 77(a) **Ramp Changing Levels**

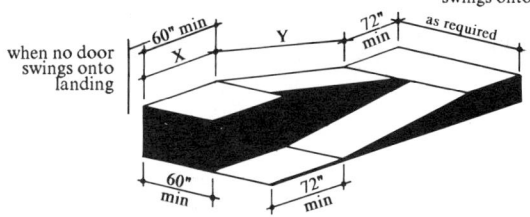

Fig. 77(b) **Switchback Ramp**

- The bottom landing and intermediate landings with a change of direction in excess of 30 degrees shall have at least a 72-inch run in the direction of the ramp. Other intermediate landings shall have a 60-inch minimum run.

CALIFORNIA ACCESS CODE • TITLE 24
ROUTE OF TRAVEL • Ramps

- The landing width shall extend past the strike edge of any door or gate 18 inches for interior ramps and 24 inches for exterior ramps.
- Doors standing in any position shall not reduce the minimum dimension of the ramp less than 42 inches or the required width more than 3 inches.

D-4.3.4 HANDRAILS
ADA: C-5.6.8

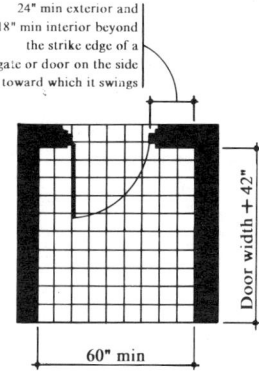

Fig. 77(c)
Ramp Door Landing

Handrails are required on ramps when the slope exceeds 1:20 and shall comply with the requirements of Sections D-4.3.4, C-5.6.8(1,4,7,8), C-6.5.2, C-6.5.3. In addition, handrails shall run along both sides of a ramp, be continuous the full length, extend at least 12 inches beyond the top and bottom of the ramp, and the ends shall be returned.

Exceptions:
1. Ramp handrails immediately adjacent to fixed seating in assembly areas.
2. Ramps serving one individual dwelling unit in Group R, Division 1 or 3 occupancies, may have one handrail, but handrails must always be provided on all open sides.
3. Curb ramps.
4. Group I, Division 1 occupancies, ramps shall have handrails.

TITLE 24 · CALIFORNIA ACCESS CODE
ROUTE OF TRAVEL · Curb Ramps

D-4.4 CURB RAMPS   ADA: C-1.2.11, C-5.1

Curb ramps shall be provided on each corner at street intersections where a pedestrian walkway crosses a curb, preferably located in the center of crosswalks. The lower end of a corner curb ramp shall terminate within a marked crosswalk where the ramp is in the center of a curb return. (Fig. 83c)

D-4.4.1 RAMP   ADA: C-5.1.3

1. **Slope**

    The slope of curb ramps shall not exceed 1:12 with flared sides no more than a 1:8 slope. The ramp shall have a smooth transition from the sidewalk to the gutter and street except the lower end shall have a maximum 1/2-inch beveled lip at 45 degrees. (Figs. 78a,b) The adjoining gutter, road surface, or accessible route's maximum slope shall not exceed 1:20 within 4 feet of the top or bottom of the curb ramp.

    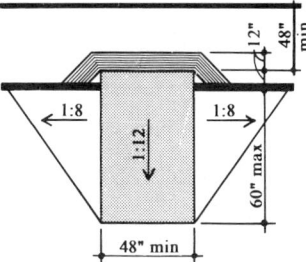

    Fig. 78(a) **Ramp Slope**

    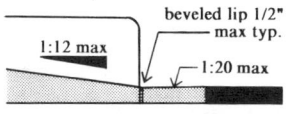

    Fig. 78(b) **Beveled Lip**

2. **Width**   ADA: C-5.1.4

    Curb ramps shall be at least 48 inches in width with a

CALIFORNIA ACCESS CODE • TITLE 24
ROUTE OF TRAVEL • Curb Ramps

single surface slope and minimum cross slope or warping. (Fig. 78a,c,d)

3. Surface ADA: C-5.1.2
The surface finish of curb ramps including flared sides shall be stable, firm, slip-resistant, and the finish shall contrast with the adjacent sidewalk.

4. Landing ADA: C-5.1.5
A level landing 48 inches long and as wide as the ramp shall be provided at the upper end of each curb ramp or the flared sides shall not exceed a 1:12 slope. (Figs. 78c)

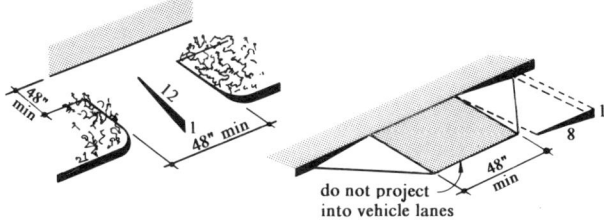

Fig. 78(c) **Returned Curb**   Fig. 78(d) **Projected Ramp**

5. Border
A 12-inch wide grooved border with grooves approximately 3/4 inch on center shall be provided at the level surface of the sidewalk along the top and each side. A grooved border shall be provided at the level surface of the sidewalk on all curb ramps located between the face of the curb and the street. (Figs. 79, 80, 81)

6. Detectable Warning ADA: C-5.1.7
Detectable warnings shall meet the requirements in Figure 82 and Section C-5.1.7 except C-3.2.2(3) is not specified. In addition, the warning area shall be located within the grooved border on ramps with less than a 1:15 slope. The

CALIFORNIA ACCESS CODE • TITLE 24
ROUTE OF TRAVEL • Curb Ramps

domes may be part of a prefabricated surface treatment, cast in place, stamped, or other approved method.

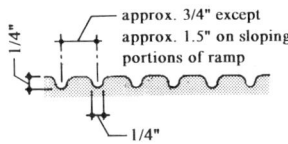

Fig. 79(a) **Groove Detail**

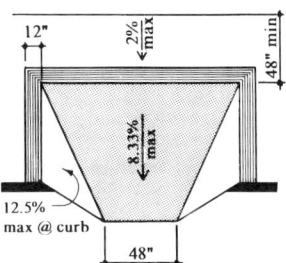

Fig. 79(b) **Recessed Ramp with Grooved Border**

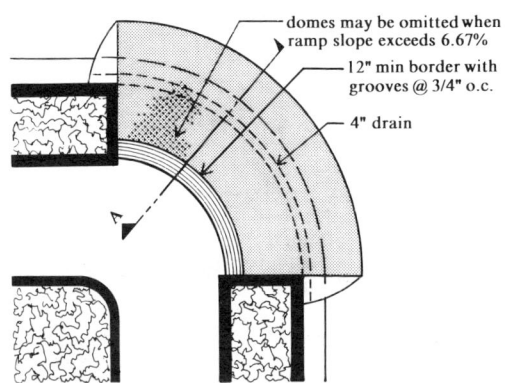

Fig. 80 **Corner Curb Ramp with Detectable Warning**

CALIFORNIA ACCESS CODE · TITLE 24
ROUTE OF TRAVEL · Curb Ramps

7. Placement ADA: C-5.1.8

Curb ramps shall comply with Sections C-5.1.8 through C-5.1.8(1) and as shown in Figure 83.

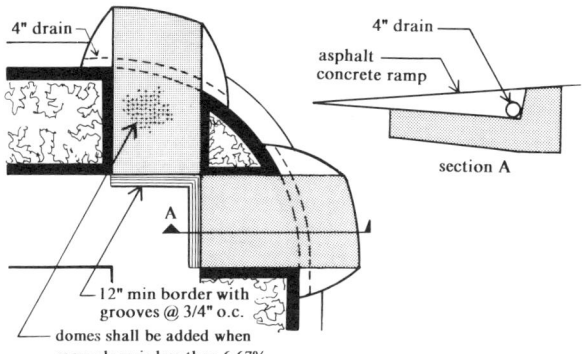

Fig. 81 **Typical Curb Ramp with Detectable Warning**

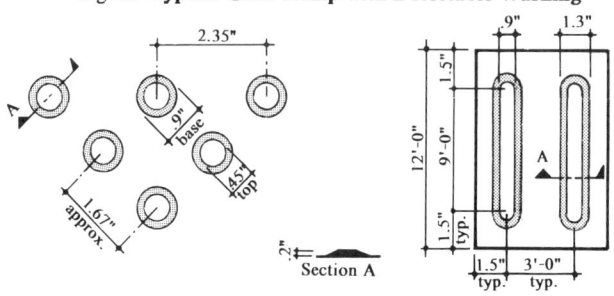

Fig. 82(a) **Truncated Domes**   Fig. 82(b) **Directional Bars**
Fig. 82 **Detectable Warnings**

CALIFORNIA ACCESS CODE • TITLE 24
ROUTE OF TRAVEL • Curb Ramps

Fig. 83 Curb Ramps

Grooves shall be used on the slope of ramps when located in the center of curb returns

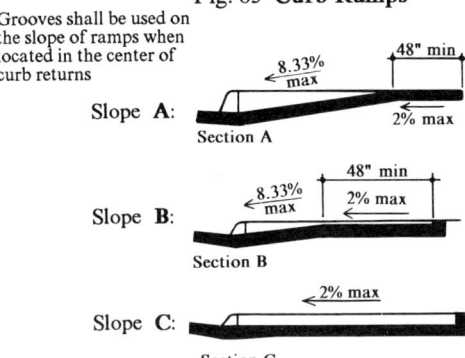

Fig. 83(a) **Slope Variations used in Curb Examples I-V**

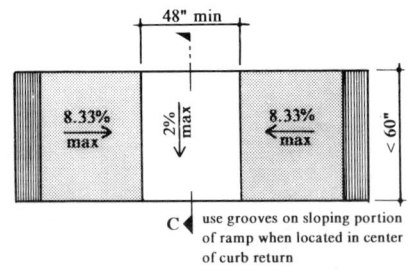

Curb Ramp Example I

CALIFORNIA ACCESS CODE · TITLE 24
ROUTE OF TRAVEL · Curb Ramps

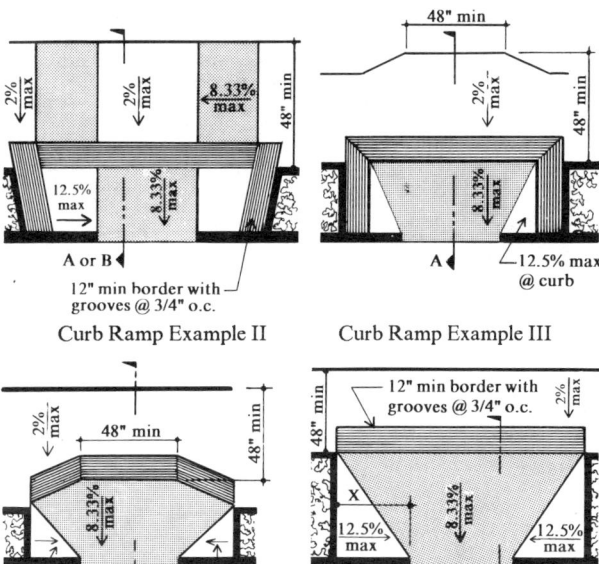

Fig. 83(b) **Curb Variations**

1. The full width of the sidewalk shall be depressed when the sidewalk is less than 5 feet wide. (Example I)
2. A ramp side slope shall be at least 3 feet when the planted area equals or is greater than the ramp length as shown by "x" in Example V.

CALIFORNIA ACCESS CODE • TITLE 24
ROUTE OF TRAVEL • Curb Ramps

Fig. 83(c) **Condition 1**

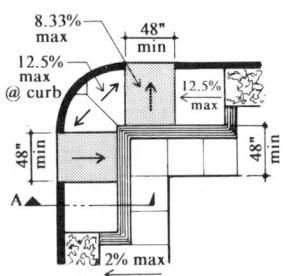

3. Examples II, IV, V allow a 2 percent sidewalk slope when a 48-inch space is not provided behind the 12-inch border. The longitudinal portion of the sidewalk may need to be depressed as shown in example II.
4. Ramps shall have a minimum 12-inch border with 1/4-inch grooves, placed 3/4-inch on center, and located on the level surface of the sidewalk as shown in Examples I-V.
5. When the distance between the curb and back of a sidewalk is too short to accommodate a ramp and a 48-inch platform, the sidewalk may be depressed in the length as shown in Examples I and II and in the width as shown in Example III.
6. A curb return may have one ramp in the center as shown in Condition 2 as an alternative to the ramp shown in Condition 1.

Crosswalk configurations must accommodate wheelchairs for ramps located in the center of curb returns. The sides of a ramp located on a curve need not be parallel. The ramp must be at least 48 inches wide with the bottom edge inside marked crossings and have a minimum 24-inch straight curb on each side of the ramp.

Fig. 83(c) **Condition 2**

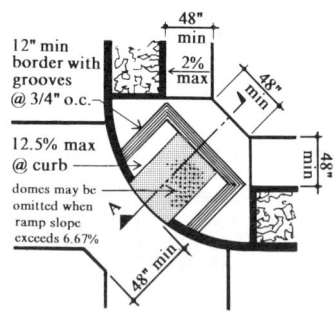

CALIFORNIA ACCESS CODE • TITLE 24
ROUTE OF TRAVEL • Curb Ramps

D-4.4.2 GRADE SEPARATIONS ADA: C-5.1.8

Pedestrian pathways crossing vehicular traffic ways that can be used safely by persons with disabilities shall have an accessible path and curb ramp that complies with the requirements of Section D-4.4, and the ramps on pedestrian grade separations shall comply with Section D-4.3. Walking surface cross-slopes shall not exceed 1/4 inch per foot and 1:12 for warped surfaces.

Exceptions
1. An exception shall be granted when the enforcing agency determines that compliance would create an undue hardship when the grade differential exceeds 14 feet due to required height clearance, grade conditions, topography, or natural barriers which prevent wheelchair accessibility. Other types of mobility impairment accessibility shall be provided when possible.
2. Existing buildings where legal or physical constraints do not allow compliance with the accessibility building standards or equivalent facilitation without creating an undue hardship.

D-5 COMMUNICATIONS

D-5.1 ALARMS
ADA: B-3.22, C-1.3.21, C-3.1

Notification alarm systems required by Section D-3.8 shall comply with Section D-5.1.

D-5.1.1 VISUAL ADA: C-3.1.3

Notification appliances for the hearing impaired shall comply with the requirements shown in Table C-3A. In addition, the appliances shall meet the requirements of the NFPA 72G in the following areas.
 a) Lobbies
 b) Corridors
 c) Restrooms
 d) Meeting rooms
 e) Multipurpose rooms
 f) Gymnasiums
 g) Band rooms
 h) Music practice rooms
 i) Occupational shops
 j) Occupied rooms where ambient noise impairs hearing an alarm
 k) Other common use rooms or areas

D-5.1.2 AUDIBLE ADA: C-3.1.2

1. **Public use**
   Audible signals shall have a sound level of at least 110 dbA at the closest hearing distance from the audible

appliance or at least 75 dBA ten feet from the appliance.

2. Private Use
Audible signals shall have at least 110dBA at the closest hearing distance from the audible appliance and at least 45dBA ten feet from the appliance.

D-5.2 DETECTABLE WARNINGS

ADA: C-1.3.22, C-3.2

Detectable warnings required by Section D-3.9 shall comply with Section D-5.2.

D-5.2.1 TEXTURE ADA: C-3.2.2

Detectable warning texture shall comply with Figure 82 and have the following features:

Surface Texture
The surface texture shall be of durable slip-resistant material comprised of raised truncated domes in a staggered pattern complying with Section C-3.2.2 and have the following features:
a) the truncated domes shall be tapered to 0.45 at the top and comply with Figure 82, and
b) the color shall be yellow, Federal Color No.33538, as shown in Table V of Standard No.595A. A 1-inch wide black strip shall separate the yellow warning area from the main walking surface where the color value contrast between both surfaces is less than 70 percent.

("Nominal" means the required dimensions within $\pm$ 0.020 inch for dome height, top diameter, and bottom diameter and $\pm$ 0.050 inch for dome spacing.)

CALIFORNIA ACCESS CODE • TITLE 24
COMMUNICATIONS • Detectable Warnings

D-5.2.2 VEHICULAR AREAS ADA: C-3.2.3

The boundaries between a pedestrian area and a vehicular area shall be defined by a 36-inch wide continuous detectable warning strip and shall comply with Section D-5.2.1 when the walking surface is not separated by curbs, railings, or other elements.

D-5.2.3 CURB RAMPS ADA: C-5.1.7

Curb ramps shall have a detectable warning strip extending the full width and depth of the curb ramp inside the grooved border for ramps with less than a 1:15 slope, or curb ramps shall comply with Section D-5.2.1 except the access code does not specify (2b). The domes may be cast in place, stamped, part of a prefabricated surface, or other similar treatment.

D-5.2.4 TRANSIT BOARDING PLATFORMS

The detectable warning texture shall extend the full length of the loading area and comply with Section D-5.2.1. Directly behind this texture and in alignment with all doors of the transit vehicles where passengers embark, the following texture shall be placed that has:
a) a width equal to the width of the transit vehicle door opening,
b) a depth of 24 to 36 inches placed at the edge of the drop-off or safe area, and
c) a texture that is
  - 1/10 inch in height tapering to 4/100 inch with bars raised 2/10 inch from the surface,
  - 1.3-inch wide raised bars 3 inches from center-to-center, and
  - the color shall be yellow and comply with Section D-5.2.1(b).

CALIFORNIA ACCESS CODE • TITLE 24
COMMUNICATIONS • Signs

D-5.3 SIGNS _{ADA: C-1.3.2, C-3.3}

Signs required by Sections D-3.10 and D-3.3.4(1b) shall comply with Section D-5.3 and sanitary facilities shall also comply with Section D-6.3.2.

D-5.3.1 INTERNATIONAL SYMBOL _{ADA: C-3.3.3(1)}

The International Symbol of Accessibility shall comply with Figures 17(a,b) and consist of a white figure on blue background, the blue equal to Color No. 15090, Federal Standard 595A. The enforcing agency may determine and approve alternate colors when the signs provide adequate direction for persons with disabilities.

D-5.3.2 SPECIFICATIONS _{ADA: C-3.3.6, C-3.3.7, C-3.3.8}

Sign characters, symbol dimensions, contrast, and Braille shall comply with Sections C-3.3.6 through C-3.3.8. The California Access Code does not place a maximum limit on the character or symbol height.

D-5.3.3 BRAILLE SYMBOLS _{ADA: C-3.3.8}

When Braille symbols are required, Contracted Grade 2 Braille shall be used. Dots shall be raised at least 1/40 inch, be 1/10 inch on center in each cell, and have 2/10-inch spacing between cells.

D-5.3.4 PLACEMENT _{ADA: C-3.3.2}

Sign placement shall comply with Section C-3.3.2. In addition, permanent room and space signs shall have raised letters accompanied by Braille complying with Section C-3.3.8 and

CALIFORNIA ACCESS CODE • TITLE 24
COMMUNICATIONS • Telephones

shall be preferably placed on the adjacent right wall when there is no wall space on the latch side.

D-5.3.5 INFORMATION SIGNS ADA: C-1.2.3

Existing buildings which have been remodeled and provide accessible sanitary facilities or an elevator shall post this information in the lobby or in the building directory.

D-5.3.6 ENTRANCE SIGNS ADA: C-1.3.2(3)

All accessible entrances shall be identified by a standard sign with additional directional signs along the approaching pedestrian pathways visible to persons with disabilities.

D-5.3.7 TRAFFIC CONTROL DEVICES

Poles having traffic control buttons shall be identified by a textured horizontal yellow band encircling the pole immediately above the control button and within 48 inches above the ground. The band shall be 2 inches in width with a 1-inch dark border above and below the yellow band.

D-5.4 TELEPHONES ADA: C-1.3.18, C-3.4

When provided, public telephones shall comply with Sections D-5.4, C-2.3.2, C-3.4.7, Figure 84, and Figures 18(a,b) with the changes noted in D-5.4.2(2a).

D-5.4.1 HEIGHT ADA: C-3.4.2

The telephone heights shall comply with Section C-3.4.2, C-2.3.3, and Figure 84. A corner telephone's operable parts shall be a maximum 54 inches high for a diagonal reach.

CALIFORNIA ACCESS CODE • TITLE 24
COMMUNICATIONS • Telephones

D-5.4.2 ENCLOSURES

Telephone enclosures shall comply with Figures 84 and 18(a,b). Figure 18 is drawn to ADAAG requirements and corresponds to the California Access Code requirements with the exception of the dimensions in number 2 below.

1. **Full-height enclosure**
   Full-height telephone enclosures shall provide at least a 30-inch entrance opening as shown in Figure 84(a).

2. **Clear Space Overhang**
   Telephones may overhang clear floor spaces as follows:
   a) **Side Reach**
      California Access Code allows up to a 19-inch overhang as shown in Figure 12(a) rather than the 10 inches specified by the ADAAG. The height of the lowest overhanging part shall be 27 inches or greater.
   b) **Forward Reach**
      The enclosure shall have a clear width of at least 30 inches when the overhang is more than 12 inches. If the enclosure clear width is less than 30 inches, the lowest overhanging part shall be equal to or greater than 27 inches above the floor.

Fig. 84 **Telelphone Clearances**

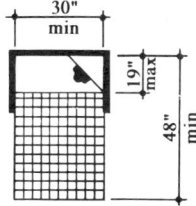

Fig 84(a) **Wheelchair Space at Enclosure**

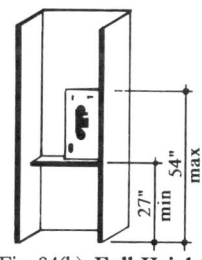

Fig. 84(b) **Full-Height Enclosures**

CALIFORNIA ACCESS CODE • TITLE 24
COMMUNICATIONS • Telephones

3. **Protruding Enclosures**
   Telephone enclosures protruding into pedestrian ways, shall comply with Section C-2.2.

D-5.4.3 TEXT TELEPHONES
ADA: B-3.2.2, C-1.2.14, C-1.3.18(3), C-3.4.9

Where required, text telephones shall comply with Sections C-1.3.18(3), C-3.4.3, C-3.4.4, C-3.4.5, C-3.4.9, and be identified with appropriate signs as displayed in Figures 17(c,d). When banks of telephones are provided, 25 percent and not less than one in each bank shall comply with Sections C-1.3.18(2) and C-3.4.8.

CALIFORNIA ACCESS CODE • TITLE 24
FACILITY AREAS • Parking

D-6 FACILITY AREAS

D-6.1 PARKING
ADA: C-1.3.3, C-4.4

Parking areas required by Section D-3.12 shall comply with Section D-6.1 and Table C-1A.

D-6.1.1 PARKING SPACES
ADA: C-1.3.3, C-4.4.4

Parking spaces shall be located at the nearest primary entrance, as practical, and meet the following requirements:

1. **Single Spaces** ADA: C-1.3.3(3,4)
   When provided, spaces shall be a total of 14 feet wide consisting of a 9-foot wide parking space with a 5-foot wide access aisle on the passenger side. Two parking spaces may be provided within a 23-foot wide space where two 9-foot wide parking spaces share one 5-foot wide center access aisle. The space shall be lined to define the specific use. Each parking space shall be at least 18 feet in length. Figs. 85(a,b).

2. **Less Than Five Spaces**
   Buildings and facilities providing less than five spaces shall provide at least one 14-foot wide space as described above. The space does not have to be designated for the exclusive use of persons with disabilities.

3. **Van-Accessible Space** ADA: C-1.3.3(5), C-4.4.4(6)
   One in every eight accessible spaces, but never less than one space, shall be designated as van accessible by signs complying with Section D-6.1.3 and have at least one 8-foot wide access aisle. All van-accessible parking spaces may be grouped on one level of a parking structure.

CALIFORNIA ACCESS CODE • TITLE 24
FACILITY AREAS • Parking

Fig. 85 Parking Spaces

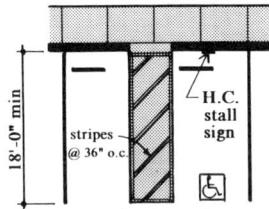

Fig. 85(a) **Single Parking Space**

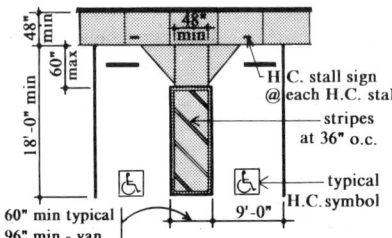

Fig. 85(b) **Double Parking Space**

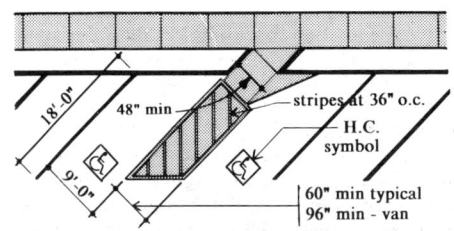

Fig. 85(c) **Diagonal Parking Space**

CALIFORNIA ACCESS CODE • TITLE 24
FACILITY AREAS • Parking

4. Design

A bumper or curb shall be provided and placed to prevent encroachment of vehicles within the access aisles of each parking area. An accessible space shall be located where persons with disabilities are not required to travel behind vehicles other than their own. An accessible route of travel shall be provided from each accessible parking space to the related facility. Curb cuts or ramps shall be provided on the route of travel where needed, but no ramp shall encroach within any parking space.

5. Slope ADA: C-4.4.4(3)

The surface slope of an accessible parking space shall be no greater than 1/4 inch per foot in any direction.

6. Exceptions

a) Ramps

A ramp at the front of an accessible space may encroach into the length if the ramp does not limit a disabled person's ability to enter or leave their vehicle as shown in Figures 85(b,c).

b) Parking Space

Parking spaces which require a disabled person to travel behind parked vehicles may be provided when the enforcing agency determines that compliance with these guidelines or equivalent facilitation would create an undue hardship.

c) Variance

A variance or waiver may be granted by the enforcing agency when they determine compliance would create an undue hardship.

D-6.1.2 PARKING STRUCTURES ADA: C-4.4.3, C-4.4.4(2)

All entrances and vertical clearances within parking structures shall be at least 8 feet 2 inches where required to access

CALIFORNIA ACCESS CODE • TITLE 24
FACILITY AREAS • Parking

designated accessible parking spaces.

Exceptions
1. An exception shall be granted when the enforcing agency determines that compliance would create an undue hardship and when equivalent facilitation is provided.
2. Existing buildings where legal or physical constraints do not allow compliance with the accessibility building standards or equivalent facilitation without creating an undue hardship.

D-6.1.3 SIGNS ADA: C-3.3.2, C-4.4.5

Each accessible off-street parking space shall be identified by the following:
1. A permanent reflectorized sign adjacent to and visible from each space which includes:
   (a) the International Symbol of Accessibility,
   (b) at least 70 square inches in size, and
   (c) the bottom sign edge shall be at least 80 inches above the finish grade when located in the path of travel.
2. Signs may be centered on an interior end-wall of a parking space at least 36 inches above the finished grade.
3. Van-accessible parking spaces shall have an additional sign stating "Van-Accessible" placed below the symbol of accessibility.
4. A conspicuous sign shall be placed at each entrance of off-street parking facilities or adjacent and visible from each accessible space. Such sign shall be 17 by 22 inches with 1 inch lettering that states, "Unauthorized vehicles parked in designated spaces not displaying distinguishing placards or license plates issued for persons with disabilities may be towed away at owner's expense. Towed vehicles may be reclaimed at _(fill in with appropriate information)_ or by telephoning _____."

CALIFORNIA ACCESS CODE • TITLE 24
FACILITY AREAS • Shower • Bath

In addition, each accessible parking space surface shall provide identification by one of the following:
1. A 36 by 36-inch blue background with a white International Symbol of Accessibility painted on the parking space surface visible to traffic enforcement officers when vehicles are properly parked in the space. (Fig. 85)
2. The parking space shall be outlined or painted blue with the International Symbol of Accessibility outline in white or other suitable contrasting color.

D-6.2 SHOWER • BATH

Shower and bathroom facilities required to be accessible by Section D-3.13 shall comply with Section D-6.2.

D-6.2.1 APPLICATION ADA: C-1.3.14, C-4.5

When provided, bathing facilities shall provide at least 2 percent but not less than one bathtub or shower accessible to persons with disabilities. When bathing facilities are provided for the public, client, or employees, at least one percent of all facilities and never less than one of each fixture including showers, bathtubs, and lockers shall comply with the standards in Section D-6.2 unless specifically exempted by other regulations herein.

D-6.2.2 BATHTUBS ADA: C-4.5.4, C-6.2

1. Application
Bathtubs required to be accessible shall comply with Section D-6.2.2 and the California Plumbing Code Section 1506.

CALIFORNIA ACCESS CODE • TITLE 24
FACILITY AREAS • Shower • Bath

2. **Bathtub Enclosures** ADA: C-6.2.5
   When provided, bathtub enclosures shall comply with Sections C-6.2.5 and D-6.2.5.
3. **Bathtub Seat** ADA: C-6.2.4, C-6.5.4
   Bathtub seats shall comply with the requirements of Section C-6.2.4.
4. **Grab Bars** ADA: C-6.2.6
   Grab bars shall comply with Sections C-6.5 and as shown in Figure 57 and grab bar reinforcement as shown in Figure 86.

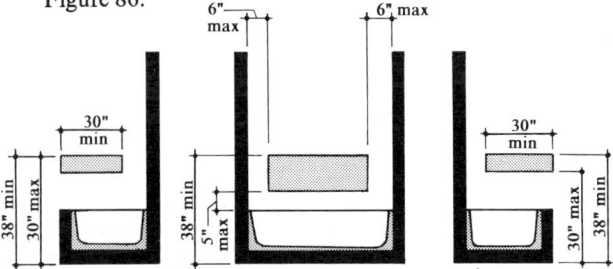

Fig. 86 **Bathtub Reinforcement**

5. **Controls** ADA: C-6.2.2
   Faucets and controls shall comply with Section C-6.3.2 and placed as shown in Figure 57.
6. **Floor Space** ADA: C-6.2.7
   A clear floor space shall be provided adjacent to accessible bathtubs as shown in Figure 58.

D-6.2.3 SHOWERS ADA: C-4.5.11, C-4.5.4, C-4.6

Shower compartments required to be accessible shall comply with Section C-6.2.3.

CALIFORNIA ACCESS CODE · TITLE 24
FACILITY AREAS · Shower · Bath

1. **Stall** ADA: C-4.6.2
   An accessible shower stall shall be 42 by 48 inches with a 36-inch entrance opening. The floors and walls shall comply with Section D-6.3.7(4).
2. **Threshold** ADA: C-4.6.4
   When used, a threshold or recessed drop shall be no more than 1/2 inch high and beveled or sloped no more than 45 degrees from the horizontal.
3. **Floor**
   The floor shall be sloped a maximum of 1/2 inch per foot toward a drain located within 6 inches of the back wall. The surface shall be Carborundum, grit-faced tile, or an equivalent slip-resistant material.
4. **Enclosure** ADA: C-4.6.5
   When provided, a shower stall enclosure shall not obstruct a person's transfer between a wheelchair and shower seat and shall comply with Section D-6.2.5.
5. **Seat** ADA: C-4.6.3
   Accessible shower stalls shall have a folding seat mounted 18 inches above the floor on the wall opposite the controls as shown in Figure 87.

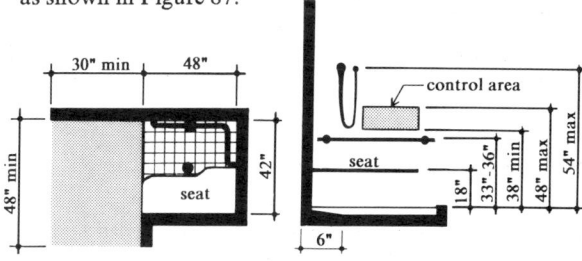

Fig. 87 **Shower Stalls**

CALIFORNIA ACCESS CODE • TITLE 24
FACILITY AREAS • Shower • Bath

6. **Soap Dish**
   An accessible shower stall shall provide a soap dish on the control wall no higher than 40 inches above the floor.
7. **Grab Bars** ADA: C-4.6.8, C-6.5.1
   Accessible shower compartments shall provide grab bars that comply with the requirements of Section C-6.5 and Figures 87 and 88. L-shaped shower grab bars shall not be less than 36 inches in length on the wall with the shower head and 24 inches long on the adjacent wall with the controls as shown in Figure 87. Grab bars shall be installed between 33 and 36 inches above the compartment floor.
8. **Hand Sprayer** ADA: C-4.6.6, C-4.6.7, C-6.2.3
   Hand held sprayers shall be placed no higher than 54 inches above the finished floor.

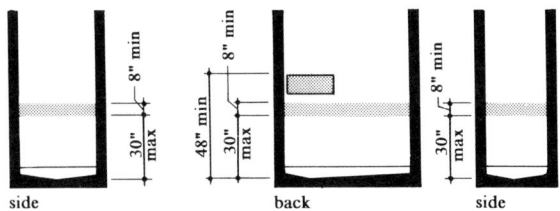

Fig. 88 **Shower Stall Area Reinforcement**

D-6.2.4 OPEN SHOWERS

When shower compartments are not provided, shower facilities for persons with disabilities shall be provided in a corner with grab bars on the adjacent walls with the seat as shown in Figure 89. The folding seat shall comply with Section D-6.2.3(5).

CALIFORNIA ACCESS CODE • TITLE 24
FACILITY AREAS • Shower • Bath

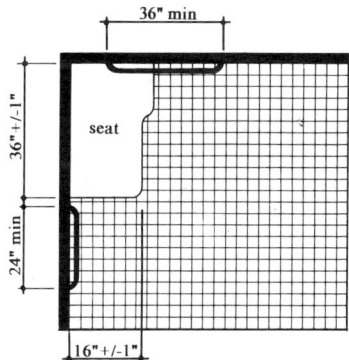

Fig. 89 **Open Showers**

D-6.2.5 SHOWER • BATHTUB ENCLOSURES

Glazing used in shower and bathtub enclosure doors and panels shall be fully tempered, laminated safety glass, or approved plastic. Glass shall be 1/4-inch laminated or at least 1/8 inch when fully tempered and pass the UBC Standard No. 54-2 test. Plastic doors and panels of enclosures shall be shatter-resistant.

D-6.2.6 LOCKERS ADA: C-1.3.15

At least one percent but not less than one of all lockers provided for the public, members, clients, employees, or participants shall be accessible to persons with disabilities and located on at least a 36-inch wide accessible path of travel.

CALIFORNIA ACCESS CODE • TITLE 24
FACILITY AREAS • Toilet Rooms

D-6.3 TOILET ROOMS   ADA: C-4.8

Toilet rooms required to be accessible by Section D-3.15 shall comply with Section D-6.3 and D-5.3.4.

D-6.3.1 APPLICATION   ADA: C-1.2.7, C-1.3.13, C-4.8, C-4.8.9

Accessible toilet facilities in dwellings, congregate housing, and guest rooms shall comply with the California Access Code. Other occupancy toilet facilities shall have at least one accessible water closet. Two accessible water closets shall be provided when there are 10 or more water closets. At least one lavatory, mirror, and towel fixture within any toilet facility shall be accessible to persons with disabilities.

When separate toilet facilities are provided for each sex, each facility shall accommodate persons with disabilities. Unisex toilet facilities shall be provided for both disabled and non-disabled persons. Facilities used solely by children may adjust the requirement heights to meet their accessibility needs.

D-6.3.2 IDENTIFICATION SYMBOLS   ADA: C-3.3.2

Doorways leading to toilet rooms shall have the following

Fig. 90 **Toilet Facility Symbols**

MEN   **UNISEX**   **WOMEN**

CALIFORNIA ACCESS CODE • TITLE 24
FACILITY AREAS • Toilet Rooms

identifying symbols centered on the door 60 inches above the floor and in a color and contrast different from the door. Men's facility doors shall have an equilateral triangle 1/4-inch thick, 12-inch sides, and a vertex pointing upward. Women's facility doors shall have a 12-inch diameter circle, 1/4-inch thick. A unisex facility door shall have a 12-inch diameter circle, 1/4-inch thick, and a 1/4-inch thick triangle with 12-inch sides inscribed and superimposed on the circle. (Fig. 90)

D-6.3.3 PASSAGEWAY ADA: C-4.8.2

Passageways leading to toilet rooms shall comply with Section D-4.1. Doorways leading to toilet facilities shall have a clear 32-inch wide opening and a minimum 60-inch clear and level floor space in the direction of the door swing and a 44-inch space away from the door swing. The measurement shall be taken at right angles from the door plane in its closed position. The width of the clear floor space shall extend 24 inches past the strike edge of exterior doorways on the swing side and 18 inches past the strike edge of interior doorways.

D-6.3.4 SINGLE ACCOMMODATION
ADA: C-1.2.8, C-4.8, C-4.9

Toilet rooms shall comply with Section D-6.3.3 and residential toilet rooms shall also comply with the regulations required by Group R occupancy in Section D-2.8.

1. **Accessible Route of Travel**
   All doors, fixtures, and controls shall be on an accessible route of travel and comply with Section C-2.1.3(1).
2. **Clear Floor Space** ADA: C-4.8.8, C-4.9.2, C-6.10.6
   A single accommodating toilet facility shall have a 30-inch wide by 48-inch long space sufficient to allow a wheelchair to enter the room and close the door. A minimum 48-inch long space shall be provided in front of the toilet.

CALIFORNIA ACCESS CODE • TITLE 24
FACILITY AREAS • Toilet Rooms

3. **Maneuvering Space** ADA: C-4.8.8
   A maneuvering space shall be provided that complies with either option in Figure 10 and be unobstructed by any swing of a door.
4. **Water Closet** ADA: C-4.5.6, C-4.8.4, C-4.9.5
   The water closet shall be placed 18 inches from the centerline of the fixture to an adjacent side wall. The other side of the water closet shall have a 28-inch minimum clear space between any adjacent fixture or a 32-inch wide minimum clear space between the water closet and the other side wall.
5. **Exception**
   A single toilet room accommodation in an existing building may provide a minimum clear floor space 36 inches wide by 48 inches long in front of the water closet.

D-6.3.5 MULTIPLE ACCOMMODATION
ADA: C-1.2.8, C-4.5.7, C-4.8.3, C-4.9, C-6.10

Multiple accommodation toilet rooms shall comply with Section D-6.3.5. When six or more stalls are provided, at least one shall comply with subparagraph 2 below and at least one additional stall shall be at least 36 inches wide with an outward swinging door and parallel grab bars that comply with Section D-6.3.6.

1. **Clear Floor Space** ADA: C-4.8.8
   The toilet room shall have a 5-foot diameter or a 56 by 63-inch clear floor space within a height of 27 inches above the floor. No doors in any position, other than the accessible toilet compartment door, shall encroach within this space more than 12 inches.
2. **Toilet Compartments** ADA: C-4.8.9, C-4.9.5
   An accessible individual toilet stall shall provide at least a 28-inch wide clear space directly adjacent to the side of a

water closet or a 32-inch clear space between the water closet and a wall on one side of the fixture. The other side of the water closet shall be 18 inches from the wall to the centerline of the water closet. A stall with an end compartment door shall have a minimum 48-inch long clear space in front of the toilet or a minimum 60-inch long clear space with a side compartment door. Grab bars shall not protrude more than 3 inches into the clear space. (Fig. 91)

a) Access Aisle

A clear 44-inch wide access aisle shall be provided to accessible toilet compartments with a 48-inch long clear space provided immediately in front of the stall measured at right angles to the door in the closed position.

b) Door

Accessible water closet compartment doors shall have a 32-inch clear end-door opening or 34-inch side-door opening when the door is positioned at a 90 degree angle from the closed position. The door shall have an automatic closing device. A clearance at the strike edge as specified in Sec-

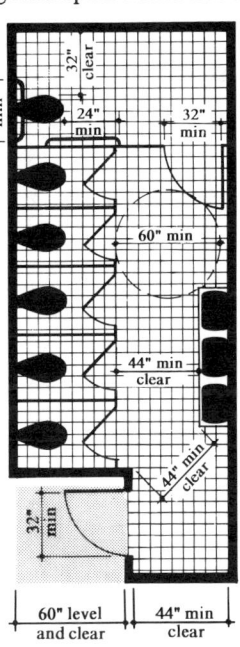

Fig. 91 **Toilet Rooms**

CALIFORNIA ACCESS CODE • TITLE 24
FACILITY AREAS • Toilet Rooms

tion D-7.1.4(2) is not required when a self-closing standard door is used that has at least a footrest clearance of 9 inches under the door. The door hardware shall be either a loop or U-shaped handle located immediately below the latch. The latch shall be sliding, flip-over, or another similar type not requiring a grasp or twist to operate.

Fig. 92 **Accessible Toilet Facilities**

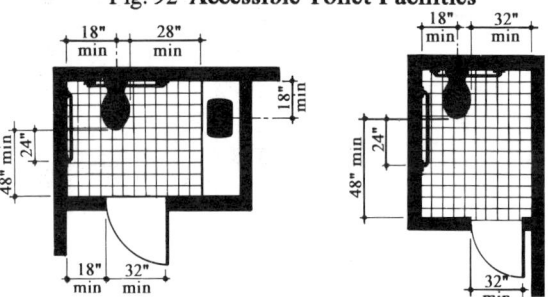

Fig. 92(a) **Single Occupancy**   Fig. 92(b) **Toilet Stall**

D-6.3.6 GRAB BARS   ADA: C-4.9.3, C-4.9.5(3), C-6.5.1, C-6.10.5

Grab bars located on each side or on one side and the back in accessible toilet stalls shall be securely attached at 33 inches above and parallel to the floor. Placement as high as 36 inches is allowed where a toilet tank prevents mounting the bars at 33 inches. Grab bars shall be at least 42 inches long and positioned with 24 inches in front of the water closet. Bars placed on the back wall shall be at least 36 inches in length. All grab bars in accessible toilet stalls shall comply with Section C-6.5 and Figures 92 and 93. Grab bar reinforcement required by Section D-2.8.4.5(2) shall comply with Figure 94.

CALIFORNIA ACCESS CODE • TITLE 24
FACILITY AREAS • Toilet Rooms

D-6.3.7 FIXTURES • ACCESSORIES

1. Urinals
ADA: C-4.5.5, C-4.8.5, C-6.9

When provided, at least one urinal shall comply with the clear floor space requirement of Section C-2.3.2 allowing a forward reach complying with Section C-2.3.3.1.

2. Lavatories
ADA: C-4.5.8, C-4.8.6, C-6.6.5

Lavatories shall comply with Section C-6.6.5 with the exception of the clear floor space extending under the lavatory which has no limitation.

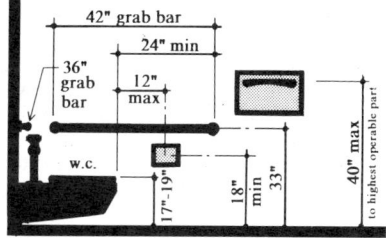

Fig. 92(c) **Side Elevation**

3. Mirrors
ADA: C-4.5.8, C-4.8.6, C-6.6.6

Mirrors for lavatories shall comply with Section C-6.6.6.

4. Walls • Floors

With the exception of structural elements, water closet and shower areas in all occupancies other

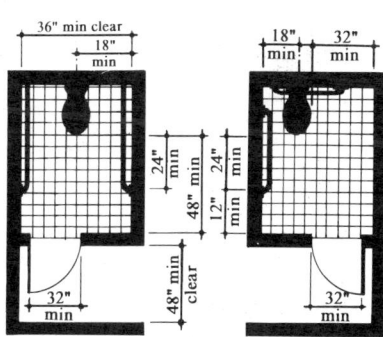

Front Transfer   Side Transfer

Fig. 93 **Equivalent Facilitation Existing Construction**

CALIFORNIA ACCESS CODE • TITLE 24
FACILITY AREAS • Toilet Rooms

than dwelling units shall finish the floors and walls with a hard, smooth, non-absorbent surface such as portland cement, concrete, ceramic tile, or other approved materials not adversely affected by moisture and in the following areas:

floors - floors with at least a 5-inch extension onto the walls

urinals - floors within 24 inches of the front and sides, walls at least 48 inches high

toilet stalls - floor and the walls to a height of at least 48 inches

showers - floor and the walls to a height of at least 70 inches above the drain inlet.

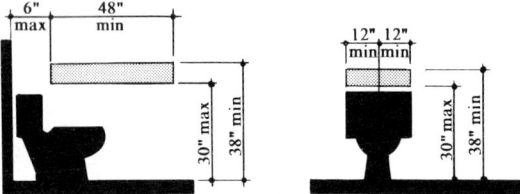

Fig. 94 **Reinforcement Areas**

5. Tissue Dispensers ADA: C-6.10.4

Toilet tissue dispensers shall be wall-mounted within 12 inches of the toilet seat's front edge. Dispensers shall not control tissue delivery or prevent a continuous flow of tissue.

6. Dispensing and Disposing Fixtures ADA: C-4.5.10, C-4.8.7

When provided, at least one of each type of dispensing or disposal fixtures shall be provided with all operable parts located within 40 inches above the finished floor including towels, sanitary napkins, and waste receptacles.

D 6.3

CALIFORNIA ACCESS CODE • TITLE 24
BUILDING ELEMENTS • Doors

D-7 BUILDING ELEMENTS

D-7.1 DOORS
ADA: C-1.2.13, C-1.3.5, C-2.1.4, C-5.2

D-7.1.1 APPLICATION ADA: C-5.2.1

All doors required to be accessible by Section D-1 shall comply with Section D-7.1.

D-7.1.2 DOORS

1. **Size** ADA: C-1.2.13(1), C-5.2.9
   Every required exit doorway shall provide at least a 36-inch wide door 80 inches high and allow a clear opening 32 inches wide when the door is in the open position. The net dimension of the exit opening shall be used when computing a specific width required by an occupancy load that complies with the CBC Section 3303(b). Group I, Division 2A, occupancies allow an exception where doorways may be 30 inches in width.

2. **Hinged**
   The doorway opening width shall be determined with the door at a 90 degree angle from the closed position.

3. **Double-leaf** ADA: C-5.2.2
   At least one leaf in a pair of doors shall have a clear 32-inch opening width when the leaf is placed 90 degrees from the closed position.

4. **Revolving** ADA: C-5.2.4
   Revolving doors shall not be used as a required accessible entrance for persons with disabilities.

CALIFORNIA ACCESS CODE • TITLE 24
BUILDING ELEMENTS • Doors

5. **Automatic** ADA: C-5.2.3

   A pair of automatically operated doors shall provide at least a 32-inch clear opening at one leaf when open at a 90 degree angle from the closed position.

   Exceptions
   1. Double-leaf and automatic door provisions do not apply in existing buildings except as otherwise required for accessibility to persons with disabilities. Doorways may have a 30-inch clear width in existing buildings if
      a) the occupant load is less than ten except Group I, Division 1 occupancies, and
      b) the occupant load is greater than 10 and compliance with Section D-7.1(1) would create an undue hardship.
   2. Existing buildings where legal or physical constraints do not allow compliance with the accessibility building standards or equivalent facilitation without creating an undue hardship.

D-7.1.3 DOOR HARDWARE   ADA: C-5.2.7

1. **Location**
   Hardware shall be centered between 30 and 44 inches above the floor for hand-activated hardware.

2. **Operation**
   Hand activated hardware shall be operable by a single effort of a lever, push-pull bar, panic bar, or other hardware designed not to require a grasp of the hardware to open, lock, or latch the door. This applies to all doors in a path of travel and exit doors in an egress direction. This also applies to individual hotel and motel unit doors except when a key operates the bolt and unlatching operation from the corridor or exterior side of the door. Large 1.25 or 2 inch bow keys shall then be used in lieu of the lever

CALIFORNIA ACCESS CODE • TITLE 24
BUILDING ELEMENTS • Doors

type hardware. The room side shall have a separate deadlock bolt activated by a lever or large thumb turn.

3. Exit Doors
Exit doors shall be operable from the inside without the use of a key or special knowledge or effort.

4. Exceptions
 1. Group B occupancies.
    A main exit consisting of a single door or pair of doors may have key-locking hardware when a durable sign is posted on or adjacent to the door stating "THIS DOOR IS TO REMAIN UNLOCKED DURING BUSINESS HOURS". The letters shall be at least one inch high on a contrasting background. The operable door(s) shall be free to swing without operation of a latching device when unlocked. This exception may be revoked for due cause by a building official.
 2. Individual dwelling unit exit doors, Group R occupancies, Division 3 congregate residences, and Group R occupancy guest rooms that have an occupant load of 10 or less may have a night latch, dead bolt, or security chain if mounted at a maximum height of 48 inches above the finished floor and openable from the inside without a key or tool.

The unlatching of any leaf shall not require more than one operation. An exit door leaf having an approved automatic flush bolt shall not have a door knob or surface mounted hardware. Manually operated edge or surface-mounted flush bolts and surface bolts are prohibited.

Exceptions
1. Group R, Division 3 occupancies
2. A pair of doors serving a room not generally occupied but needed for the movement of room equipment may have a manually-operated edge or surface bolt. The inactive leaf does not require a door closer.

CALIFORNIA ACCESS CODE • TITLE 24
BUILDING ELEMENTS • Doors

D-7.1.4 LANDINGS

A door shall have a floor landing on each side of the door regardless of the occupant load.

1. Exit Doors ADA: C-5.2.10
The floor or landing length on each side of an exit door shall be level and clear at least 60 inches in the direction of the door swing and 48 inches on the other side of the doorway when measured at right angles from the door in the closed position. The length may be 44 inches on both sides of the doorway in Group R occupancies.

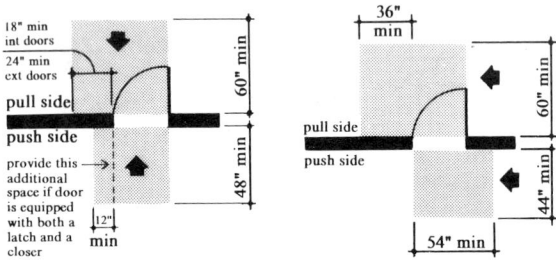

Fig. 95(a) **Front Approach**   Fig. 95(b) **Latch Approach**

2. Floor Clearance ADA: C-5.2.10, C-2.3.2
Figures 95(a-c) shows the minimum clear and level floor space required at doors that are not automatic or power assisted. The width shall extend 24 inches beyond the strike edge of all exterior doors and 18 inches for all interior doors including power-assisted and automatic doors.

3. Doors in Series ADA: C-5.2.6
The space between two doors in a series, other than at a required exit stairway, shall comply with Section C-5.2.6.

CALIFORNIA ACCESS CODE • TITLE 24
BUILDING ELEMENTS • Doors

Additional maneuvering space of 12 inches on latch doors and 18 inches on doors with no closers shall be provided on the swing side of the door.

4. **Stair enclosure**

   The landing to a smokeproof enclosed stairway does not have to be 60 inches long.

Fig. 95(c) **Hinge Approach**

5. **No Landing**

   Adequate lighting and a sign posted on the door stating "Danger! Stairway—No Landing" or equivalent wording shall be provided at existing stairways with no landing.

D-7.1.5 THRESHOLDS
ADA: C-1.2.13(2), C-5.2.8, C-5.4.4

Thresholds shall not be more than 1/2 inch above the floor and shall comply with the level change requirements of Section C-5.4.4. (Fig. 96)

D-7.1.6 OPERATION
ADA: C-5.2.12

The pull or push effort applied at right angles to hinged doors or at the center plane of sliding or folding doors shall not exceed a maximum 8.5-pound force for exterior doors and 5-pound force for interior doors. Automatic

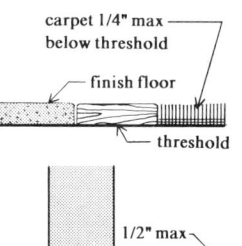

Fig. 96 **Threshold Details**

CALIFORNIA ACCESS CODE • TITLE 24
BUILDING ELEMENTS • Doors

door operators or other compensating devices are allowed to meet the above standard. The allowable force to operate a fire door may be increased to the minimum allowable by the appropriate administrative authority but shall not exceed a 15-pound force.

D-7.1.7 DESIGN

Except for automatic and sliding doors, doors shall have a smooth surface along the bottom 10 inches to allow a wheelchair footrest to open the door safely. Narrow-frame doors shall provide a 10-inch high smooth panel on the push side of the door to allow a wheelchair footrest to open the door safely. (Fig. 97)

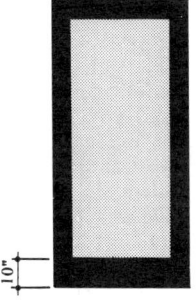

Fig. 97 **Door Design**

D-7.1.8 TURNSTILES ADA: C-5.2.4

An accessible door or gate for persons with disabilities shall be provided where a turnstile is used to control the access to a facility. The door or gate shall be within 30 feet of the turnstile entrance, unlocked during business hours, and shall not activate a publicly audible alarm system. A clear 32-inch wide space shall be provided at pedestrian controls such as posts or rails.

D-7.1.9 EXCEPTIONS

The requirements of Sections D-7.1.2, D-7.1.3, D-7.1.6, and D-7.1.7 shall not apply when physical constraints or equivalent facilitation in compliance with these building standards create an undue hardship in existing buildings.

CALIFORNIA ACCESS CODE • TITLE 24
BUILDING ELEMENTS • Stairs

D-7.2 STAIRS   ADA: C-1.3.6, C-5.7

Stairways in accessible buildings and facilities shall comply with Section D-7.2.

D-7.2.1 STEPS   ADA: C-5.7.2, C-5.7.3

Stair nosing shall not project more than 1.5 inches beyond the face of the riser below. Treads shall be slip-resistant and have a smooth, rounded, or chamfered exposed edge with no abrupt edge at the nosing. Open risers are not permitted unless an exception is granted
a) when the enforcing agency determines that compliance would create an undue hardship and when equivalent facilitation is provided, or
b) in existing buildings where legal or physical constraints do not allow compliance with the accessibility building standards or equivalent facilitation without creating an undue hardship.

D-7.2.2 STRIPING

Striping shall be provided to alert the visually impaired. The upper approach and lower tread of each stair shall have at least a 2-inch wide contrasting color strip placed parallel to and not more than 1 inch from the step nosing. (Fig. 98) The striping shall be slip-resistant like the treads. In addition, outside stairways shall also have the striping on all treads. The striping may be painted strips.

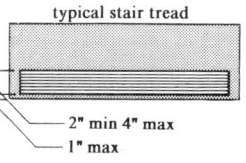

Fig. 98 **Striping Detail**

CALIFORNIA ACCESS CODE • TITLE 24
BUILDING ELEMENTS • Stairs

D-7.2.3 HANDRAILS ADA: C-1.2.12, C-6.5.1, C-5.7.4

Handrails shall comply with the following requirements.

1. **Placement**
   Stairways shall have handrails on each side. In individual dwelling units in Group R, Division 1 or 3 occupancies, a stairway may have only one handrail except handrails shall be provided on all open sides. Private stairways 30 inches or less in height may have one handrail.

2. **Intermediate Handrail**
   Stairways exceeding 88 inches wide shall provide an intermediate handrail for each 88-inch width of stairway.

3. **Configuration**
   Handrails shall comply with Sections C-5.7.4(5-7). In areas where a handrail extension would create a hazard along the direction of the stair, the extension may be rounded or returned smoothly to the floor. On continuous stairs from landing to landing, the inner handrail shall be continuous and need not extend onto the landing.

4. **Handrail Features** ADA: C-6.5.2, C-6.5.3
   Handrails shall comply with Sections C-6.5.2 and C-6.5.3.

5. **Exceptions:**
   a) An exception shall be granted on 3 and 4 above when the enforcing agency determines that compliance would create an undue hardship and when equivalent facilitation is provided, or
   b) Existing buildings where legal or physical constraints do not allow compliance with the accessibility building standards or equivalent facilitation without creating an undue hardship.

CALIFORNIA ACCESS CODE • TITLE 24
BUILDING ELEMENTS • Stairs

D-7.2.4 SIGNS ^{ADA: C-3.3.2}

An identification sign shall be placed at each enclosed stairway floor landing in buildings with four or more stories and with two or more stories for OSA/ACS requirements. The sign shall meet the following requirements:

1. **Identify**
   - stairway
   - roof access
   - floor level
   - upper or lower terminus of the stairway
2. **Presentation**
   - raised Arabic numerals
   - raised braille symbols
   - comply with Section D-5.3
3. **Location**
   Identification signs shall be placed approximately 5 feet above the landing and be readily visible with the door open or closed or be placed approximately 5 feet above the landing adjacent to the strike side of the door as required by OSA/ACS.

CALIFORNIA ACCESS CODE • TITLE 24
FIXTURES • Automated Teller Machines

D-8 FIXTURES

D-8.1 AUTOMATED TELLER MACHINES

D-8.1.1 APPLICATION ADA: C-1.3.20, C-6.1.1

An automated teller machine (ATM) is any electronic information processing device structurally affixed to a building or other structure including a point-of-sale machine which is used by a financial or other business entity for the primary purpose of executing financial transactions between itself and its customers. An ATM site is the immediate area to which one or more ATM is or will be installed. Section D-8.1.1 applies to ATMs used by the public in grocery stores, ticket sales, and other business entities but not card reading devices at vehicle facilities and fuel pumps. ATMs provided for the public shall comply with Section D-8.1.

Exceptions:
1. ATMs located at accessible individual checkstands in grocery stores and retail outlets. AMTs must be accessible when (a) located away from individual checkstands and (b) located at accessible checkstands.
2. An exception shall be granted when the enforcing agency determines that compliance for an existing ATM undergoing an alteration would create an undue hardship and when equivalent facilitation is provided.
3. Existing buildings where the legal or physical constraints do not allow compliance with the accessibility building standards or equivalent facilitation without creating an undue hardship.

4. Drive-up only ATMs are not required to comply with Section D-8.1.
5. Card reading devices at vehicle fuel pumps and facilities are not required to comply with Section D-8.1.

D-8.1.2 CONTROLS ^{ADA: C-6.3.2}

Controls for user activation shall comply with the requirements of Section C-6.3.2.

D-8.1.3 REACH RANGES ^{ADA: C-6.1.3, C-2.3.3}

The clearance and reach range at free standing or built-in ATM units not having a clear space under them shall comply with the following:

1. **One ATM**
   Where one ATM is provided at a location, it shall meet the specifications of Sections C-6.1, C-6.3.3, and C-6.3.4. (It is the intent of the OSA to amend this provision by emergency regulation if the Department of Justice amends their federal regulation.)
2. **Two ATMs**
   Where two ATMs are provided at a location, one shall comply with Sections C-6.3.3, C-6.3.4, and C-2.3.3(1). The other units height or display height is not required to comply with these requirements.
3. **Three ATMs or more**
   Where three or more ATMs are provided at a location, two shall meet the requirements for two ATMs preceding. The others shall comply with Sections C-6.3.3 and D-8.1.4.

CALIFORNIA ACCESS CODE • TITLE 24
FIXTURES • Automated Teller Machines

D-8.1.4 ALTERNATE SIDE REACH

Where a side reach is required for ATMs, the following provisions can be used as an alternative to the side reach requirements of Section C-2.3.3(2).

1. **Reach depth of 10 inches or less.**
   The maximum height above the floor shall be 54 inches when the reach depth does not exceed 10 inches.
2. **Reach depth more than 10 inches.**
   The maximum height above the floor shall comply with Figure 99 when the reach depth exceeds 10 inches.

The reach depth to the operable parts of any control shall be measured from the vertical plane perpendicular to the edge of the unobstructed clear floor space at the farthest protrusion of the ATM or its surrounding unit.

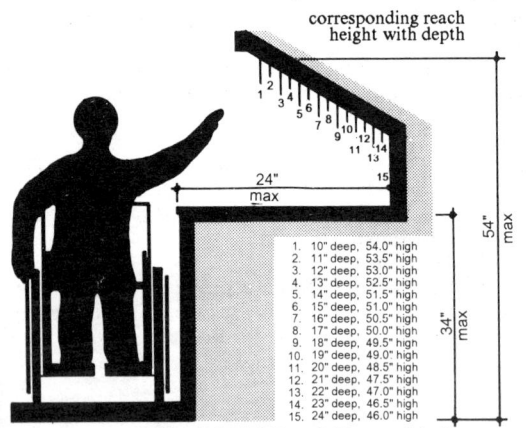

1. 10" deep, 54.0" high
2. 11" deep, 53.5" high
3. 12" deep, 53.0" high
4. 13" deep, 52.5" high
5. 14" deep, 51.5" high
6. 15" deep, 51.0" high
7. 16" deep, 50.5" high
8. 17" deep, 50.0" high
9. 18" deep, 49.5" high
10. 19" deep, 49.0" high
11. 20" deep, 48.5" high
12. 21" deep, 47.5" high
13. 22" deep, 47.0" high
14. 23" deep, 46.5" high
15. 24" deep, 46.0" high

Fig. 99 **ATM Reach Range Limits**

CALIFORNIA ACCESS CODE • TITLE 24
FIXTURES • Automated Teller Machines

D-8.1.5 DISPLAY

LED, Cathode Ray, or other screen devices for viewing shall be positioned for usability and visibility by persons sitting in a wheelchair at approximately a 45-inch eye level and comply with the following:

1. **Vertical Mounted Screen**
   The center line of screens shall be a maximum of 52 inches above grade when mounted vertical or tipped within 30 degrees away from the user.
2. **Angle Mounted Screen**
   The center line of screens shall be a maximum of 44 inches above grade when mounted vertical or tipped between 30 to 60 degrees away from the user.
3. **Horizontal Mounted Screen**
   The screen center line shall be a maximum of 34 inches above grade when mounted at an angle between 60 and 90 degrees away from the user.

ATMs are exempt from Section D-8.1.5 if the ATM is unregulated in height required by Section D-8.1

D-8.1.5 VISION IMPAIRMENT ADA: C-6.1.4

ATMs shall comply with Section C-6.1.4 to accommodate those with vision impairments.

D-8.2 CONTROLS   ADA: C-1.3.19, C-6.3, C-6.4.3

Controls and operating devices shall comply with the requirements of Section C-6.3 and Sections 210-50(e), 380-8(c), and 760-8.1 of the California Electrical Code for electrical installation.

CALIFORNIA ACCESS CODE · TITLE 24
FIXTURES · Drinking Fountains · Fixed Seating

D-8.3 DRINKING FOUNTAINS
ADA: C-1.3.17, C-6.4

When provided, drinking fountains shall be positioned within alcoves at least 32 inched wide, 18 inches deep, and shall not encroach into pedestrian pathways. (Fig. 99)

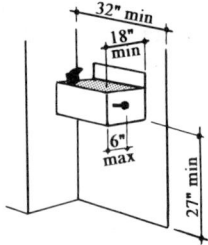 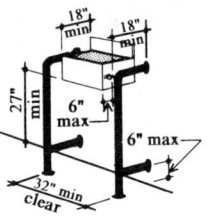

Fig. 100(a) **Alcove**   Fig. 100(b) **Wing Wall**
Fig. 100 **Drinking Fountains**

D-8.4.1 APPLICATION
ADA: C-1.3.11, C-6.7.1, C-7.5

Fixed seating, tables, and counters required to be accessible shall comply with Sections C-1.3.11 and C-6.7 with the exception that knee clearance is not required at checkstands.

D-8.4 FIXED SEATING · COUNTERS

D-8.4.2 WORK SURFACE HEIGHT
ADA: C-6.7.4

Work surface heights shall be between 28 and 34 inches above the floor. At least 5 percent and never less than one of each type of station shall have a counter at least 36 inches

CALIFORNIA ACCESS CODE • TITLE 24
FIXTURES • Fixed Seating • Counters

each type of station shall have a counter at least 36 inches long with a maximum height between 28 and 34 inches where a single counter contains more than one transaction station.

D-8.4.3 AISLES

Each building area where installed seats, tables, equipment, merchandise, or similarly provided fixtures and materials shall have an access aisle leading to an exit. Access aisles and every aisle serving one side of a fixture shall be at least 36 inches wide and 42 inches wide when serving both sides. The minimum width shall be measured at the farthest point from an exit and increased by 1.5 inches for each 5 feet in length toward the exit including across aisles or a foyer. Continental seating side-aisles shall not be less than 44 inches wide.

D-8.5 VENDING MACHINES
ADA: C-7.5.7

Vending machines shall comply with the control and operating mechanism requirements of Section D-8.2.

INDEX

A

access aisle, 7
accessibility, 7, 49
   alteration, 18, 65, 281
   assembly facilities, 96, 136, 239
   auxiliary aids, 50
   bath facilities, 86, 98, 148, 191, 204, 325
   buildings, 64
   communication, 51
   corridors, 283, 294
   curb ramps, 88, 306
   dining facilities, 243
   doors, 93, 166, 292, 337
   dressing rooms, 86, 97
   drinking fountain, 99, 195
   elevators, 82, 87, 94, 172, 295
   employee areas, 82, 288
   entrances, 92, 143, 284
   maximum extent, 18
   minimum requirements, 81
   new construction, 18
   parking, 90, 144, 290, 321
   path of travel, 65
   platform lift, 87, 284
   primary function area, 85
   priority order, 66
   ramps, 88, 285, 303
   reach range, 117, 131
   religious facilities, 245
   rescue assistance, 95, 107
   route of travel, 89, 105, 283
   seating, 97, 350
   service entrance, 25
   shower stall, 151, 291, 327
   signs, 124, 147, 286, 289, 317
   stairs, 93
   storage, 154, 291
   symbol, 17
   telephones, 88, 99, 131, 133, 134, 290, 318
   toilet rooms, 86, 97, 156, 208, 291, 330
   wheelchair space, 96, 287
accommodations
   public, 21
ADA, 4, 8
   enforcement, 69
   implementation, 64, 73
   law, 37
   violation, 62, 72
ADAAG, 8
administration
   authority, 8
   enforcing agency, 15
   entity, 23
   official, 26
aids
   auxiliary, 9, 96
   interpreter, 23
   volume controls, 133

INDEX

aisle
　access, 7, 351
alarms
　audible, 120, 314
　auxiliary, 122
　minimum requirements, 288
　vibrator, 122
　visual, 120, 314
alteration, 8, 65
　barriers, 59
　bath facilities, 86
　cost, 66
　curb ramps, 88
　doors, 88
　dressing room, 86
　elevators, 85, 87
　exceptions, 283
　historic property, 102, 288
　limitations, 281
　maximum extent, 18
　minimum requirements, 282
　performing area, 86
　ramps, 88
　sleeping units, 215
　telephones, 88
　toilet rooms, 86
　undue burden, 28, 282
　unfeasible, 27
　valuation, 282
alternatives
　barrier removal, 10, 32
animal, 25
architect, state, 234

architecture
　compliance, 63
　discrimination, 63
assembly areas, 136, 239, 254
　A-occupancy, 238
　auditoriums, 239
　club rooms, 243
　dining areas, 243
　entrances, 244
　exceptions, 239, 241, 242, 243
　listening system, 138
　minimum requirements, 96
　performing areas, 137, 241
　public areas, 241
　religious facilities, 245
　route of travel, 136
　seating, 53, 86, 136, 242, 244
　sport facility, 241
　sport participation areas, 242
　theaters, 239
　ticket booths, 239, 241
　toilet rooms, 245
　wheelchair space, 96, 136, 239
assistive facilities
　auxiliary aids, 9
　interpreter, 23
　listening system, 96, 138, 246
　signs, 247
　TDD, 27
　text telephone, 27
　volume control, 133
ATM, 9
　application, 346

354

INDEX

clear space, 190
controls, 347
exceptions, 346
minimum requirements, 101
reach range, 347
screen, 348
vision impairment, 190, 349
auxiliary aids, 9, 51
alarms, 120, 314
alternatives, 52
courses, 56
education facility, 55
exception, 52
listening system, 96, 138, 246
services, 51
warning system, 101

B

barrier
architectural, 9
communication, 12
barrier removal, 10, 58
achievable, 23
alteration, 59
alternatives, 10, 32
cinema, 61
fixtures, 60
good faith effort, 16, 32
maximum, 18
obligation, 60
plan, 32
priority order, 59
ramps, 61
remedies, 61
tax credits, 27
transportation, 57
undue burden, 28
bath facilities
application, 148, 325
bathtubs, 149, 191, 325
doors, 149
dwelling, 276, 277
fixtures, 150
lavatories, 149, 200
lockers, 329
minimum requirements, 98, 291
mirrors, 149
shower stall, 149
toilets, 149, 206
unisex, 86
urinal, 149, 335
wheelchair space, 148, 326
bathtubs
application, 149
enclosure, 191, 326, 329
faucet, 191
grab bars, 192, 326
seat, 191, 197, 199, 326
wheelchair space, 193
bench
dressing rooms, 142
building
accessibility, 64
adaptability, 8

INDEX

addition, see alteration
alteration, 281
assembly, 9
egress, 95, 284
entrances, 92, 143, 284
ground floor, 16
level, 26
multi-family, 272
multi-story, 273
official, 10
owner, 11
parks, 267
tenant, 11
building code, *"see code"*
building department
enforcement, 235
building elements, 15
accessibility, 7
curb ramps, 163
doors, 166, 292, 337, 342
elevators, 82, 94, 172, 295
floor, 180, 292
ramps, 182
stairs, 93, 186, 343
windows, 189
building fixtures
ATM, 190, 346
bathtubs, 191, 325
dispensers, 336
drinking fountain, 99, 195, 349
fixed seating, 350
grab bars, 197, 326, 328, 334
handrails, 197, 344
lavatories, 200, 335
lockers, 329
merchandise display, 99
mirrors, 335
sink, 204
telephones, 99, 318
urinals, 335
work stations, 350

C

California
  access code, 231
  Title 24, 231
  UBC amendments, 234
care facilities
  alteration, 220
  application, 219, 262
  entrance, 221, 262
  hospitals, 219, 261
  medical, 219
  minimum requirements, 81, 261
  nursing homes, 219, 261
  offices, 263
  parking, 92
  patient bedroom, 221, 263
  prisons, 262
  rehabilitation, 219
  sanitariums, 262
  toilet room, 221, 264
  treatment areas, 263

INDEX

carpet, 181
civil action
    Attorney General, 70
    authority, 70
    enforcement, 70
    injunctive relief, 69
    penalties, 20, 32
civil rights
    legislation, 11
clear spaces
    door openings, 107
    doorway, 170
    floor, 11, 115
    height, 113
    pedestrian traffic, 113
    protruding objects, 110
    route of travel, 106
    telephone, 133
    toilet rooms, 157
    wheelchair space, 109, 114, 137
club
    private, 21
code, 11
    application, 232
    California Access Code, 231
    certification, 10, 74
    minimum requirements, 231
    model, 18, 78
    state fire, 233
    submittal, 74
    submitting official, 26
    UBC, 28
    validity, 236
code certification
    application, 74
    code, 74
    denied, 76
    equivalency, 11
    preliminary, 21, 77
    procedure, 74
code classification
    A-occupancy, 238
    B-occupancy, 248
    E-occupancy, 256
    H-occupancy, 259
    I-occupancy, 261
    M-occupancy, 264
    R-occupancy, 267
commerce, 12
    clause, 12
commercial facility, 12
    lodging, 214
    mercantile, 222, 250
    offices, 249
    requirements, 38
    restaurants, 224, 243
    sports, 241
    theater, 239
common areas, 12, 273
communication, 51
    alarms, 314
    barrier, 12
    detectable warnings, 123, 315
    interpreter, 23
    listening system, 96

INDEX

lodging facilities, 213
nondiscrimination, 5
rescue assistance, 109
signs, 85, 89, 109, 124, 317
tactile, 27
TDD, 27
telephones, 88, 99, 131, 290, 318
text telephone, 27
compliance, 32
  alterations, 18
  Attorney General, 70
  law, 37
  maximum, 18
  new construction, 18
  undue burden, 28
  violation, 72
construction, 63
  cost, 66
  discrimination, 63
  exceptions, 64
  infeasibility, 27
  minimum requirements, 81
  new, 18
  site, 25
  standards, 13
controls
  ATM, 347
  elevators, 297
  minimum requirements, 101
  operating, 19, 193, 349
  reach range, 194
  showers, 153
  volume, 133
  wheelchair space, 194
corridors, 284, 294
  exception, 295
cost
  disproportionate, 14, 66
  tax credits, 27
  undue burden, 28
  valuation threshold, 281
counters, 350
  dwelling, 276
  work surface, 350
crosswalk
  grade separation, 19
curb ramps, 13, 163, 266
  alteration, 88
  border, 307
  curb cut, 13
  detectable warning, 102, 164, 289, 307, 316
  exceptions, 313
  flared sides, 164
  grade separation, 19, 166, 313
  landing, 307
  marked crossings, 17
  placement, 166
  ramp, 23, 164, 306
  slope, 88, 163, 183, 306
  surface, 163, 307

INDEX

D

detectable warning, 13, 123, 315
   curb ramp, 164, 289, 307, 316
   minimum requirements, 102, 289
   pools, 124
   truncated domes, 123
   vehicle area, 124, 315

disabled person
   cane techniques, 111
   disability, 14
   reach range, 131
   service animal, 25
   visually impaired, 111

discrimination, 4
   administrative control, 45
   architecture, 63
   Attorney General, 70
   construction, 63
   enforcement, 15
   equal benefits, 44
   equal opportunity, 42
   equal participation, 42
   insurance, 39
   law, 37
   violation, 72

doors
   automatic, 9, 167, 338
   B occupancy, 339
   bath facilities, 149
   closer, 170
   design, 342
   double-leaf, 166, 337
   dressing rooms, 142
   exceptions, 338, 339, 342
   gates, 167
   hardware, 168, 338
   kick plate, 17
   minimum requirements, 93, 166, 292
   opening, 88, 169, 337
   opening force, 171
   passage, 19, 337
   power-assisted, 20
   R occupancy, 339
   revolving, 167, 337
   series, 167
   thresholds, 88
   toilet room, 156
   turnstile, 167, 342

doorways
   clear spaces, 170
   dwelling, 273
   landing, 292, 340
   route of travel, 107
   thresholds, 168, 341

dormitory, 14, 270

dressing rooms, 142
   bench, 142
   doors, 142
   mercantile facility, 252
   minimum requirements, 97

INDEX

    mirrors, 142
    wheelchair space, 143
drinking fountain
    application, 195, 349
    controls, 196
    minimum requirements, 99
    wheelchair space, 196
dwelling, 14
    adaptable, 8, 273
    grab bars, 279
    lavatory, 279
    multi-family, 18, 272
    shower, 278

E

education facilities, 38, 256
    auxiliary aids, 55
    courses, 54, 56
    laboratory rooms, 258
    libraries, 257
elevators, 68
    application, 172, 295
    bank, 15
    call buttons, 173, 297
    car, 295
    communication, 179, 298
    control panel, 175
    exception, 68, 295, 299
    floor area, 177
    floor designations, 172, 296, 298
    handrails, 296
    illumination, 172, 296
    lanterns, 174, 298
    lobby, 299
    location indicator, 176
    minimum requirements, 82, 87, 94, 284
    operation, 177
    platform lift, 26, 87, 182, 300
    reopening device, 178, 297
    signal timing, 178, 296
    smoke-detection, 299
    standby power, 299
employee
    employment, 4
employee areas
    minimum requirements, 82, 288
    sales station, 250
    work station, 29, 202, 350
enforcement, 15, 69
    agencies, 235
    Attorney General, 70
    building department, 235
    civil action, 69
    court, 70
entity, 21
    private, 21
    public, 23
    religious, 24
entrances, 15
    application, 143
    assembly areas, 244
    care facility, 262, 263, 268

INDEX

doors, 93
dwelling, 273
level, 21
minimum requirements, 92, 284
primary, 21
route of travel, 143
service, 25, 143
undue burden, 285
escalator, *"see elevators"*
exceptions
   alteration, 283
   animals, 58
   assembly areas, 239
   ATM, 346
   auxiliary aids, 52
   B occupancy, 339
   construction, 64
   corridors, 295
   curb ramps, 313
   dining areas, 243
   discrimination, 46
   doors, 338, 339, 342
   elevator, 68, 237, 295, 299
   floor, 293
   handrails, 305, 344
   park buildings, 265
   parking, 323, 324
   performing area, 241
   platform lift, 300
   private club, 21, 38
   privately funded, 237
   protruding objects, 287
   public entities, 38
   R occupancy, 339
   religious facility, 38
   toilet rooms, 292, 332
exits
   minimum requirement, 95, 284
   rescue assistance, 95, 287

F

facilitation
   equivalent, 15, 134
facility, 16
   areas, 136
   assembly areas, 96, 136, 239
   bath facilities, 98, 148
   care facilities, 16, 219
   club rooms, 243
   commercial, 12
   dining areas, 243, 255
   dressing rooms, 97
   E occupancy, 256
   education facilities, 256
   egress, 95, 284
   elements, 163
   employee areas, 288
   exceptions, 242, 243
   factories, 254
   fences, 264
   food preparation areas, 245
   food service aisles, 244
   full-time care, 261

INDEX

H occupancy, 259
hazardous material, 259
I occupancy, 261
libraries, 209, 257
locker rooms, 242
lodging, 267
M occupancy, 264
medical, 219
mercantile, 222, 250
offices, 249
parking, 145, 290, 321
parks, 265
private, 264
public service, 254
public use, 253
R occupancy, 267
religious facility, 245
restaurants, 224, 255
self-service areas, 244
services, 253
shopping center, 25
sport facility, 241
sport participation area, 242
toilet rooms, 97, 245, 291, 330
transportation, 227
warehouse, 254
fire-resistant, 16
floor
    alcove, 115
    carpet, 181
    clear space, 11, 115, 137
    exceptions, 293
    grating, 181
    level change, 180
    minimum requirements, 292
    surface, 105, 137, 180
function area
    entrance, 21
    minimum requirements, 85
    primary, 21
funded
    construction, 23
    multi-family, 272
    privately, 21, 233
    publicly, 232

G

grab bars, 16
    application, 197
    bathtub, 192
    dwelling, 279
    showers, 154
    size, 197
    spacing, 197
    structural strength, 199
    surface, 199
    toilet rooms, 334
    toilets, 159, 207
grating, 181
guard rail, 16

INDEX

H

handrails
  application, 197
  exceptions, 305, 344
  extensions, 88
  ramps, 184, 305
  size, 197
  spacing, 197
  stairs, 187, 344
  structural strength, 199
  surface, 199
hardship, 29, 282
  entrances, 285
hazard materials, 259
historic property, 17, 67
  alteration, 102
  alternatives, 103
  minimum requirements, 102, 288
  qualified, 102
  state officer, 103

I

insurance
  nondiscrimination, 39
international symbol
  accessibility, 17, 289, 317

K

kick plate, 17
kitchen
  dwelling, 273
  lodging, 270

L

landlord
  obligation, 38
  path of travel, 66
laundry room
  dwelling, 277
lavatories, 149, 157
  application, 200
  faucets, 200
  height, 200
  mirrors, 201
law
  civil rights, 11
  conflict, 40
  enforcement, 15, 69
  implementation, 73
  landlord, 38
  obligation, 37
  tenant, 38
libraries, 257
  aisles, 209
  application, 209
  checkout area, 210

INDEX

    minimum requirements, 81
    reach range, 210
    reading areas, 209
    stacks, 209
lift, *"see platform lift"*
listening system
    assembly areas, 96, 138
    exceptions, 247
    religious facility, 246
    types, 138
    volume control, 133
loading zone, 90, 144, 291
lockers, 329
    exception, 242
lodging
    adaptable unit, 273
    alarms, 211, 270
    application, 210, 267
    bath facilities, 271
    choice, 269
    commercial facilities, 214
    common areas, 211, 270
    communication devices, 213
    dormitory, 270
    funding, 272
    guest rooms, 269
    kitchens, 270
    minimum requirements, 81, 211
    multi-family, 272
    multi-story, 273
    recreational facilities, 271
    social services, 216
    telephones, 211
    transient, 28, 269

M

mercantile
    application, 222
    ATM, 101, 251
    check-out areas, 223, 250
    counters, 222
    display, 99
    dressing room, 86, 252
    minimum requirements, 81, 250
    security bollards, 224, 251
mezzanine, 18
minimum requirements, 81, 281
    alarms, 288
    alteration, 83, 281
    assembly areas, 96, 239
    controls, 101
    curb ramps, 88
    design, 81
    detectable warning, 102, 289
    dining areas, 243
    doors, 93
    elevators, 82, 87, 94, 284
    employee areas, 82, 288
    entrances, 92, 244
    exits, 284
    floor, 292
    food service aisles, 244

INDEX

   impracticable, 82
   locker rooms, 242
   parking, 290
   performing area, 86
   platform lift, 87, 300
   ramps, 88, 285
   rescue assistance, 287
   route of travel, 89, 283
   seating, 86, 239, 242, 244
   self-service areas, 244
   signs, 85, 289
   special use, 81
   sport facilities, 241
   stairs, 93
   telephones, 290
   temporary structures, 82
   toilet rooms, 242, 245
   warning system, 101
   wheelchair space, 287
mirrors, 157
   bath facilities, 149
   dressing room, 142
   lavatory, 201
   toilet rooms, 335

N

non-ambulatory, 19
noncompliance
   penalties, 20
nondiscrimination, 42, 72
   conduct, 45
   equal benefits, 44
   equal opportunity, 42
   equal participation, 42
   public accommodation, 43

O

obligation
   barrier removal, 60
   landlord/tenant, 38
   law, 37
   path of travel, 66
occupancy
   care facilities, 219
   group, 237
   group A, 238
   group E, 256
   group H, 259
   group I, 261
   group M, 264
   group R, 267
   libraries, 209
   mercantile, 222
   multi-family, 18
   restaurants, 224
   special use, 81
office facilities, 249

P

parking, 147
   access aisle, 145
   accessibility, 90

INDEX

care facilities, 92, 290
design, 323
exceptions, 323, 324
facilities, 145
loading zones, 90, 144, 291
minimum requirements, 90, 290
parks, 266
ramps, 323
signs, 147, 324
spaces, 91, 144, 145, 321, 323
structure, 323
valet, 90, 291
van, 91, 146, 321
parks
  buildings, 267
  campsites, 266
  parking, 266
  rest areas, 266
  toilets, 267
  trails, 267
path of travel, 19, 105
  also see route of travel
  alterations, 65
  corridors, 284, 294
  cost, 66
  entrance, 21
  exterior, 286
  grade separation, 19, 313
  grating, 181
  landlord, 66
  obligation, 66
  priority order, 66
  protruding objects, 110, 286
  ramps, 23, 182, 285, 303
  surface, 180
  tenant, 66
pedestrian traffic, 19
  circulation, 11
  grade separation, 19
  marked crossings, 17
  route of travel, 19, 105
  walkway, 20
  wheelchair space, 113
penalty, 20
  court, 70
  noncompliance, 32
platform lift
  application, 300
  exceptions, 300
  landings, 301
  minimum requirements, 87, 284
  operation, 182, 302
  ramp, 302
  safety, 301
  special access, 26
priority order
  standards, 233
protruding objects, 286
  exceptions, 287
  projection, 110
public
  use, 23
public accommodation, 21
  animals, 58

INDEX

construction, 63
nondiscrimination, 5, 43
place, 20
residence, 67
special use, 49, 81
transportation, 56
violation, 62

R

ramps, 23
  alteration, 88
  application, 303
  barrier removal, 61
  curb ramps, 164, 306
  exterior, 184
  guard rail, 16
  handrails, 184, 305
  landings, 183, 303
  minimum requirement, 88, 182, 285
  platform lift, 302
  protection, 184
  slope, 88, 183, 303
  surface, 183
reach range
  ATM, 347
  controls, 194
  from wheelchair, 117
regulations
  enforcement, 235
  Fire Marshal, 233
  law, 37
  modifications, 57
  priority order, 233
religious facilities, 24, 245
rescue assistance
  area, 9, 24, 107
  communication, 109
  emergency egress, 107
  minimum requirements, 95, 287
  non-ambulatory, 19
  signs, 109
  stairs, 109
  wheelchair space, 109
residence
  congregate, 13
  public accommodation, 38
responsibility
  law, 37
  owner, 11
  tenant, 11
restaurants
  A-occupancy, 243
  aisles, 226
  application, 224
  B-occupancy, 255
  counters, 225
  dining areas, 225
  food preparation, 245
  minimum requirements, 81
  raised platforms, 227
  seating, 244

INDEX

    self-service areas, 226, 244
    service lines, 226, 244
    vending machines, 227
route of travel, 105, 283
    accessible, 7
    also see *"path of travel"*
    application, 105
    assembly areas, 136
    corridors, 284, 294
    door, 19
    doorways, 107
    egress, 14, 107
    emergency exits, 107
    exterior, 286
    grade separation, 313
    grating, 181
    height, 113
    location, 107
    marked crossings, 17
    minimum requirements, 89, 283
    multiple, 286
    path, 19
    pedestrian traffic, 113
    protruding objects, 110, 286
    ramps, 182, 285, 303
    rescue assistance, 107
    slope, 105
    stairs, 186
    surface, 105, 180
    wheelchair space, 106

S

seat
    bathtub, 197
    shower, 151, 152, 154, 197
    structural strength, 199
seating, 137
    assembly areas, 97, 136, 239
    dining areas, 244
    minimum requirements, 86, 97, 350
    sport facilities, 242
    tables, 202
shelves
    dwelling, 276
shopping center, 25
showers
    application, 149, 291, 325, 326
    bathtub, 191
    controls, 153
    curb, 152, 327
    dwelling, 278
    enclosures, 152, 327, 329
    floor, 327
    grab bars, 154, 328
    hand sprayer, 328
    open, 328
    roll-in, 215
    seat, 151, 197, 199, 327
    size, 151
    stall, 150, 327

INDEX

signs, 25
   application, 124, 317, 318
   Braille, 131, 317
   dimensions, 130
   finish, 130
   handset symbol, 125
   hearing loss, 127
   illumination, 127
   international symbol, 125, 286, 289, 317
   minimum requirements, 85, 89, 286, 289, 317
   parking, 147, 324
   pictograph, 131
   placement, 124, 125, 317
   raised characters, 131
   rescue assistance, 109
   stairs, 345
   symbols, 126, 131
   toilet rooms, 85, 330
sinks, 204
   wheelchair space, 204
site, 25
   accessibility, 7
   improvement, 25
slope
   cross, 13
   curb ramps, 163
   route of travel, 105
   running, 24, 183
space
   accessible, 8
   occupiable, 19

stairs
   exterior, 189
   handrail, 88, 187, 344
   minimum requirements, 93, 186
   nosing, 186, 343
   rescue assistance, 95, 109, 287
   riser, 24, 186, 343
   signs, 345
   striping, 343
   tread, 28, 186, 343
standards
   construction, 13
   Fire Marshal, 233
states, 26
storage
   application, 154
   fixed, 98
   hardware, 154
   hazardous material, 259
   minimum requirements, 98, 291
   reach range, 155
   wheelchair space, 154
structural
   frame, 26
   infeasibility, 27
   strength, 199
surface
   cross slope, 13
   grating, 181
   running slope, 24, 183

INDEX

symbols
  international, 17

T

taxes
  credits, 27
TDD, 27, 52
telephones
  accessories, 133, 134
  alternative, 134
  application, 131, 318
  bank, 101
  closed circuit, 11
  controls, 133
  enclosures, 319
  floor space, 133
  minimum requirements, 99, 290
  portable, 134
  reach range, 131
  text, 27, 52, 88, 99, 134, 320
  volume control, 99, 133
tenant
  obligation, 38
terminology, 7
ticket booths, 239, 241
toilet rooms, 18
  aisle, 333
  application, 156, 330
  assembly areas, 245
  dispensers, 336
  doors, 156, 331, 333
  dwelling, 277
  exceptions, 292, 332
  fixtures, 157
  grab bars, 334
  lavatories, 157, 200, 335
  lodging, 270, 272
  minimum requirements, 97, 291
  mirrors, 157, 335
  multiple accommodation, 332
  paper dispensers, 207
  restaurants, 245
  signs, 85, 330
  single accommodation, 331
  stall, 87, 156, 159, 160, 332
  symbols, 331
  toilets, 156, 332
  unisex, 86, 157
  urinal, 156
  walls, floors, 335
  wheelchair space, 157, 331, 332
toilets, 149, 156, 206
  grab bars, 159, 207
  multiple, 18, 332
  paper dispensers, 207, 336
  portable, 98
  stall, 149, 156, 159
  wheelchair space, 208
transportation, 56, 227
  barrier removal, 56, 57
  detectable warning, 316

INDEX

minimum requirements, 81
nondiscrimination, 4
platform, 23
public, 26
terminal, 28

U

undue burden, 282
    entrances, 285
urinals, 149, 156, 205, 335
    wheelchair space, 205

V

valuation threshold, 281
    alteration, 282
vehicle
    accessibility, 73
    vehicular way, 29
    warning strip, 124
vending machines, 227, 351
violation, 72
    ADA, 62

W

walkway
    detectable warnings, 123
    grating, 181
    marked crossings, 17
    pedestrian traffic, 113
    protruding objects, 110, 286
    surface, 180
warning system
    alarms, 120, 314
    detectable warning, 123, 289, 307, 315
    emergency, 101
wheelchair, 29
    reach range, 117, 131
wheelchair lift, see platform lift
wheelchair space
    assembly areas, 96, 136, 239, 244
    bath facilities, 193, 326
    clear space, 115
    controls, 194
    drinking fountain, 196
    lavatories, 200
    minimum requirements, 287
    pedestrian traffic, 113
    religious facilities, 245
    rescue assistance, 109
    route of travel, 106
    sink, 204
    tables, 201
    toilet room, 157, 208, 331, 332
    turning space, 114, 143
    urinals, 205
windows, 189

NOTES

Amendment 93-3

The **California Access Code** was adopted at the Building Standards Commission meeting on March 5, 1993. The new revisions (■) are:

- *Delete the "**primary entrance**" definition and the word "**primary**" when used with entrance in Sections D-2.2.3.2, D-2.5.2, and D-3.3.4.*

- **"publicly funded"** and **"privately funded"** (Delete definitions.)

- Fig. 91 **Toilet Rooms** *change accessible side door dimension from 32" to 34" to conform with text.*

- **D-2.2.4.5(6) Usage Fee** *(Add the following)*
  No surcharge shall be placed on any particular individual, or group of individuals, with a disability to cover the cost of such equipment.

- **D-2.3.2.6 FACTORIES · WAREHOUSES** *(Add the following.)*
  Factories and warehouses shall also conform to the provisions of Section D-2.1 and D-2.1, Exception 2, for multistory buildings. *[Change the wording* "entry level" *to* "level entry" *under Section D-2.3.3.6(b).]*

- *Replace* **Exception 1(b) of Section D-3.3.4 Entrances · Exits** *with:*
  (b) Exits in excess of those required by Section D-3.5 that are 24" above grade. The door shall have a warning sign of inaccessibility that complies with Section D-5.3.

- **D-7.1.4(1) LANDINGS** *(Add the following.)*
  Exception:
  A 44" minimum length opposite the direction of the door swing is allowed when:
  1) the door has no latch and a wheelchair approach can be made from the latch side; or
  2) the door has no latch or closer and a wheelchair approach can be made from the hinge side.

- **D-8.1.1, Exception 5** and the **ATM** *definition's last sentence shall be changed to read* "An ATM does not include card reading devices at motor vehicle fuel pump islands or fuel facilities."

D-8.1.3 REACH RANGES (*Replaces Sections D-8.1.3 and D-8.1.4*)

1. One ATM at a location
The ATM shall meet the specifications of Section C-6.1 as follows:
  a) The clear floor space shall allow a wheelchair forward approach, parallel approach, or both to the machine.
  b) Controls reached from the **forward approach** shall comply with Section C-2.3.3(1)
  c) Controls reached from the **parallel approach** shall be placed as follows:
   The reach depth to the operable parts of any control shall be measured from the vertical plane perpendicular to the edge of the unobstructed clear floor space at the farthest protrusion of the ATM or its surrounding unit.
   - **Reach depth of 10 inches or less:** The maximum height above the floor shall be 54 inches when the reach depth does not exceed 10 inches.
   - **Reach depth more than 10 inches:** The maximum height above the floor shall comply with Figure 99 when the reach depth exceeds 10 inches.
  d) Access to controls with a possible **forward and parallel** approach shall be within one of the reach ranges of (b) or (c).
  e) At least one ATM **bin** of each type provided for supplies, waste, or other uses shall comply with the applicable reach range of (b), (c) or (d).
  f) At least one of each function **control** type shall comply with this section. When a control is identified by tactile markings, all controls shall be so identified.

2. Two ATMs at location
Two ATMs shall provide one that complies with Section D-8.1.3(1) except the highest operable part shall be no higher than 48 inches. The second ATM and it's display are not regulated to height.

3. Three ATMs or more at location
Two ATMs shall comply with Section D-8.1.3(1) when more than two ATMs are provided. At least 50% of all ATMs exceeding the first two shall comply with Section D-8.1.3(1). No height restrictions are placed on those not required to comply. All provided features shall be equally represented among the accessible ATMs.

NOTES

ADA REGISTRATION FORM

Please register me for updates.

Name: _____

Company: _____

Address: _____

City: _____ State: ____ Zip: _____

Phone: ( ) _____

Profession or business: _____

I am also interested in the following:

☐ SELF-SURVEY KIT

☐ ADA SURVEYED DECAL

ACR Group
P. O. Box 720808
San Diego, CA 92172

ADA

♿

SURVEYED

T